Critical Readings in **Social Psychology**

Darren Langdridge and Stephanie Taylor

OPEN UNIVERSITY PRESS
McGraw - Hill Education

Published by

Open University Press
McGraw-Hill House
Shoppenhangers Road
Maidenhead
SL6 2QL

in association with

The Open University
Walton Hall
Milton Keynes
MK7 6AA

First published 2007.

Edited and designed by The Open University.

Typeset by The Open University.

Printed and bound in the United Kingdom by CPI, Bath.

This book forms part of an Open University course DD307 *Social psychology: critical perspectives on self and others*. Details of this and other Open University courses can be obtained from the Student Registration and Enquiry Service, The Open University, PO Box 197, Milton Keynes MK7 6BJ, United Kingdom: tel. +44 (0)870 333 4340, email general-enquiries@open.ac.uk

http://www.open.ac.uk

ISBN 0 33522 104 1/ISBN 978 0 3352 2104 2 (pb)

ISBN 0 33522 106 8/ISBN 978 0 3352 2106 6 (hb)

1.1

Contents

Preface

The editors of this book would like to thank all the chapter authors for their insightful contributions to the book, as well as the authors of all the previously published writings from which the readings have been selected. In addition, because this book was produced for The Open University's Social Sciences course DD307 *Social psychology: critical perspectives on self and others*, the editors would like to acknowledge the special contributions from colleagues at The Open University: other members of the DD307 course team, Karen Hagan, Wendy Hollway, Mary Horton-Salway, Caroline Kelly, Helen Lucey, Ann Phoenix and Bianca Raabe; External Assessor, Valerie Walkerdine; Associate Lecturer and Student Critical Readers, Sally Ann Gallagher, Geoff Harris, Marie Ann Lavelle, Harriette Marshall, Kate Pearson, Anna Sarphie, Annette Thomson; Course Manager, Ann Tolley; Editorial Media Developer, Kathleen Calder; Media Project Manager, Lynne Downey; Copublishing Media Developer Margrit Bass; Psychology Department Office Manager, Lynda Preston; and the secretarial team from the Psychology Office in Social Sciences, Sarah Pelosi and Elaine Richardson.

Darren Langdridge and Stephanie Taylor

Chapter 1

Introduction

by Stephanie Taylor, The Open University

Introduction

Contemporary social psychology encompasses a range of theoretical positions, research approaches and purposes. Its interest and dynamism derives in a large part from this complexity and its background. This book has been designed to contribute in several ways to your understanding of the discipline.

One of these is through the topics of the central chapters: close relationships, attitudes, attribution, intragroup processes, intergroup processes, conformity and individual differences. These have been selected by the British Psychological Society as central to the discipline. The book is organised as a combination of textbook and reader. Each chapter presents contrasting approaches to its topic through two or three extracts from previously published material, supported by the author's commentary. Taken together, the central chapters will therefore give you an overview of the key areas of academic work in contemporary social psychology and the debates associated with them.

The book will also show you how debate and criticism are part of the ongoing processes through which social psychology continues to change and develop. This is not a simple 'before' and 'after' story of critique producing changes; the book aims to present a more complex narrative. For example, many of the chapters contain an earlier and a later reading, but you should not assume that the earlier work has inevitably been superseded by the later approach; they may now represent two separate lines of social psychological work. You should also be aware that the readings are 'snapshots' of work which has continued to develop and diversify, and this applies as much to a position which some authors refer to as 'mainstream' as to alternative approaches, although this book focuses more on the latter.

In many of the chapters, the author refers to the work presented in the first reading as 'mainstream'. It is certainly possible to tell a binary story of social psychology in which a period of crisis and change led to the divergence of work into mainstream and other work (e.g. Hollway, 2006; Stainton-Rogers, 2003, p. xv). When authors make this distinction, they are generally referring to the contemporary mainstream as the areas of social psychological theory and research associated with the largest amounts of research funding, the highest-status journals, and the largest number of departments and academics, especially in the USA. In this binary story, the 'other' work to the mainstream is sometimes discussed as an area or even a sub-discipline in its own right, referred to as 'critical psychology' or 'critical social psychology': there is considerable overlap between the two terms since one of the features which 'critical' writers emphasise is the importance of the particular, socially situated nature of experience and behaviour (e.g. Gough and McFadden, 2001, pp. 10–11); arguably, critical psychology is necessarily social.

However, this is an oversimplified account since social psychology is constantly changing. This means that what is referred to by some as 'mainstream' social psychology develops partly by taking account of critiques from 'critical social psychology' (see, for example, Parkinson, 2007). Furthermore, critical social psychology has developed over time to be as varied as mainstream social psychology so that the terms refer to areas that are both broad and internally differentiated. In addition, some areas which are largely encompassed in the critical social psychology category, such as discursive psychology, have gained popularity and prestige and are less likely to have to explain why they are a necessary part of social psychology, while some areas of mainstream social psychology fall into disfavour over time. The critical–mainstream binary is sometimes used to refer to differences in methodology (largely an experimental/quantitative-qualitative differentiation). Nonetheless, as I discuss below, this further distinction is also problematic, and it frequently breaks down since experimental social psychology sometimes employs qualitative methods and some critical social psychology uses quantitative methods. It is, therefore, important to recognise that the binary between 'mainstream' and 'critical' social psychologies may sometimes be a useful working distinction, but it is not fixed and clear-cut.

Writers on critical psychology point to a series of debates and contrasting positions which it will be useful to keep in mind while you are reading this book. (I outline these below.) These writers emphasise the breadth and complexity of work encompassed in the term 'critical'. Prilleltensky and Nelson (2002), for instance, suggest that critical psychology is better understood as an *approach* rather than a field in itself. Similarly, Ros Gill suggests that 'the critical in critical social psychology refers both to a political project and an epistemological stance' (quoted in Hepburn, 2003, p. 222). I discuss these claims in more detail in the next section.

In general, therefore, the book presents critique and contrasting positions in relation to different topics, avoiding any simple division between 'mainstream' and 'critical'. As you read, you should be aware that both terms have a shifting reference, as do many other terms you will encounter throughout this book. This again reflects the complexities of the contemporary academic field of social psychology and the debates that take place in its journals, conferences and funding bodies. The chapters present some of the academic history or genealogy of the discipline, including the inevitable untidiness of that history.

A further feature of the book is the range of voices that is included. The author of each chapter has written an introduction, commentary and conclusion. These support the previously published readings from other sources. In addition to the various 'teaching' voices, in the readings themselves you will encounter the specialist vocabulary and often distinctive prose styles associated with different areas of social psychology, and also different social periods. This variety is an intended and important feature of the book. It gives another indication of the breadth of the discipline and it will provide you with useful experience of reading different kinds of psychology texts. But, even more importantly, the terminology that the texts use and even the ways that they are written are markers of the authors' theoretical positions. As just one example, psychology texts were conventionally written in the impersonal style associated with science. In contrast, many (but not all) contemporary social psychologists refer to 'I' in order to introduce themselves into their writing – both as a contrast to scientific conventions and a challenge to the neutral authority which the scientific style implies. This is therefore another way in which the range and complexity of contemporary social psychology is presented.

The remainder of this introductory chapter presents a brief summary of the contrast positions already mentioned, some advice on using the book effectively for your own study and then an overview of the content of the central chapters.

Critical contrasts

Writers who identify 'critical social psychology' as a separate sub-discipline (e.g. Gough and McFadden, 2001; Hepburn, 2003; Stainton-Rogers, 2003) draw attention to a number of contrasting positions which it will be useful to keep in mind while you are reading. These include differences in research practice, the underlying practical methods and the assumptions involved in creating new knowledge in social psychology. Other contrasts relate to the purpose of the research and the larger project of psychology.

You are almost certainly aware of the distinction between quantitative and qualitative research. At its simplest, this refers respectively to research which produces countable findings, which can be presented as statistics, and research in which the findings have some other form. A more complicated distinction might be that between description and interpretation. Many theorists, including phenomenologists, would challenge whether the two *can* be neatly distinguished (see Reading 4.2); however, I raise the distinction here as a useful way to begin thinking about several issues. The distinction is relevant to the kind of knowledge claims which are made in research and therefore to the 'epistemological stance' referred to by Gill (quoted in Hepburn, 2003). For example, it could be argued that both a survey, which produces quantitative findings (see Reading 2.1), and observations (see Readings 3.1, 4.1, 5.1 and 8.1), which might be either counted or described in words, are intended to represent some external 'real world'. This contrasts with research, such as social constructionist research (see Phoenix, 2006), which does not assume such straightforward representation but explicitly acknowledges the presence of the researcher within the research process (see Readings 6.2 and 7.2) and her or his role in interpreting data, whether these are in a quantitative form, like statistics, or are qualitative data such as observations (see Reading 2.2) or talk or written text (see Readings 3.3 and 6.2).

This also relates to the issue of whether objectivity is possible in research, a point which critical psychologists have challenged (e.g. Gough and McFadden, 2001, p. 17). It is, of course, an assumption of scientific research that objectivity is not only possible but necessary, in order to eliminate bias and distortion and to produce reliable findings which can be checked by replicating the research. The contrasting position is that research, like any other human activity, takes place within a wider socio-historical context and is shaped by it; as Michael Billig puts it 'no social psychology is value free, for all social psychology reflects the cultural climate in which it is produced' (Reading 6.2). A number of chapters and readings in this book draw attention to the importance of researchers' world views as part of this context (see Readings 3.3, 5.2, 7.2 and 8.2). They suggest that objectivity is, in Viv Burr's words, 'an unattainable fiction' (Chapter 7) and also one which can distort research findings because it involves a denial of the researcher's situatedness and its effect on what is being studied.

In general, critical social psychologists are more likely to use research methods that are commonly described as 'interpretive'. You should be aware, however, that the reverse is not necessarily true; many interpretive researchers would not categorise their work as 'critical'. Where they do adopt the label, as with Margaret Wetherell and Nigel Edley's 'critical discursive psychology' (Wetherell, 1998; Edley, 2001), it is generally intended to mark their concern with issues of power and inequality in contemporary social contexts (part of the 'political project' which Gill refers to).

Critical social psychologists have challenged the use of experiments, to the extent that one writer, Wendy Stainton-Rogers, suggests that the discipline is now divided between the two camps: 'experimental' and 'critical' (Stainton-Rogers, 2003). An experiment may be conducted in either a laboratory or a real world context (see Readings 2.1, 4.1, 6.1). Its distinctive feature is that it involves an element of control. In addition, it generally models the world in terms of variables. (Some other research also does this, such as surveys (see Reading 2.1).) The causes or influences which operate in a situation are distinguished and considered separately or in limited and specific combinations. There seems to be a definite contrast here with the view of an untidier world, such as that proposed by psychoanalytic or discursive researchers, which is characterised by overlapping and contradictory influences and more complicated causes that need a lot of unravelling.

However, the researcher's model or theory should not be confused with the *purpose* of the research. On the one hand, there is research that attempts to model and predict. The researchers may be well aware of the complexity of the social world, and indeed, have perhaps taken some seemingly intractable social problem as a starting point (see Chapters 6 and 7). But, they then put much of the detail aside in order to devise an experiment that can explore some practical explanation or intervention (see Readings 3.2, 6.1 and 7.1). On the other hand, there is research that has almost the opposite purpose: it draws attention to complexity, explores it and seeks to make multiple connections (see Readings 4.2 and 7.2). This is a particular feature of discourse analytic or discursive research (see Readings 3.3, 5.2 and 6.2). Discursive psychologists are especially concerned with the 'local' meanings which operate in a specific situation. They challenge the emphasis on rationality in cognitive–experimental research. Psychoanalytic research (see Reading 2.2) goes further and considers the unconscious meanings which people bring to a new situation from their experience.

This discussion of the purpose of research raises the question of the larger project of social psychology. Two authors who work in the cognitive–experimental tradition suggest that 'the shared mission of all psychologists' is 'understanding the causes of behaviour' (Eagly and Chaiken, 1993, p. 216). Many social psychologists have looked in particular at the behaviour of groups and also the impact of the group on the behaviour of an individual. These concerns are obviously relevant to two of the central topics in social psychology: prejudice and group conflict (see Chapters 3, 6 and Reading 5.2).

Writers on critical social psychology have suggested rather different projects for the discipline. The term 'critical' psychology was originally coined to draw attention to issues of power (Prilleltensky and Nelson, 2002) and is linked to a Marxist critique (see Hepburn, 2003, Chapter 3). I have already mentioned the criticism of research which, in the classic scientific tradition (see Readings 4.1 and 8.1), aims to be objective; critical psychologists argue that objectivity is not a neutral, a-political position but one which, by obscuring inequalities, such as those associated with gender, sexuality, social class, race and ethnicity, can contribute to their perpetuation. In addition, there is a strong argument that issues of power and inequality are even more relevant to psychology than other academic disciplines because the work of psychologists has been so closely implicated with institutional and social definitions of normality and pathology (see Chapter 8) (e.g. Rose, 1989, 1996). It can therefore be seen to have contributed to the exercise, and possible abuse, of power in certain institutional contexts, such as mental hospitals, prisons and schools (see Chapter 8).

I have suggested that critical psychology is in some senses inevitably social because of its emphasis on the socially situated nature of findings and the locatedness of individuals. This is in direct contrast to research which attempts to establish universals, for example of behaviour and personality (see Readings 2.1, 3.2 and 8.1). Critical social psychologists turn from the more external view of the person which is often associated with experimental and survey work to what Gough and McFadden (2001, p. 93) have defined as 'the actual experience of selfhood', subjectivity. This term is linked to both the 'subject' of psychoanalysis (see Reading 2.2) and the 'subject position' which Michel Foucault invoked in his account of how we derive our identities from where we are located within a larger socio-cultural context (as opposed to carrying separate identities contained within us) (see Hepburn, 2003, pp. 61–5 for a discussion of Foucault). Hepburn has suggested that subjectivity is a central issue for critical psychology (p. 134). This book will demonstrate that the delineation and exploration of subjectivity – for example, whether it is rational or unconscious, fragmented or unified (see Readings 2.2 and 3.3) –

has become a major project for many social psychologists (Hollway, 2006) and perhaps *the* alternative to a concern with the causes of behaviour.

Using this book

You are probably aware that a textbook does not need to be read straight through from start to finish, like a novel. While I hope that you have begun by reading this introduction, you will also find it useful to return to the points I make here, including the chapter summaries in the next section, to assist your reading of the central chapters. Each of these chapters has a 'club sandwich' structure: there is a slice of discussion by the chapter author at the beginning, in the middle and at the end (the introduction, commentary and conclusion) and two different 'fillings' (three for Chapter 3) in the form of previously published readings. These readings have a range of publication dates; full details of the original source are given at the end of each reading. They also have very different styles, so you are likely to notice the transition between one part of the chapter and the next; you may need to slow down, or read more closely, depending on the density and formality of each reading. You may find it useful to flick through the whole chapter before starting to read it in order to check what it contains. There are also activities before the readings which contain focus questions. These are intended to assist your reading by drawing your attention to the most important points. Each chapter is relatively self-contained, but you may want to use this introduction, the conclusion (Chapter 9) and the index to the book to help you draw out some common themes and other connections.

The chapters

In this section I summarise the central chapters of the book and point to some of the links between them. You may want to return to it to guide your reading of each chapter.

Chapter 2, by Shelley Day Sclater, presents two contrasting perspectives on close relationships in adulthood. Reading 2.1, by Steve Duck, is concerned in particular with 'courtship' as a phase in couple or partner relationships. The reading is largely descriptive, summarising the patterns revealed in a large number of studies, many involving surveys or other empirical work that have produced quantitative data. It considers the cultural context of relationships, such as the expectations attached to 'courtship', although you may note that there is a tacit assumption that the prevailing culture in the wider sense is Western/North American, 'Anglo' and Christian. Reading 2.1 contains little acknowledgement of national, ethnic or religious differences. The reading also focuses mainly on heterosexual relationships.

The chapter author, Sclater, presents Duck's work as a traditional psychological approach and contrasts it with an extract from the work of Nancy Chodorow, Reading 2.2, who takes a psychoanalytic approach. An interesting point about Reading 2.2 is that, although the critical perspective presented by Chodorow's work was first published at roughly the same time (1978) as the Duck reading was first published (1981), psychoanalytic theorising has a longer history than social psychology itself. However, its use in social psychology is relatively new (Hollway, 2006, Chapter 2) and is generally distinguished with the term 'psychosocial' or 'social psychoanalytic'.

Chodorow is particularly interested in gender differences in the ways that people relate and their expectations of relationships. Her argument is that men's and women's different experience of being parented, by the mother and the father, carries through into differences in their adult relationships, with partners, friends and their own children. Sclater suggests that Chodorow's work offers a critical perspective on the study of relationships in several ways. The focus on gender identities contrasts with the kind of scientific approach which would generalise about people as uniform, statistically equivalent individuals without considering the different experiences of women (or gay, lesbian, bisexual and trans people, or people of colour, or those from minority religious or ethnic groups). As discussed above, this more conventional scientific approach risks ignoring and denying the experience of anyone in a disadvantaged or subordinate social position. Chodorow's work also challenges a generalised model of the individual in another way, by emphasising people's interconnectedness and interdependence; this is a particular view of subjectivity. Sclater emphasises how a psychoanalytic approach acknowledges each person as an individual subject, uniquely located by biography and culture, which structure their experiences of close relationships.

Chapter 3, by Stephanie Taylor, contains three readings from previously published material on the topic of attitudes. Readings 3.1 and 3.2, by Richard LaPiere and Icek Ajzen respectively, are in the broad tradition of cognitive experimental work. Although they employ different definitions and concepts of an attitude and different research methods, they are linked in their research questions and their larger project, namely, the precise connection between attitudes and behaviour. The second is an example of a 'scientific' social psychological study to devise possible interventions to produce changes in people's behaviour. Reading 3.3, by Jonathan Potter and Margaret Wetherell, is a critique of this kind of research from the perspective of discourse analysis or, as it is now more usually called, discursive psychology.

Discursive approaches have developed relatively recently in social psychology (see also Readings 5.2 and 6.2). The example you read here, first published in 1987, is a challenge to cognitive experimental work. However, as I point out in the chapter, discursive psychology has not had a significant impact on cognitive experimental attitude research, which has continued to develop in the direction presented in the first two readings. In many respects, Reading 3.3 represents the start of a different area of social psychological work with its own concerns, including subjectivity.

Readings 3.1 and 3.3 are concerned with attitudes to others and are part of the major tradition of social psychological work on prejudice and group conflict. They present research from very different socio-historic contexts (North America in the 1930s and New Zealand in the 1980s); and in Reading 3.3, this context is central to the analysis. Reading 3.3 also discusses a more conventional survey study which shows how ethnocentric conceptualisations and assumptions can become built into social psychological methods. This final reading therefore shows two different approaches to ethnicity – first as a category and second as a discursive resource.

Chapter 4, by Darren Langdridge, takes a classic psychological problem, the fundamental attribution error (FAE), and presents two alternative approaches to the question: why are we more likely to explain an event as caused by (the internal disposition of) an actor rather than the wider context (or external situation)?

Reading 4.1, by Lee Ross, considers the FAE as a scientific problem. Ross presents this approach in a perhaps surprising way, through an account of how, in his view, 'ordinary people' perceive and understand the world. Ross's title refers to 'the intuitive psychologist' and his view is that the ordinary person *is* a scientist, specifically an intuitive scientific psychologist who approaches the world rationally. As in scientific research, obtaining knowledge of the world involves three tasks: causal judgement, social inference and prediction; it is developed through the progressive accumulation and refinement of detail. A complex situation is reduced to a relatively small number of variables. Interestingly, although Ross is working within a broadly experimental tradition of social psychology, he also criticises experimental work in some detail. He points out, for example, that the distinction between 'situation' and 'disposition' is not always clear-cut.

Ross's model of the person is therefore of a rational, neutral observer, just like the ideal model of a scientific psychologist, and the one which critical psychologists have questioned. The 'ordinary' person Ross discusses is definitely masculine: the 'man in the street' and 'psychological man'. It is, of course, a (somewhat outdated) writing convention to use masculine terms as general referents; however, it also raises again the problem considered by Frances Cherry in a later chapter (see Reading 7.2) of how generalisation omits certain 'stubborn particulars', such as gender, which may be highly relevant to a situation.

Reading 4.2, by Darren Langdridge and Trevor Butt, considers the FAE from a different perspective, that of phenomenology. As the authors point out, this is not a new way of thinking but one which has recently been revived in social psychology. They begin by summarising more conventional research on the FAE, showing how it has been dominated by the experimental method. They then outline a phenomenological approach as an alternative. This involves a focus on immediate experience rather than rational information processing. This might sound a rather individualistic and detached approach, like the kind of separation from mundane reality commonly associated with meditation or other 'transcendent' states. However, according to the existential phenomenology advocated by the philosopher Merleau-Ponty, experience is both 'embodied and intersubjective', which denies a separation, or dualism, of body and mind, or of individual and social. Our relationship with the world cannot be broken down into separate parts but involves all of these aspects simultaneously. This assumption has several implications. Interpretation or the acquisition of knowledge is not the final result of several steps of rational information processing, as cognitive approaches might imply (see Reading 3.2), but the instantaneous perception of a phenomenon within the social world, with all the complexity that implies. In contrast to Ross's model of the person as scientist, for Langdridge and Butt the ordinary person is more like a certain kind of qualitative analyst who does not attempt to edit down experience but to embrace all its rich detail. Finally, as Langdridge puts it, 'all social psychological phenomena must be understood in context, being inseparable from the persons situated in a particular culture, time and place'. This is, then, another argument against distinguishing description and interpretation; 'facts' cannot exist separately from their social meanings.

The fifth and sixth chapters focus on one of the classic concerns of social psychology, the group. In **Chapter 5**, Ann Phoenix discusses *intra*group processes, that is, those internal to the group, among the people who comprise it. In **Chapter 6**, Steve Brown discusses *inter*group processes, or those between groups. Phoenix begins her chapter with a review of previous research on groups, dividing this into several broad categories. Her typology provides a useful overview and shows how different groups 'have often raised different social psychological issues and are associated with different ... processes, theories and methods'. She also reminds us, once again, how categories and terms are fluid and have to be related to the specific context of use: 'group' can mean many different things. She suggests that the common feature of groups is that they are *seen*, by themselves or others, 'to constitute a group or entity': the term she uses for this is 'entitativity'. Reading 5.1 is on 'groupthink', a largely negative phenomenon defined by the reading's author, Irving Janis, on the basis of observations (e.g. of an anti-smoking group in a clinic) and also of historical records of policy-making groups. The approach of this research is descriptive rather than interpretive. In contrast, the second reading, by Jonathan Potter and Steve Reicher, steps back from a particular group, a community, and considers how it is differently interpreted and defined, on different occasions and by insiders and outsiders. Reading 5.2 uses a discourse analytic approach (although a somewhat different one to the earlier example in Reading 2.3, which was also co-authored by Potter). The two readings in Chapter 5 exemplify contrasting purposes or projects, even though both are concerned with people in groups.

The introduction to Chapter 6, by Steve Brown, provides a further overview of research on groups and repeats a point made in Chapter 5, that social psychologists have generally assumed that the group has a negative influence on the individual. The chapter then presents the historical background to the social identity theory (SIT) of the relations between groups, one of the most influential theories in contemporary social psychology and the basis of a considerable amount of cognitive experimental work. It introduces the work of one of the major figures of social psychology, Henri Tajfel. Reading 6.1, by Henri Tajfel and John Turner, gives an overview of previous cognitive research and theorising on groups and then outlines SIT. A particular aim of this theory was to explain violence towards groups defined by race and ethnicity.

Reading 6.2, by Michael Billig, is a critique of the theory. It begins by locating Tajfel's work within its specific particular socio-historical context and indicates the idea he was arguing against, that human conflict is the consequence of people reverting to irrational biological instincts. Tajfel was concerned to emphasise the rational basis of conflict between groups. Billig, in turn, draws attention to the limitations of the model of the rational person that underlies cognitive theories. He suggests that the study of conflict needs to consider both emotion and power; otherwise, there is a danger of ignoring the intensity of the hatred involved in bigotry and also its ideological nature, linked to the political context in which it occurs. Reading 6.2 is an example of a particular kind of discursive psychology pioneered by Billig, called 'rhetorical psychology'.

Chapter 7, by Viv Burr, presents two contrasting pieces of work prompted by the same events, the highly publicised account of how people who heard or directly witnessed a fatal attack did not attempt to intervene to save the victim. Reading 7.1, by John Darley and Bibb Latané, describes a series of experiments devised to explore the circumstances in which bystander intervention is more or less likely. The chapter raises again the question of whether action, or in this case, failure to act, should be attributed to individuals or to circumstances (you may want to make comparisons with Chapters 4 and 8). As Burr discusses, one of the researchers' aims was to counter the suggestion that the bystanders in the original case were personally at fault and that other individuals in the same situation would have acted differently. She points out some of the strengths of experimental research illustrated by the reading: its aim to produce objective, unbiased findings which hold across different social contexts.

I have already mentioned the counter-argument, that objectivity is never achievable in research and, furthermore, that in attempting to be objective, researchers risk distorting a problem by oversimplifying it and omitting relevant considerations linked to the specific socio-historical context. Reading 7.2, by Frances Cherry, presents this position in detail. She suggests that Darley and Latané's experiments ignore the gendered aspect of the original attack, reflecting contemporary attitudes towards violence against women. A similar argument can be made with respect to racial issues. Of course, experiments could be devised to include these aspects, and Burr describes some, but these still, inevitably, involve simplification. Burr suggests that the kind of qualitative research favoured by, among others, feminist researchers like Cherry, would foreground meanings which experimentalists might ignore. But there is an even wider aspect to the problem. Cherry also draws out how a researcher is influenced by her or his own socio-historical context and may have difficulty thinking beyond prevailing values and views of the world. (This point is also made by Billig, in Reading 6.2, which I quoted earlier. You might, at this point, like to look back to Reading 3.1 and consider how far it reads as a product of its socio-historical context.) In other words, any research, including experimental studies, involves interpretation, and reflects the extent to which the researcher is, inescapably, part of the same context that she or he is researching. Part of good research practice is therefore to acknowledge this locatedness and actively consider how it has shaped the research; this is what is meant by 'reflexivity'.

Chapter 8, by Trevor Butt, returns in a different way to the causes of people's behaviour. The chapter presents two contrasting theories of personality. The first, trait theory, is concerned with 'placing the individual with respect to a number of trait dimensions that are thought to underpin behaviour' (Butt, 2006). This is, of course, similar to the way that we might informally interpret people and connect what they *do* to the kinds of people they *are* (e.g. reliable or unreliable). Reading 8.1 is by Hans Eysenck and Stanley J. Rachman, who suggest that personality is not a matter of absolute categories (e.g. 'you are an introvert' or 'you are a neurotic person') but of dimensions ('you are more/less strongly introverted' or 'neurotic' etc.). Traits are assumed to be biologically based, enduring and universal; for instance, Eysenck and Rachman suggest that an Ancient Greek typology ('melancholic', 'choleric' and so on) corresponds to the traits identified in modern factor analytic studies. This is a scientific psychology in which people are measured and classified on the basis of empirical work. It is also the basis of the psychometric work which is now widely used in occupational psychology.

The chapter goes on to challenge Eysenck's theory. Butt suggests that the traits the authors discuss may in fact be 'in the eye of the beholder'; in other words, how we interpret other people may be less a reflection of the traits they possess and the kinds of people they are than of our own world view. This would suggest that a study of personality should consider difference in another way, in terms of how people perceive and construct the world, including other people. This is the focus of a different theoretical approach, George Kelly's personal construct theory, which is the basis of Reading 8.2 by Phillida Salmon. In Reading 8.2, Salmon challenges British educational policy which attempts to classify pupils according to their scores in tests. She suggests that this fails to take account of the more important differences in world view which Kelly's theory considers. She then discusses the difficulty people have in changing their world views. She sees learning as part of living, and more specifically as 'the shifting of meanings within an essentially personal system of understandings' (Salmon, 2003). Salmon emphasises that this is not an easy process: 'learning carries personal risks' because it challenges the whole way in which someone views the world. She proposes a technique to assist this which acknowledges 'the personal, idiosyncratic meaning' of educational progress, and allows the learner to define that progress.

There are a number of striking differences from the theory presented in Reading 8.1. First, what people do is explained not in terms of their traits but their view of the world. Second, Salmon, following Kelly, does not attempt to define the differences between people in terms of norms or a continuum between fixed points. The range of possibilities she considers is much more open ended, and perhaps infinite. Third, while both readings refer to the practical applications of theory (Eysenck and Rachman discuss people with problems of mental health and criminality; Salmon's aim is to help pupils in schools), Salmon is concerned not with the classification of differences but with understanding.

I have noted that Eysenck and Rachman's purpose is to find out where people with particular problems (mental illness, criminality) are located within a larger population mapped through experimental and statistical studies. As with any classification system, this assumes a tidy and stable world in which people can be neatly allocated to fixed places. You can probably see some of the larger implications, and problems, of this assumption. One is its potential for pathologising individuals by ascribing a negative label to them. One of Salmon's aims is to challenge this kind of pathologising. She adopts a constructivist approach which is concerned with the individual but could perhaps be criticised for underplaying the commonalities of people's experience. (You might find it interesting, at this point, to look back to Reading 2.1 and consider the patterns in people's behaviour which that research detected.) Butt's response is to extend Kelly's theory one step further. He suggests that people's understandings or constructs are derived from their social worlds, and he returns us therefore to individual differences as an issue for social psychology.

The final chapter of the book, **Chapter 9**, the conclusion, returns to some of the issues of this introduction and then looks ahead to the future of social psychology.

References

Butt, T. (2006) 'Individual differences' in Langdridge, D. and Taylor, S. (eds) *Critical Readings in Social Psychology*, Maidenhead, Open University Press/ Milton Keynes, The Open University.

Eagly, A. and Chaiken, S. (1993) *The Psychology of Attitudes*, Fort Worth, Harcourt Brace College Publishers.

Edley, N. (2001) 'Analysing masculinity: interpretative repertoires, subject positions and ideological dilemmas' in Wetherell, M., Taylor, S. and Yates, S. (eds) *Discourse as Data: A Guide for Analysis*, London, Sage.

Gough, B. and McFadden, M. (2001) *Critical Social Psychology: An Introduction*, Houndsmills, Hampshire/New York, Palgrave.

Hepburn, A. (2003) *An Introduction to Critical Social Psychology*, London, Sage.

Hollway, W. (2006) 'Methods and knowledge in social psychology' in Hollway, W., Lucey, H. and Phoenix, A. (eds).

Hollway, W., Lucey, H. and Phoenix, A. (eds) (2006) *Social Psychology Matters*, Maidenhead, Open University Press/Milton Keynes, The Open University.

Merleau-Ponty, M. (1962) *Phenomenology of Perception*, trans. C. Smith, London, Routledge.

Prilleltensky, I. and Nelson, G. (2002) *Doing Psychology Critically: Making a Difference in Diverse Settings*, Basingstoke, Palgrave.

Rose, N. (1989) *Governing the Soul: The Shaping of the Private Self*, London, Routledge.

Rose, N. (1996) *Inventing Our Selves: Psychology, Power and Personhood*, Cambridge, Cambridge University Press.

Salmon, P. (2003) 'A psychology for teachers' in Fransella, F. (ed.) *International Handbook of Personal Construct Psychology*, Chichester, Wiley.

Stainton-Rogers, W. (2003) *Social Psychology; Experimental and Critical Approaches*, Maidenhead, Berkshire/Philadelphia, Open University Press.

Wetherell, M. (1998) 'Positioning and interpretative repertoires: conversation analysis and post-structuralism in dialogue', *Discourse & Society*, vol. 9, no. 3, pp. 387–412.

Further reading

The texts by Hepburn and by Gough and McFadden, listed in the references, are both recommended as an introduction to critical social psychology. The collection *Social Psychology Matters* (Hollway et al., 2006) is the companion text to this book for The Open University course DD307 *Social Psychology: Critical Perspectives on Self and Others*.

Chapter 2

Close relationships

by Shelley Day Sclater, University of East London

Introduction

Close personal relationships are the bedrock of human existence. From our earliest dependencies in infancy, through the knocks and bumps of childhood, the angst of adolescence, the responsibilities of adulthood and the challenges of ageing, close relationships are central to our lives. They strongly influence not only the quality of our lives, but also who we are and who we might become. Unsurprisingly, then, the whys and wherefores of personal relationships have long attracted human attention. Novelists, artists, poets, playwrights and philosophers have explored their vicissitudes and their mysteries. And social scientists too have made their own distinctive contribution to this enterprise. The area of close relationships is now a flourishing field of psychosocial research.

It is of course no accident that social scientists should have increasingly focused on close relationships, as societies in the developed world have witnessed such dramatic changes in relationship patterns since the Second World War. There is ample evidence – both demographic (documented, for instance, in *Population Trends*) and in relation to attitudes (see, for example, successive editions of the *British Social Attitudes* survey) – that shows both changes and continuities in family patterns and attitudes towards relationships since the 1950s. For example, the increasing prevalence of divorce, the declining popularity of marriage, the increase in cohabitation, and in numbers of children being born outside of marriage are frequently mentioned as indicators of dramatic social change in how we 'do' close relationships (Haskey, 1996, pp. 7–24; Jamieson, 1998; Lewis, 1999, pp. 355–64).

Sociologists too have highlighted the changing meanings of intimacy in a world that has increasingly valued individualism and choice (see, for example, Giddens, 1992; Beck and Beck-Gernsheim, 1995). Recognition of and respect for diversity in relationships have brought a critical appraisal of the traditional exclusive focus on white, heterosexual families and a move instead towards inclusion, with increasing attention to both so-called 'non-traditional' relationships, such as those among gay men and lesbians, and the sometimes distinctive relationship patterns in different cultural and ethnic groups. Alongside these academic developments, the immense popularity of 'pop psych' self-help books such as John Gray's *Men are from Mars, Women are from Venus* (1993) is testimony to the widespread fascination that intimacy holds for many people in all walks of life.

Within mainstream psychology, the study of close relationships has grown out of an older concern with interpersonal and group processes, and much work has been done on affiliation and friendship, attraction – particularly physical and sexual attraction – and love. Psychologists, for their part, have focused on exploring the factors that influence the formation and maintenance of close relationships, their 'success' and 'failure', and the fall-out when things go wrong (Buunk, 1996; Malim and Birch, 1998). In this chapter, we will be discussing two main perspectives on close relationships – a mainstream psychological approach, and a 'critical' perspective represented by a psychoanalytic approach.

There are several significant differences between these two approaches. It is most important to note that each approach has a different set of ontological and epistemological assumptions within its theoretical framework, though these are rarely made explicit. Further, each paradigm generates its own distinctive kinds of research questions and uses its unique range of methodologies to address them.

The hallmark of a mainstream psychological approach to close relationships may be summarised as the application of tried and tested psychological methods to the objective study of close relationships, with the aim of discovering the general principles that govern relationship formation, maintenance and dissolution. As a result of systematic research, psychologists working within a mainstream paradigm have identified a range of factors of general significance in relationships. They have generated theories of how the various factors fit together, and which can be used to explain relationship processes and predict relationship patterns. For example, it has been shown that one of the simplest determinants of interpersonal attraction is proximity: the people whom, by chance, you see and interact with the most often are most likely to become your friends and lovers. This is referred to as the *propinquity effect* (Berscheid and Reis, 1998). Theories not only enable us to explain research findings, they also alert us to the aspects of the world that don't fit, and thus to the need for further research and new theory. Thus, the propinquity effect does not explain all there is to be explained about interpersonal attraction, since it is obvious that we don't become friends, or fall in love, with everyone who happens to be near us on a daily basis. As a result, psychologists have looked for further factors that underlie our choice of friends and mates, and have generated theories about, for example, the importance of *similarities* in terms of background, interests, values and so on, and theories about *physical attractiveness* which help to build a more complete picture of the fundamentals of close relationships.

The first, 'classic', reading (Reading 2.1 – an extract from *Relating to Others* (Duck, 1999)) is a good example of the psychological work on close relationships within the mainstream paradigm, but one which recognises the need to take account of a multiplicity of factors. Since the 1990s, psychological research into personal relationships has enjoyed an increasing popularity. Steve Duck was the founding editor of the *Journal of Social and Personal Relationships*. He has long been a leader in the field and has been highly influential in shaping the landscape of psychological work on personal relationships.

ACTIVITY 2.1

As you read the following extract, consider these points:

■   What evidence does the reading provide for Duck's interdisciplinarity?

■   What kinds of evidence does Duck present for his claim that there are some general principles that operate in social and personal relationships?

■   What significance might context have on the formation and dynamics of close relationships (including date, nation)?

Reading 2.1 is from a classic book published in 1999 by Steve Duck, whose work helped to establish the study of personal relationships as a field in psychology.

READING 2.1

'Developing a steady and exclusive partnership'

Most people develop a relationship with a life-partner at some point in their lives [...]. While the earliest research on this topic examined the types of people who married (for example, by recording their race, religion, economic class, and so on), more recent work has explored the processes of courtship itself and has been more concerned with courtship progress and courtship styles than with the broad social categories that are associated with stable or unstable marriages. [...] The focus on long-term relationships of heterosexuals has also now been supplemented with discussion of gay and lesbian relationships (Huston and Schwartz 1995), including work on the stability and dissolution of such relationships (Kurdek 1991, 1992). [...] Yet, as Huston and Schwartz (1995) note, we still know relatively little about gay and lesbian experience in serious relationships or networks of maintenance and commitment. Even in the heterosexual literature, most research looks only at young couples. Young people are not the only ones who marry, especially now that the increasing divorce rate releases older individuals to enter second marriages and create blended families (Coleman and Ganong 1995). The results of studies reported below, however, are invariably derived from subjects below the age of 30 and one can only assume that the results would have been different had the subjects been older. For instance, second marriages usually follow a briefer courtship than do first marriages (Coleman and Ganong 1995; Notarius 1996; Sher 1996) [...].

Courting disaster: some early research approaches

Because courtship is a halfway house between casual dating on the one hand and a stable, exclusive relationship on the other, a fairly natural assumption within our cultural belief system is that some force operates to drive it forward or give it momentum. Readers should note, also, the value judgements that are associated with this topic and this style of research into it. Those value-laden styles of thinking – which still pervade our common-sense view – assume that people who stay in relationships are 'successes' and people who leave them or are left by partners have 'failed'. Indeed Umberson and Terling (1997) analysed both in-depth interviews and survey data and showed that the symbolic meaning of relationships is a significant reason for the deep distress felt during their dissolution. [...] Such cultural judgements also can affect the feelings of those who enter non-normative relationships (Huston and Schwartz 1995). [...] There are strong cultural endorsements for certain types of relationship conduct [...].

A corollary of this value-laden approach is that people celebrate lengthy relationships (e.g., by ceremonial marking of silver wedding anniversaries or re-enactment of vows; Braithwaite and Baxter 1995). [...] On the other hand, overlengthy courtships are viewed with scepticism and a culture has its own views of the appropriate length of time between first meeting and exclusive commitment [...].

Our cultural models for relationships offer, as the engine for courtship progress and relationship 'success', the notion of love for one's partner: as love grows, this 'theory' would claim, so the relationship deepens and broadens; eventually the two partners realize that they were 'made for each other' and become exclusive or move into a live-in-lover relationship of some kind. Although this force has probably been implicit in many approaches to courtship progress, love is clearly experienced in a cultural context and is not a pure emotion felt and expressed the same way all over the world (Beall and Sternberg 1995). It is also experienced in a practical context and people who have affairs or people who are gay or lesbian or bisexual feel pressures not to reveal their love to 'outsiders' in public in the same way that single heterosexual people feel perfectly free to do (Huston and Schwartz 1995; Carl 1997; Shackelford and Buss 1997).

[...]

Some theories see love as a relatively unique emotion and they typologize its manifestations into different varieties that are broadly distinct from each other. Thus Lee (1973) and Hendrick and Hendrick (1993) identify [...] six basic types of love, ranging from self-sacrificing love of the kind shown by Christ and Gandhi to the passionate/romantic/erotic love shown by almost everyone else. [...] some theories [...] create structural hierarchies by mixing other variables, like commitment, passion and intimacy, each of which is itself a different thing from love, but which can be mixed together with the others in order to create different forms of love (Barnes and Sternberg 1997). [...]

Zeifman and Hazan (1997) have recently reviewed the research suggesting that adult styles of loving may be similar to those noted by workers on childhood attachment. Ainsworth et al. (1978), working with children, proposed that there are three styles of attachment and many researchers have used these as their guide: *secure attachment* and loving are characterized by confidence and security in intimacy, while *avoidant attachment* and the avoidant style of loving are characterized by lack of acceptance of others, avoidance of closeness and discomfort with intimacy. The final style, *anxious/ambivalent attachment* and the anxious/ambivalent style of loving, are characterized by dependency and a certain amount of insecurity coupled with feelings of lack of appreciation. A fourth style suggested by Bartholomew (1990) is a result of differentiating avoidance of intimacy into two: a *fearful style* that is characterized by a conscious desire for social contact which is inhibited by fear of its consequences; and a *dismissive style* that is characterized by a defensive denial of the need or desire for social contact. Fuendeling (1998) indicates that such styles of loving are indeed associated with particular styles of regulating or responding to affect and emotion. [...]

[...] In the work on courtship that has preceded the recent work on the nature and description of love, theories about its nature are often undeveloped or implicit, and they broadly assume that we know what it is and that it promotes satisfaction and development in courtship. Adopting such an approach either explicitly or implicitly, much early research was devoted to the discovery of static or global factors that predicted love and assumed that this led more or less directly to courtship progress or marital success. Among a [...] predictable list of such factors are [...] the matching of partners' characteristics; the partners' demographic origin or background; and their personality characteristics, specifically the influence of partner similarities or individual differences that pre-existed the courtship.

[...]

Early research therefore proposed essentially that the specific stimuli or characteristics of persons best predicted the progress of courtship or were the best correlates of ultimate stability and satisfaction in marriage. The question addressed by such research was: what sorts of people get into the most stable and happy relationships? The old answers tended to refer to religion, economic background, race, age, intelligence, and so on (Levinger 1965). It was repeatedly found, for instance, that couples who married young were likely to experience instability in marriage and had a higher risk of divorce [...].

More recent researchers have explored different sorts of stable relationships. For example, Cunningham and Antill (1995) have examined POSSLQs (People of Opposite Sex Sharing Living Quarters), the new term for cohabitation, a growing and widely occurring form of relationship. However as Cunningham and Antill (1995: 150) note: 'We know far more about the demographics and attitudes of those who cohabit than about the ways they weave their lives together, define the meaning of their relationships and, in general, go about the business of enacting connection.' Younger people are more likely to cohabit than are older people; the experience of parental divorce increases the likelihood of a person cohabiting; and women (but not men) who cohabit are more likely to divorce. There is also a disturbing tendency for increased violence in cohabiting relationships (West 1995). Cohabitors are likely to score lower on romanticism scales, but also are now much more likely to marry eventually, whereas 20 years ago cohabitors tended to be people with attitudes opposed to marriage and to score higher in measures of unconventionality (Cunningham and Antill 1995).

In tandem with studies about partners' demographic characteristics, past experiences and habits, researchers have looked at other global personal characteristics, such as personality factors, as predictors not only of original choice but also of 'success' in the eventual relationship (Notarius 1996; Sher 1996). These reviews indicated that the psychologically distressed, the neurotic, the highly ambitious individual and the person with a rigid defensive style were likely to be 'unsuccessful' in marriage, whether that meant a higher likelihood of divorce or merely higher levels of conflict (Gottman 1994). Notarius (1996), however, indicated that the skills of relating – the words, thoughts, emotions, and their management – are better predictors of specific outcomes of stable relationships than are demographic or other personal characteristics of the individual partners. [...]

How 'courtship' grows: some basic views

[...] the present chapter focuses [...] on the ways in which the partners *manage* the dating and the courtship process. Such management depends not only on the characteristics of individuals, the ways in which a culture predisposes couples to approach the enterprise, and the pathways or landmarks that it expects them to follow or pass, but also on the specific ways in which couples manage conflict, triumph, and disaster (Klein and Johnson 1997) and the manner in which they deal with other practical issues like the balance between the relationship and other life-concerns such as career (Crouter and Helms-Erickson 1997).

Conflict in courtship used to be regarded as a problem, [...] and the researcher's job was conceived as directed to finding ways of reducing it (e.g., Haley 1964). [...] Since conflict was regarded as an indication of instability in a relationship, its frequency was often used as a barometer of the relationship's stability or progress (Haley 1964). By contrast, Lloyd and Cate (1985) showed that some conflicts had beneficial effects on relationships. For example, when couples argued not about 'personal stuff' but about the ways in which to carry out the roles of partnership, their arguments led, as often as not, to a compromise or to a good resolution of the issue that then led to a smoother, more agreeable and more satisfactory conducting of the relationship. [...] A large part of 'making a relationship work' is precisely the practical joint construction of a shared experience and routine (Duck 1994). Thus not all conflict will hinder a relationship: some sorts of conflict promote relational growth by being a major part of the process of relationship creation. [...]

By contrast, researchers looked at intimacy and assumed that it underlay successful relationships; the intimate feelings of men and women were assumed to be not only comparable but probably identical as far as scientific scrutiny was concerned, a view now cast into some doubt (e.g., Wood 1993). Only recently have new approaches to intimacy and distance begun to uncover sex differences and similarities in intimacy (Canary and Emmers-Sommer 1997) and it is clear that the progress of a courtship is affected by the degree to which the two individuals differ in their conceptualization and operationalization of intimacy. Instead of being a simple independent variable that operates on the dependent variable of courtship growth, intimacy is itself influenced by courtship progress and has complex interconnections with courtship development, courtship outcomes and subsequent marital 'success or failure' (Crohan 1996; Veroff et al. 1997).

Such research also assumed that one marriage was much like another and therefore that 'a marriage' was essentially the same kind of institution and the same kind of experience for everyone [...] On this view [...] there is a right way to do it and other ways are wrong, inexpert, or misguided (Prusank et al. 1993). Even that view, however, tacitly assumes that satisfaction with a courtship is not based simply on love, since couples will be able to compare themselves to the social ideal and could judge their satisfaction and success partly in terms of fulfilment of that ideal (Simmel 1950) or in terms of peer pressure [...]. Such views are fostered by very extensive literatures about romance, not only popular magazines, but also the very widespread romance novels available in supermarkets (Sterk 1986).

An alternative early idea was proposed by Murstein (1971, 1976, 1977) in an approach known as S-V-R theory (for stimulus-value-role). The notion here is that at first couples are influenced by one another's stimulus features (looks, for example) but subsequently concern themselves with the match between their values, attitudes, and so on. Finally, the important feature that concerns them is the role behaviour that they perform: for instance, whether their respective performances of the role of husband and wife complement one another sufficiently to make a satisfactory working unit for the total relationship. [...]

Clearly, some of the pioneering explorations of relationship development both answered some questions and raised other, more difficult, ones for future researchers to explore. Such work helped to uncover the difficulties with the belief that courtship success was determined by the two partners' attributes at the outset of the relationship, and that successful courtship is conflict-free [...].

Is 'courtship' any different from any other relationship?

If we look at a courtship as a process and as a *practical* issue rather than as a *state* of relationship or as a *type* of relationship, we can see that it has many parts and we can consider the research in that light – just as we can examine our own assumptions in the light of that new way of seeing things. First, courting or even long-term dating couples have special feelings for one another but only one part of the relationship involves that set of emotions. Courtship and marriage are probably the only types of voluntary relationship that have an exclusivity about them: part of the whole business of courtship is the cutting off of other sexual relationships and the devotion of oneself to a specific partner. Naturally, that fact has several important implications but also important to bear in mind is that as a couple develops increased closeness in relationships so, too, is it also trying out a new *way of life*, with which its other aspects of life must be fitted or accommodated.

Courtship typically takes place particularly at one period in the life cycle. Typically, courtship partners are aged between approximately 16 and 26. [...] It is not just that one has feelings of love for a courtship partner, then, but that one is also aware of the appropriateness of the time to express and execute those feelings. Courtship takes place in a period which is known to last until a certain time of life after which the opportunity for courtship diminishes, as people see their 'marketability' for a first marriage or long-term partnership decreasing dramatically with increasing age. Often this makes partners think very carefully about such questions as 'Is this my last chance?' or 'Should I commit myself just now when other, more suitable partners may come along? I'm still young yet...'. It may be too early to get married to someone you love and have known for a year if you both still happen to be 20, but you might feel that the time is just right if you are both 25, even if the loving feelings are of the same strength in both cases. If courtship were about love and nothing else, these issues would not strike people as forcefully as they often do.

The importance of this point is accentuated by the special nature of courtship as a testing relationship *en route* to a known goal (long-term partnership) which allows partners greater leeway to end the courtship if it gets into trouble. When a friendship gets into trouble, the partners may just let things lie fallow for a while; by contrast, partners in a courtship will rarely be content merely to ignore or set aside troubles, problems or dissatisfactions with their relationships. Once they suspect that their relationship is not working they will probably at least talk about that (Acitelli 1988) and they may decide to end the relationship. Marriage is intended to be an exclusive relationship that lasts for life and the purpose of courtship is to test out a future marriage. Thus, if a courtship seems to be working enjoyably, one stays in it, yet if it does not work, one leaves in order to have a better chance to find a more congenial one. [...]

Courtship and others' expectations

Another point about courtship has to do with the organization of the relationship (McCall 1988). Courtship, being a kind of recognizable relationship with a known social form and known expectancies [...], has a certain predictability not only for the partners themselves but also for parents and friends. Once one partner has been introduced to the other partner's parents and friends he or she becomes enmeshed in the social network and its own characteristic set of expectancies about the relationship.

[...] Furthermore, such social influences can take the control of the relationship out of the hands of the partners themselves and some actions in a relationship may be deferred [...] because of the fear that people other than the partner may find out, disapprove, or be upset. For instance, friends or parents may get angry or may disapprove if the unmarried courting partners enter obviously into a sexual relationship and, for example, want to sleep in the same bedroom when they stay at the parents' home. Equally, couples may be influenced by social networks to expect certain activities in their relationship. [...] such influences can affect even the existence of the relationship as well as the behaviour in it; on the one hand is the claim of a 'Romeo and Juliet effect' that may occur in relationships where parents disapprove (Driscoll et al. 1972): i.e., couples may pull closer together in the face of parental opposition to the relationship [...]. Other authors are more qualified and claim that, whatever the immediate response, the ultimate result is that parental opposition (or very strong opposition from friends) is more likely to predict the break-up of the relationship (Parks and Eggert 1991). One thing that is certain is that the approval of other people is important and 'noticeable': whether we are eventually swayed by it or not, we cannot ignore it very easily. Indeed, Burger and Milardo (1995), who studied 25 wives and their husbands [...] indicated that couples who are well integrated in their networks are also more stable as a couple.

The relational context provided by religious background can also be relevant here since, for instance, Catholics may progress more slowly in courtship or may stay in unhappy marriages for longer periods of time because of their religious convictions and the influence of these upon their beliefs about the conduct of relationships. [...] couples may get into greater conflicts with one another because of differences in their religious beliefs about the sexual components of courtship and how those aspects should be managed (Cunningham and Antill, 1995).

Organization of the relationship is also done with reference to cultural prescriptions [...]. Being in a known type of relationship for which strong social expectations exist, couples can, therefore, evaluate their progress towards normality and the approved endpoint or style of relationship (Fitzpatrick and Badzinski 1985). [...] Part of the process of courtship furthermore involves the partners becoming attached to the socially defined role of 'being a couple', as well as coming to love the partner (Cate and Lloyd 1992). It takes a considerable amount of effort and accommodation for couples to work out the difficulties of becoming a couple that shares living space, develops routines for doing chores, accommodates one another's needs for privacy and for intimacy, and deals with the requirements of managing sexual interaction (Herold et al. 1998; O'Sullivan and Gaines 1998). [...]

Other aspects of courtship: [...] sex (and possibly violence)

Courtship is different from friendship because it raises the issue of sexuality. Couples who fall in love may feel sexual needs that have to be dealt with in a way that satisfies them, yet does not upset outside observers. While promiscuity is tolerated in some societies, most have restrictive rules about sexual interaction. Persons or couples are not free to decide for themselves the limits of their sexual conduct and habits but are expected to abide by the formal rules of the society. [...] The norms about relationship conduct are not always formalized, however, and are often embodied in 'social pressure' from peers or parents, even in the form of gossip that can make a person's position awkward and thereby bring them back into line (Bergmann, 1993). [...]

[...] During courtship, obviously, the management of sexual behaviour is an increasingly significant aspect of the relationship. Christopher and Cate (1985) explored the different pathways to sexual intimacy taken by couples moving from first date through casual dating to considering becoming an exclusive couple to actually becoming one. Couples who pass rapidly through the progression (and who may even have sexual intercourse on their first date) experience not only greater feelings of love for one another but also much higher rates of conflict. For couples who move more slowly up the sexual intimacy scale, the increases in intimacy are also associated with increases in conflict, and it seems quite clear that intimacy and conflict go hand in hand in many ways.

Dating violence

As dating intimacy increases so too does violence between partners, as if the positive and negative elements in the relationship are jointly increased. In the case of married couples rather than dates, Kenrick and Trost (1997) suggest that violence occurs when it is in the reproductive interest of the involved persons – husbands who kill their wives most usually do so from jealous concern over reproductive rights whereas women who kill their husbands most often do so to protect themselves and their children. Accordingly Kenrick and Trost note that dating violence is less severe but more prevalent than spousal homicide. Although some studies (e.g., Makepeace 1981; Cate et al. 1982) report a figure around 20 per cent, Deal and Wampler (1986) report results of a survey showing that 47 per cent of individuals had experience of violence in a dating relationship at some point – the majority of such cases being reciprocal, with both partners being violent at the same time. We should be curious about why the figures disagree – and why disagreements are constantly noted and reported by reviewers (e.g., Cate and Lloyd 1992). Clearly there are some problems about the status of respondents' reports – not everyone wants to admit to perpetrating violence or being the victim of it – but there are also different definitions of it, some of it being 'symbolic' (such as threatening to hit or hurt someone, but without any real intention to carry out the threat). Not everyone who threatens violence actually does carry out the threat or even means the threat seriously or literally, as parents of young children often exemplify: the threat of punishment itself is often enough to induce obedience. Given such problems, still unresolved in this complex literature, it is interesting that Deal and Wampler's (1986) figures for non-reciprocal violence indicate that it was the male partner who was three times as likely to report being the victim, a finding very similar to that reported by Rosen and Stith (1995). There are various ways of interpreting this finding, one being that men and women differ in their expectations of being on the receiving end of violence and report only those cases where these expectations are exceeded. Another interpretation is that men, for some reason, feel more secure about admitting to being on the receiving end of violence. A third is that men regard more minor experiences as 'violence'. Fourthly, there could be a 'gendering effect', with female assertiveness being interpreted by a male partner as aggressive or violent, whereas the same behaviour in a man is perceived 'merely' as an expression of male assertiveness. A fifth possibility is that females do resort to physical violence when frustrated, because they have had fewer opportunities to engage in other, non-violent, forms of assertive display.

On a related theme, Marshall and Rose (1987) found that some 74 per cent of couples report having expressed violence at some point while somewhere around 60 per cent had received violence at some point in an adult relationship. [...] Obviously these figures imply that violence is very common and a question we need to explore in future is whether the experience of violence is especially associated with certain points in a relationship or with particular styles of relationship management or certain types of partners. [...]

Organization of the relationship

Given all that is going on in the background, it is clear that courtships are not simply about the development of feelings for one another, even if that were a simple thing in itself. We should instead ask what it is that develops in courtship on the basis of all these expectations, attitudes, and differences in perspective. Researchers are now increasingly taking the view that what really happens is that people get themselves sorted out as a functioning couple (Veroff et al. 1997), although this is also accompanied by some important reorganization of thought, attribution, and cognitive schemas (Fletcher and Fitness 1993) as well as changes in the form of intimacy (Prager and Buhrmester 1998). As we explore courtship as an interpersonal process that is placed within a network context (Milardo and Allan 1997), and a set of other issues to do with work and everyday life in general (Chan and Margolin 1994), so it becomes clear that a major part of the process of courtship deals with the creation and organization of activities in the relationship, and such socially informative issues as whether the woman will change her surname on marriage (Kline et al. 1996). A considerable part of courtship involves the sharing of time together and, of course, the couple has to work out the means of achieving this for themselves. Huston et al. (1981) gathered recollections of courtship in 50 couples who were in a first marriage of 10 months' duration or less. The couples drew graphs to indicate changes in the likelihood that they would marry as they reviewed the period before they eventually did marry. After completing such a graph the subjects also filled out an activity checklist in respect of activities such as leisure, instrumental activity (such as shopping), and affectional activity. The research showed that courtship breaks down into four major types which differ not only in the speed with which the couple decides to get married but also in terms of their distribution of activity. Accelerated–arrested couples begin with a high level of confidence in the probability of marriage and then slow down their final progression to marital commitment. However, such couples are closely tied to one another emotionally and affectionally. They also spend most of their leisure time together and they typically segregate tasks and chores into those performed by the man and those performed by the woman. Accelerated couples start off somewhat more slowly but follow a steady track towards eventual marriage. They are typically the most close couples emotionally and also share many instrumental activities. Intermediate couples evolve slowly but steadily and do not really experience much turbulence or difficulty until the very end of the whole process. They are rather disaffiliated from one another, having weaker emotional and affectional ties; they spend considerable time alone, do not act particularly affectionately with one another and are quite separate and segregated in their performance of instrumental tasks. Prolonged couples are turbulent and difficult most of the time and their progress to eventual marriage is slow. Like the intermediate couples, they are quite unbonded affectionally, do not spend a lot of leisure time together, and typically segregate their roles in performing instrumental tasks.

So what is going on in these different courtships? In the longer ones the distinguishing feature is that the couple spends less time on joint activities and may not express strong feelings for one another consistently, either. The main point, however, is that there is an important integration between the development of feeling and the creation of joint patterns of activity for the spending of leisure time together.

[...]

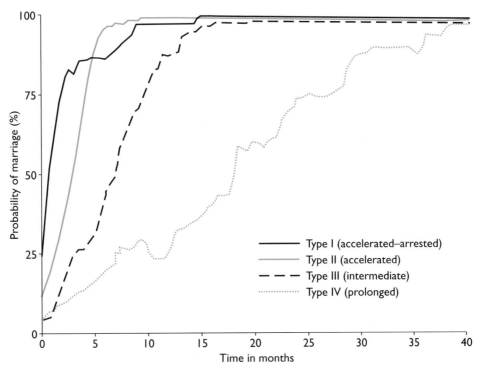

Figure 1   Average trajectories to marriage for relationship types
                (Source: Huston et al. in Duck and Gilmour (eds) 1981, p. 67)

References

Acitelli, L.K. (1988) 'When spouses talk to each other about their relationship', *Journal of Social and Personal Relationships*, vol. 5, pp. 185–99.

Ainsworth, M.D.S., Blehar, M.C., Waters, E. and Wall, S. (1978) *Patterns of Attachment: A Psychological Study of the Strange Situation*, Hillsdale, NJ, Erlbaum.

Barnes, M.L. and Sternberg, R.J. (1997) 'A hierarchical model of love and its prediction of satisfaction in close relationships' in Sternberg, R.J. and Hojjat, M. (eds) *Satisfaction in Close Relationships*, New York, Guilford.

Bartholomew, K. (1990) 'Avoidance of intimacy: an attachment perspective', *Journal of Social and Personal Relationships*, vol. 7, pp. 147–78.

Beall, A. and Sternberg, R. (1995) 'The social construction of love', *Journal of Social and Personal Relationships*, vol. 12, pp. 417–38.

Bergmann, J.R. (1993) *Discreet Indiscretions: The Social Organization of Gossip*, New York, Aldine de Gruyter.

Braithwaite, D.O. and Baxter, L.A. (1995) '"I do" again: the relational dialectics of renewing marriage vows', *Journal of Social and Personal Relationships*, vol. 12, pp. 177–98.

Burger, E. and Milardo, R.M. (1995) 'Marital interdependence and social networks', *Journal of Social and Personal Relationships*, vol. 12, pp. 403–15.

Canary, D.J. and Emmers-Sommer, T. (1997) *Sex and Gender Differences in Personal Relationships*, New York, Guilford.

Carl, W.J. (1997) 'Relationship gumbo: understanding *bricolage* and the creation of personal relationships as a definitional process', paper presented to the Annual

Convention of the International Network on Personal Relationships, Oxford University, Ohio, June 1997.

Cate, R.M., Henton, J., Koval, J., Christopher, F.S. and Lloyd, S.A. (1982) 'Premarital abuse: a social psychological perspective', *Journal of Family Issues*, vol. 3, pp. 79–90.

Cate, R.M. and Lloyd, S.A. (1992) *Courtship*, Newbury Park, Sage.

Chan, C.J. and Margolin, G. (1994) 'The relationship between dual-earner couples' daily work mood and home affect', *Journal of Social and Personal Relationships*, vol. 11, pp. 573–86.

Christopher, F.S. and Cate, R.M. (1985) 'Premarital sexual pathways and relationship development', *Journal of Social and Personal Relationships*, vol. 2, pp. 271–88.

Coleman, M. and Ganong, L.H. (1995) 'Family reconfiguration following divorce' in Duck and Wood (eds) (1995).

Crohan, S.E. (1996) 'Marital quality and conflict across the transition to parenthood in African American and White Couples', *Journal of Marriage and the Family*, vol. 58, pp. 933–44.

Crouter, A.C. and Helms-Erickson, H. (1997) 'Work and family from a dyadic perspective: variations in inequality' in Duck et al. (1997).

Cunningham, J.D. and Antill, J.K. (1995) 'Current trends in nonmarital cohabitation: in search of the POSSLQ' in Wood and Duck (eds) (1995).

Deal, J. and Wampler, K.S. (1986) 'Dating violence: the primacy of previous experience', *Journal of Social and Personal Relationships*, vol. 3, pp. 457–71.

Driscoll, R., Davies, K.E. and Lipetz, M.E. (1972) 'Parental interference and romantic love: the Romeo and Juliet effect', *Journal of Personality and Social Psychology*, vol. 24, pp. 1–10.

Duck, S.W. (1994) *Meaningful Relationships: Talking, Sense, and Relating*, Thousand Oaks, Sage.

Duck, S.W. (ed.) with Dindia, K., Ickes, W., Milardo, R.M., Mills, R.S.L. and Sarason, B. (1997) *Handbook of Personal Relationships* (2nd edn), Chichester, Wiley.

Duck, S.W. and Gilmour, R. (eds) (1981) *Personal Relationships 2: Developing Personal Relationships*, London, Academic Press.

Duck, S.W. and Wood, J.T. (eds) (1995) *Understanding Relationship Process 5: Confronting Relationship Challenges*, Thousand Oaks, Sage.

Fitzpatrick, M.A. and Badzinski, D. (1985) 'All in the family' in Miller, G.R. and Knapp, M. L. (eds) *Handbook of Interpersonal Communication*, Beverly Hills, CA, Sage.

Fletcher, G.J.O. and Fitness, J. (1993) 'Knowledge structures and explanations in intimate relationships' in Duck, S.W. (ed.) *Understanding Relationship Processes 1: Individuals in Relationships*, Newbury Park, Sage.

Fuendeling, J.M. (1998) 'Affect regulation as a stylistic process within adult attachment', *Journal of Social and Personal Relationships*, vol. 15, pp. 291–322.

Gottman, J.M. (1994) *What Predicts Divorce?* Hillsdale, NJ, Erlbaum.

Haley, J. (1964) 'Research on family patterns: an instrument measurement', *Family Process*, vol. 3, pp. 41–65.

Hendrick, S.S. and Hendrick, C. (1993) 'Lovers as friends', *Journal of Social and Personal Relationships*, vol. 10, pp. 459–66.

Herold, E.S., Maticka-Tyndale, E. and Mewhinney, D. (1998) 'Predicting intentions to engage in casual sex', *Journal of Social and Personal Relationships*, vol. 15, pp. 502–16.

Huston, M. and Schwartz, P. (1995) 'Lesbian and gay male relationships' in Wood and Duck (eds) (1995).

Huston, T.L., Surra, C.A., Fitzgerald, N.M. and Cate, R.M. (1981) 'From courtship to marriage: mate selection as an interpersonal process' in Duck and Gilmore (eds) (1981).

Kenrick, D.T. and Trost, M.R. (1997) 'Evolutionary approaches to relationships' in Duck et al. (1997).

Klein, R. and Johnson, M. (1997) 'Strategies of couple conflict' in Duck et al. (1997).

Kline, S.L., Stafford, L. and Miklosovic, J.L. (1996) 'Women's surnames: decisions, interpretations and associations with relational qualities', *Journal of Social and Personal Relationships*, vol. 13, pp. 593–617.

Kurdek, L. (1991) 'The dissolution of gay and lesbian relationships', *Journal of Social and Personal Relationships*, vol. 8, pp. 265–78.

Kurdek, L.A. (1992) 'Relationship stability and relationship satisfaction in cohabiting gay and lesbian couples: a prospective longitudinal test of the contextual and interdependence models', *Journal of Social and Personal Relationships*, vol. 9, pp. 125–42.

Lee, J.A. (1973) *The Colours of Love: An Exploration of the Ways of Loving*, Ontario, New Press.

Levinger, G. (1965) 'Marital cohesiveness and dissolution: an integrative review', *Journal of Marriage and the Family*, vol. 27, pp. 19–28.

Lloyd, S.A. and Cate, R.M. (1985) 'The developmental course of conflict in dissolution of premarital relationships', *Journal of Social and Personal Relationships*, vol. 2, pp. 179–94.

McCall, G.J. (1988) 'The organizational life cycle of relationships' in Duck et al. (1997).

Makepeace, J.M. (1981) 'Courtship violence among college students', *Family Relations*, vol. 30, pp. 97–102.

Marshall, L. and Rose, P. (1987) 'Gender stress and violence in the adult relationships of a sample of college students', *Journal of Social and Personal Relationships*, vol. 4, pp. 299–316.

Milardo, R.M. and Allan, G.A. (1997) 'Social networks and marital relationships' in Duck et al. (1997).

Murstein, B.I. (1971) 'Critique of models of dyadic attraction' in Murstein, B.I. (ed.) *Theories of Attraction and Love*, New York, Springer.

Murstein, B.I. (1976) *Who Will Marry Whom?*, New York, Springer.

Murstein, B.I. (1977) 'The Stimulus–Value–Role (SVR) theory of dyadic relationships' in Duck, S.W. (ed.) *Theory and Practice in Interpersonal Attraction*, London, Academic Press.

Notarius, C. (1996) 'Marriage: will I be happy or sad?' in Vanzetti, N. and Duck, S.W. (eds) *A Lifetime of Relationships*, Pacific Grove, CA, Brooks Cole.

O'Sullivan, L.F. and Gaines, M.E. (1998) 'Decision making in college students' heterosexual dating relationships: ambivalence about engaging in sexual activity', *Journal of Social and Personal Relationships*, vol. 15, pp. 347–64.

Parks, M.R. and Eggert, L.L. (1991) 'The role of social context in the dynamics of personal relationships' in Jones, W.H. and Perlman, D. (eds) *Advances in Personal Relationships*, vol. 1, London, Jessica Kingsley.

Prager, K.J. and Buhrmester, D. (1998) 'Intimacy and need fulfilment in couple relationships', *Journal of Social and Personal Relationships*, vol. 15, pp. 435–69.

Prusank, D., Duran, R. and Delillo, D.A. (1993) 'Interpersonal relationships in women's magazines: dating and relating in the 1970s and 1980s', *Journal of Social and Personal Relationships*, vol. 10, pp. 307–20.

Rosen, K.H. and Stith, S.M. (1995) 'Women terminating abusive dating relationships: a qualitative study', *Journal of Social and Personal Relationships*, vol. 12, pp. 155–60.

Shackelford, T.K. and Buss, D.M. (1997) 'Anticipation of marital dissolution as a consequence of spousal infidelity', *Journal of Social and Personal Relationships*, vol. 14, pp. 793–808.

Sher, T.G. (1996) 'Courtship and marriage: choosing a primary relationship' in Vanzetti, N. and Duck, S.W. (eds) *A Lifetime of Relationships*, Pacific Grove, Brooks/Cole.

Simmel, G. (1950) *The Sociology of Georg Simmel* (trans. K. Wolff), New York, Free Press.

Sterk, H. (1986) 'Functioning fictions: the adjustment rhetoric of Silhouette romance novels', unpublished PhD thesis, University of Iowa.

Umberson, D. and Terling, T. (1997) 'The symbolic meaning of relationships: implications for psychological distress following relationship loss', *Journal of Social and Personal Relationships*, vol. 14, pp. 723–44.

Veroff, J., Young, A.M. and Coon, H.M. (1997) 'The early years of marriage' in Duck et al. (1997).

West, J. (1995) 'Understanding how the dynamics of ideology influence violence between intimates' in Duck and Wood (eds) (1995).

Wood, J.T. (1993) 'Engendered relationships: interaction, caring, power, and responsibility in intimacy' in Duck, S.W. (ed.) *Understanding Relationship Processes 3: Social Contexts of Relationships*, Newbury Park, Sage.

Wood, J.T. and Duck, S.W. (eds) (1995) *Understanding Relationship Processes 6: Under-studied Relationships: Off the Beaten Track*, Thousand Oaks, Sage.

Zeifman, D. and Hazan, C. (1997) 'A process model of adult attachment formation' in Duck et al. (1997).

(Duck, 1999, pp. 57–72)

Commentary

One of the hallmarks of Duck's work is his avowed commitment to *interdisciplinarity* (Duck, 1999, pp. xi–xii). He recognises that explaining personal relationships necessarily leads us beyond the confines of the discipline of psychology, as traditionally conceived. He sees an interdisciplinary approach as necessary because the issues involved are too complex to be confined within the boundaries of any single discipline. As a result, he advocates cooperation between experts from such diverse disciplines as social psychology and sociology, developmental psychology, communication studies, and family studies, and recognises too that clinical and community psychology have an important contribution to make. His influential *Handbook of Personal Relationships* (Duck, 1997 [1988]) has sections devoted to these different disciplines, but the overriding framework is social psychology. Reading 2.1, taken from *Relating to Others* (Duck, 1999), introduces personal relationships as a field of study in its own right. It offers a perspective based on the historical development of the area from its early roots in social psychology to the broader interdisciplinary study that it is fast becoming.

A second notable feature of Duck's work is his desire to study relationships as they happen in everyday life. He is wary of placing too much emphasis on the results of traditional controlled experiments and laboratory-based studies which, although they have their place in psychological research, necessarily have limitations for understanding relationship processes in the real world. The third significant feature of Duck's approach is to highlight the ways in which personal relationships have both precursors and consequences that go beyond the relationships themselves. For example, relationships both depend on and influence self-presentation, identity management and meaning construction (see, for example, the essays in Duck, 1997).

Finally, Duck does believe that there are some general principles that operate in social and personal relationships, and that it is possible to uncover those by systematic research. He is interested in the nature of interpersonal behaviour face to face, the individual and social forces that affect communication in social interaction, and the thoughts, feelings and actions that make up the process of relating to others. At the same time, he recognises that relationships do not occur in a vacuum, but that they are positioned in broader social, cultural, economic and political contexts which fashion them in different ways.

Reading 2.2 (from Chodorow, 1999 [1978]) presents a significant contrast to the approach of the first reading. Unlike quantitative social psychology, psychoanalysis is not an objective science that seeks, through empirical means, to uncover relationships between quantifiable variables. Instead, it is an interpretive enterprise, concerned primarily with human experience, the stories that people tell about their lives, and the (sometimes contradictory) layers of meaning that underlie our perceptions and motivations (Henriques et al., 1988; Hollway and Jefferson, 2000a, 2000b). If mainstream psychology is interested in what we can systematically observe – and measure – about relationships, the psychoanalytic approach proceeds from a theory that postulates unobservables – specifically unconscious processes – as powerful, though hidden, influences on our behaviour and relationships. The unconscious is a complex concept, and is not susceptible to the kinds of 'measurement' that mainstream psychology most often uses.

Because it departs so radically from psychology's traditional concerns with objectivity and quantification, psychoanalysis has not yet found its place within mainstream psychology. Indeed, it is fair to say that if psychoanalysis is a 'science' at all, it is certainly a disputed one, and one concerned with interpretations and meanings rather than measurements. For this reason, psychoanalytic theories are difficult, if not impossible, to either verify or falsify in the traditional ways. Moreover, psychoanalysis comprises several different theoretical strands, each with different emphases and premises. For example, a Freudian approach to intimacy would foreground the Oedipus complex; an object relations approach (derived from the work of Melanie Klein and Donald Winnicott) instead emphasises the significance of pre-Oedipal relationships (see, for example, Craib, 2001, Chapters 5 and 6; Minsky, 1996, Chapters 2, 3, 8 and 9). An approach based on the re-reading of Sigmund Freud by French psychoanalyst Jacques Lacan is informed by a concern with language and cultural symbols (Craib, 2001, Chapter 9; Minsky, 1996, Chapters 4 and 10). What these different theoretical frameworks have in common, however, are a recognition of the importance of unconscious processes, the significance of early relationships and a concern with the relationships between gender identities and capacities for intimacy.

The application of psychoanalytic theories to close relationships involves a recognition that the most important influences on human behaviour derive from unconscious processes to which we can have no direct access. The main aim of a psychoanalytic approach is to explore the multiple layers of meaning as they are embedded in our significant relationships from infancy onwards, exerting their influence on all our close relationships.

The second, 'critical', reading (Reading 2.2, from Chodorow, 1999 [1978]) represents an example of a psychoanalytic approach based on object relations theory which is a peculiarly British variant of psychoanalysis. It is taken from Nancy Chodorow's highly influential *The Reproduction of Mothering: Psychoanalysis and the Sociology of Gender.* Chodorow was not centrally concerned with close relationships in adulthood, but set out to explain the persistence of gendered inequalities in society. Her work, however, as you will see, has major implications for how we think about adult intimacy. Using object relations theory, she traces the social structural power relations of gender back to our relational experiences in earliest infancy and shows how they exert a determining influence on all our intimate relationships. She argues that, because it is women who mother, girls and boys each follow particular developmental trajectories towards adult femininities and masculinities and it is in this process that the psychological constellations underlying gendered inequalities are laid down. The most notable feature of Chodorow's approach is the centrality of gender.

ACTIVITY 2.2

As you read the following extract, consider these points:

- Think about whether the different insights that Chodorow offers could be applied to the approach used by Duck. Could they be used to enhance it? Or are there obstacles on both sides that would have to be overcome?

- What is the basis of Chodorow's argument that men and women cannot fulfil each other's relational needs? What do men want? What do women want?

Reading 2.2, taken from Nancy Chodorow's book *The Reproduction of Mothering*, is an example of a psychoanalytic approach to close relationships. This was chosen by *Contemporary Sociology* in 1999 as one of the ten most influential books of the last twenty-five years.

Chodorow, 'The psychodynamics of the family'

Oedipal asymmetries and heterosexual knots

[...] Because women mother, the development and meaning of heterosexual object-choice differ for men and women. The traditional psychoanalytic account of femininity and masculinity begins from this perception. [...]

According to psychoanalytic theory, heterosexual erotic orientation is a primary outcome of the oedipus complex for both sexes. Boys and girls differ in this, however. Boys retain one primary love object throughout their boyhood. For this reason, the development of masculine heterosexual object choice is relatively continuous (Deutsch, 1969 [1925]) [...]. In theory, a boy resolves his oedipus complex by repressing his attachment to his mother. He is therefore ready in adulthood to find a primary relationship with someone *like* his mother. When he does, the relationship is given meaning from its psychological reactivation of what was originally an intense and exclusive relationship – first an identity, then a 'dual-unity,' finally a two-person relationship.

Things are not so simple for girls [...] (Deutsch, 1969 [1925]). Because her first love object is a woman, a girl, in order to attain her proper heterosexual orientation, must transfer her primary object choice to her father and men. This creates asymmetry in the feminine and masculine oedipus complex, and difficulties in the development of female sexuality, given heterosexuality as a developmental goal.

For girls, just as for boys, mothers are primary love objects. As a result, the structural inner object setting of female heterosexuality differs from that of males. When a girl's father does become an important primary person, it is in the context of a bisexual relational triangle. A girl's relation to him is emotionally in reaction to, interwoven and competing for primacy with, her relation to her mother. A girl usually turns to her father as an object of primary interest from the exclusivity of the relationship to her mother, but this libidinal turning to her father does not substitute for her attachment to her mother. Instead, a girl retains her preoedipal tie to her mother (an intense tie involved with issues of primary identification, primary love, dependence, and separation) and builds oedipal attachments to both her mother and her father upon it. [...]

For girls, then, there is no absolute change of object, nor exclusive attachment to their fathers. Moreover, a father's behavior and family role, and a girl's relationship to him, are crucial to the development of heterosexual orientation in her. But fathers are comparatively unavailable physically and emotionally. They are not present as much and are not primary caretakers, and their own training for masculinity may have led them to deny emotionality. Because of the father's lack of availability to his daughter, and because of the intensity of the mother-daughter relationship in which she participates, girls tend not to make a total transfer of affection to their fathers but to remain also involved with their mothers, and to oscillate emotionally between mother and father.

The implications of this are twofold. First, the nature of the heterosexual relationship differs for boys and girls. Most women emerge from their oedipus complex oriented to their father and men as primary *erotic* objects, but it is clear that men tend to remain *emotionally* secondary, or at most emotionally equal, compared to the primacy and exclusivity of an oedipal boy's emotional tie to his mother and women. Second, because the father is an additional important love object, who becomes important in the context of a relational triangle, the feminine inner object world is more complex than the masculine. This internal situation continues into adulthood and affects adult women's participation in relationships. [...]

Because mother and father are not the same *kind* of parent, the nature and intensity of a child's relationship to them differ as does the relationship's degree of exclusiveness. Because children first experience the social and cognitive world as continuous with themselves and do not differentiate objects, their mother, as first caretaking figure, is not a separate person and has no separate interests. In addition, this lack of separateness is in the context of the infant's total dependence on its mother for physical and psychological survival.

The internalized experience of self in the original mother-relation remains seductive and frightening: Unity was bliss, yet meant the loss of self and absolute dependence. By contrast, a child has always differentiated itself from its father and known him as a separate person with separate interests. And the child has never been totally dependent on him. Her father has not posed the original narcissistic threat (the threat to basic ego integrity and boundaries) nor provided the original narcissistic unity (the original experience of oneness) to a girl. Oedipal love for the mother, then, contains both a threat to selfhood and a promise of primal unity which love for the father never does. A girl's love for her father and women's attachment to men reflect all aspects of these asymmetries.

Men cannot provide the kind of return to oneness that women can. Michael Balint argues that the return to the experience of primary love – the possibility of regressing to the infantile stage of a sense of oneness, no reality testing, and a tranquil sense of well-being in which all needs are satisfied – is a main goal of adult sexual relationships [...] (Balint, [1952a [1935]]). He implies though [...] that women can fulfill this need better than men, because a sexual relationship with a woman reproduces the early situation more completely and is more completely a return to the mother. Thus, males in coitus come nearest to the experience of refusion with the mother [...] (Balint, [1952b]).

Women's participation here is dual. (Balint is presuming women's heterosexuality.) First, a woman identifies with the man penetrating her and thus experiences through identification refusion with a woman (mother). Second, she *becomes* the mother (phylogenetically the all-embracing sea, ontogenetically the womb). Thus, a woman in a heterosexual relationship cannot, like a man, recapture as *herself* her own experience of merging. She can do so only by identifying with someone who can, on the one hand, and by identifying with the person with whom she was merged on the other. The 'regressive restitution' (Balint's term) which coitus brings, then, is not complete for a woman in the way that it is for a man.

Freud speaks to the way that women seek to recapture their relationship with their mother in heterosexual relationships (Freud, 1931). He suggests that as women 'change object' from mother to father, the mother remains their primary internal object, so that they often impose on their relation to their father, and later to men, the issues which preoccupy them in their internal relation to their mother. They look in relations to men for gratifications that they want from a woman. Freud points to the common clinical discovery of a woman who has apparently taken her father as a model for her choice of husband, but whose marriage in fact repeats the conflicts and feelings of her relationship with her mother. [...]

But children seek to escape from their mother as well as return to her. Fathers serve in part to break a daughter's primary unity with and dependence on her mother. For this and a number of other reasons, fathers and men are idealized (Chasseguet-Smirgel, 1964; Grunberger, 1970 [1964]). A girl's father provides a last ditch escape from maternal omnipotence, so a girl cannot risk driving him away. At the same time, occupying a position of distance and ideological authority in the family, a father may be a remote figure understood to a large extent through her mother's interpretation of his role. This makes the development of a relationship based on his real strengths and weaknesses difficult. Finally, the girl herself has not received the same kind of love from her mother as a boy has. Mothers experience daughters as one with themselves; their relationships to daughters are 'narcissistic,' while those with their sons are more 'anaclitic.'

Thus, a daughter looks to her father for a sense of separateness and for the same confirmation of her specialness that her brother receives from her mother. She (and the woman she becomes) is willing to deny her father's limitations (and those of her lover or husband) as long as she feels loved (Kephart, 1967; Rubin, 1970). She is more able to do this because his distance means that she does not really know him. [...]

[...] Since the girl's relationship to her father develops later, her sense of self is more firmly established. If oedipal and preoedipal issues are fused for her, this fusion is more likely to occur in relation to her mother, and not to her father. Because her sense of self is firmer, and because oedipal love for her father is not so threatening, a girl does not 'resolve' her oedipus complex to the same extent as a boy. This means that she grows up more concerned with both internalized and external object-relationships, while men tend to repress their oedipal needs for love and relationship. At the same time, men often become intolerant and disparaging of those who can express needs for love, as they attempt to deny their own needs (Chasseguet-Smirgel, 1964; Grunberger, 1970 [1964]).

Men defend themselves against the threat posed by love, but needs for love do not disappear through repression. Their training for masculinity and repression of affective relational needs, and their primarily nonemotional and impersonal relationships in the public world make deep primary relationships with other men hard to come by (Booth, 1972; Komarovsky, 1974). [...]

Women have not repressed affective needs. They still want love and narcissistic confirmation and may be willing to put up with limitations in their masculine lover or husband in exchange for evidence of caring and love. This can lead to the denial of more immediately felt aggressive and erotic drives. [...]

As a result of the social organization of parenting, then, men operate on two levels in women's psyche. On one level, they are emotionally secondary and not exclusively loved – are not primary love objects like mothers. On another, they are idealized and experienced as needed, but are unable either to express their own emotional needs or respond to those of women. [...]

This situation is illuminated by sociological and clinical findings. Conventional wisdom has it, and much of our everyday observation confirms, that women are the romantic ones in our society, the ones for whom love, marriage, and relationships matter. However, several studies point out that men love and fall in love romantically, women sensibly and rationally (Baum, 1971; Hochschild, 1975; Kephart, 1967; Rubin, 1975). Most of these studies argue that in the current situation, where women are economically dependent on men, women must make rational calculations for the provision of themselves and their (future) children. This view suggests that women's apparent romanticism is an emotional and ideological response to their very real economic dependence. On the societal level, especially given economic inequity, men are exceedingly important to women. The recent tendency for women to initiate divorce and separation more than men as income becomes more available to them (and as the feminist movement begins to remove the stigma of 'divorcee') further confirms this.

[...]

[...] Women have acquired a real capacity for rationality and distance in heterosexual relationships, qualities built into their earliest relationship with a man. Direct evidence for the psychological primacy of this latter stance comes from findings about the experience of loss itself. George Goethals reports the clinical finding that men's loss of at least the first adult relationship 'throws them into a turmoil and a depression of the most extreme kind' (1973, p. 96) [...] in which they withdraw and are unable to look elsewhere for new relationships. He implies, by contrast, that first adult loss may not result in as severe a depression for a woman, and claims that his women patients did not withdraw to the same extent and were more able to look elsewhere for new relationships. [...]

[...] My account stresses that women have a richer, ongoing inner world to fall back on, and that the men in their lives do not represent the intensity and exclusivity that women represent to men. Externally, they also retain and develop more relationships. It seems that, developmentally, men do not become as emotionally important to women as women do to men.

Because women care for children, then, heterosexual symbiosis has a different 'meaning' for men and women. Freud originally noted that 'a man's love and a woman's are a phase apart psychologically' (1933, p. 134). He and psychoanalytic thinkers after him point to ways in which women and men, though usually looking for intimacy with each other, do not fulfil each other's needs because of the social organization of parenting. Differences in female and male oedipal experiences, all growing out of women's mothering, create this situation. Girls enter adulthood with a complex layering of affective ties and a rich, ongoing inner object world. Boys have a simpler oedipal situation and more direct affective relationships, and this situation is repressed in a way that the girl's is not. The mother remains a primary internal object to the girl, so that heterosexual relationships are on the model of a nonexclusive, second relationship for her, whereas for the boy they recreate an exclusive, primary relationship.

As a result of being parented by a woman, both sexes look for a return to this emotional and physical union. A man achieves this directly through the heterosexual bond, which replicates the early mother-infant exclusivity. He is supported in this endeavor by women, who, through their own development, have remained open to relational needs, have retained an ongoing inner affective life, and have learned to deny the limitations of masculine lovers for both psychological and practical reasons.

Men both look for and fear exclusivity. Throughout their development, they have tended to repress their affective relational needs, and to develop ties based more on categorical and abstract role expectations, particularly with other males. They are likely to participate in an intimate heterosexual relationship with the ambivalence created by an intensity which one both wants and fears – demanding from women what men are at the same time afraid of receiving.

As a result of being parented by a woman and growing up heterosexual, women have different and more complex relational needs in which an exclusive relationship to a man is not enough. [...] In addition, the relation to the man itself has difficulties. Idealization, growing out of a girl's relation to her father, involves denial of real feelings and to a certain extent an unreal relationship to men. The contradictions in women's heterosexual relationships, though, are due as much to men's problems with intimacy as to outcomes of early childhood relationships. Men grow up rejecting their own needs for love, and therefore find it difficult and threatening to meet women's emotional needs. As a result, they collude in maintaining distance from women.

The cycle completed: mothers and children

Families create children gendered, heterosexual, and ready to marry. But families organized around women's mothering and male dominance create incompatibilities in women's and men's relational needs. In particular, relationships to men are unlikely to provide for women satisfaction of the relational needs that their mothering by women and the social organization of gender have produced. The less men participate in the domestic sphere, and especially in parenting, the more this will be the case.

Women try to fulfil their need to be loved, try to complete the relational triangle, and try to reexperience the sense of dual unity they had with their mother, which the heterosexual relationship tends to fulfil for men. This situation daily reinforces what women first experienced developmentally and intrapsychically in relation to men. While they are likely to become and remain erotically heterosexual, they are encouraged both by men's difficulties with love and by their own relational history with their mothers to look elsewhere for love and emotional gratification.

One way that women fulfil these needs is through the creation and maintenance of important personal relations with other women. Cross-culturally, segregation by gender is the rule: Women tend to have closer personal ties with each other than men have, and to spend more time in the company of women than they do with men. In our society, there is some sociological evidence that women's friendships are affectively richer than men's (Booth, 1972). In other societies, and in most subcultures of our own, women remain involved with female relatives in adulthood (Booth, 1972; Bott, 1957; Gans, 1967; Komarovsky, 1962; Rosaldo and Lamphere, 1974; Stack, 1974; Young and Willmott, 1966 [1957]). [...]

However, deep affective relationships to women are hard to come by on a routine, daily, ongoing basis for many women. Lesbian relationships do tend to recreate mother-daughter emotions and connections (Deutsch, 1944; Rich, 1976; Wolff, 1971), but most women are heterosexual. This heterosexual preference and taboos against homosexuality, in addition to objective economic dependence on men, make the option of primary sexual bonds with other women unlikely – though more prevalent in recent years. In an earlier period, women tended to remain physically close to their own mother and sisters after marriage, and could find relationships with other women in their daily work and community. The development of industrial capitalism, however – and the increasingly physically isolated nuclear family it has produced – has made these primary relationships more rare and has turned women (and men) increasingly and exclusively to conjugal family relationships for emotional support and love (Young and Willmott, 1966 [1957]).

[...] Given the triangular situation and emotional asymmetry of her own parenting, a woman's relation to a man *requires* on the level of psychic structure a third person, since it was originally established in a triangle. A man's relation to women does not. His relation to his mother was originally established first as an identity, then as a dual unity, then as a two-person relationship, before his father ever entered the picture.

[...] On the level of psychic structure, [...] a child completes the relational triangle for a woman. Having a child, and experiencing her relation to a man in this context, enables her to reimpose intrapsychic relational structure on the social world, while at the same time resolving the generational component of her oedipus complex as she takes a new place in the triangle – a maternal place in relation to her own child.

[...]

[...] On a less conscious, object-relational level, having a child recreates the desired mother-child exclusivity for a woman and interrupts it for a man, just as the man's father intruded into his relation to his mother. Accordingly, as Benedek, Zilboorg, and Bakan suggest, men often feel extremely jealous toward children[1] (Benedek, 1949, 1959; Zilboorg, 1973 [1944]; Bakan, 1966). These differences hold also on the level of sexual and biological fantasy and symbolism. A woman, as I have suggested, cannot return to the mother in coitus as directly as can a man. Symbolically her identification with the man can help. However, a much more straightforward symbolic return occurs through her identification with the child who is in her womb [...] (Ferenczi, 1968 [1924]). The last act of this regression (return into the uterus) which the man accomplishes by the act of introjection in coitus, is realized by the woman in pregnancy in the complete identification between mother and child (Deutsch, 1969 [1925]).

For all these reasons, it seems psychologically logical to a woman to turn her marriage into a family, and to be more involved with these children (this child) than her husband. By doing so, she recreates for herself the exclusive intense primary unit which a heterosexual relationship tends to recreate for men. She recreates also her internalized asymmetrical relational triangle. [...]

This account indicates a larger structural issue regarding the way in which a woman's relation to her children recreates the psychic situation of the relationship to her mother. This relationship is recreated on two levels: most deeply and unconsciously, that of the primary mother-infant tie; and upon this, the relationship of the bisexual triangle. Because the primary mother-infant unit is exclusive, and because oscillation in the bisexual triangle includes a constant pull back to the mother attachment, there may be a psychological contradiction for a woman between interest in and commitment to children and that to men. Insofar as a woman experiences her relationship to her child on the level of intrapsychic structure as exclusive, her relationship to a man may therefore be superfluous.

[...]

On the level of the relational triangle [...] there can be a contradiction between women's interest in children and in men. This is evident in Freud's suggestion that women oscillate psychologically between a preoedipal and oedipal stance [...]. Deutsch points out that a man may or may not be psychologically necessary or desirable to the mother-child exclusivity. When she is oriented to the man, a woman's fantasy of having children is 'I want a child by him, *with him*'; when men are emotionally in the background, it is 'I want a *child*' (Deutsch, 1944).

Women come to want and need primary relationships to children. These wants and needs result from wanting intense primary relationships, which men tend not to provide both because of their place in women's oedipal constellation and because of their difficulties with intimacy. Women's desires for intense primary relationships tend not to be with other women, both because of internal and external taboos on homosexuality, and because of women's isolation from their primary female kin (especially mothers) and other women.

As they develop these wants and needs, women also develop the capacities for participating in parent-child relationships. They develop capacities for mothering. Because of the structural situation of parenting, women remain in a primary, preoedipal relationship with their mother longer than men. They do not feel the need to repress or cut off the capacity for experiencing the primary identification and primary love which are the basis of parental empathy. [...] The preoedipal relational stance, latent in women's normal relationship to the world and experience of self, is activated in their coming to care for an infant, encouraging their empathic identification with this infant which is the basis of maternal care.

Mothering, moreover, involves a double identification for women, both as mother *and* as child. The whole preoedipal relationship has been internalized and perpetuated in a more ongoing way for women than for men. Women take both parts in it. Women have capacities for primary identification with their child through regression to primary love and empathy. Through their mother identification, they have ego capacities and the sense of responsibility which go into caring for children. In addition, women have an investment in mothering in order to make reparation to their own mother (or to get back at her) (Klein, 1964 [1937]). [...]

Women develop capacities for mothering from their object-relational stance. This stance grows out of the special nature and length of their preoedipal relationship to their mother; the nonabsolute repression of oedipal relationships; and their general ongoing mother-daughter preoccupation as they are growing up. It also develops because they have not formed the same defenses against relationships as men. Related to this, they develop wants and needs to be mothers from their oedipal experience and the contradictions in heterosexual love that result.

The *wants and needs* which lead women to become mothers put them in situations where their mothering *capacities* can be expressed. At the same time, women remain in conflict with their internal mother and often their real mother as well. The preoccupation with issues of separation and primary identification, the ability to recall their early relationship to their mother – precisely those capacities which enable mothering – are also those which may lead to over-identification and pseudoempathy based on maternal projection rather than any real perception or understanding of their infant's needs. Similarly, the need for primary relationships becomes more prominent and weighted as relationships to other women become less possible and as father/husband absence grows. Though women come to mother, and to be mothers, the very capacities and commitments for mothering can be in contradiction one with the other and within themselves. Capacities which enable mothering are also precisely those which can make mothering problematic.

Gender personality and the reproduction of mothering

[...]

Institutionalized features of family structure and the social relations of reproduction reproduce themselves. A psychoanalytic investigation shows that women's mothering capacities and commitments, and the general psychological capacities and wants which are the basis of women's emotion work, are built developmentally into feminine personality. Because women are themselves mothered by women, they grow up with the relational capacities and needs, and psychological definition of self-in-relationship, which commits them to mothering. Men, because they are mothered by women, do not. Women mother daughters who, when they become women, mother.

Notes

1   This is not to deny the conflicts and resentments which women may feel about their children.

References

Bakan, D. (1966) *The Duality of Human Existence: Isolation and Communion in Western Man*, Boston, Beacon Press.

Bakan, D. (1968*) Disease, Pain and Sacrifice: Toward a Psychology of Suffering*, Boston, Beacon Press.

Balint, M. (1952a [1935]) 'Critical notes on the theory of the pregenital organizations of the libido' in Balint, M. (ed.) *Primary Love and Psycho-Analytic Technique,* London, Hogarth Press.

Balint, M. ([1952b]) 'Perversions and genitality' in Balint, M. (ed.) *Primary Love and Psycho-Analytic Technique*, London, Hogarth Press.

Baum, M. (1971) 'Love, marriage and the division of labor', *Sociological Inquiry*, vol. 41, no. 1, pp. 107–17.

Benedek, T. (1949) 'Psychosomatic implications of the primary unit, mother-child', *American Journal of Orthopsychiatry*, vol. 19, no. 4, pp. 642–54.

Benedek, T. (1959) 'Parenthood as a developmental phase: a contribution to the libido theory', *Journal of the American Psychoanalytic Association*, vol. 7, no. 3, pp. 389–417.

Booth, A. (1972) 'Sex and social participation', *American Sociological Review*, vol. 37, pp. 183–93.

Bott, E. (1957) *Family and Social Network: Roles, Norms and External Relationships in Ordinary Urban Families*, London, Tavistock Publications.

Chasseguet-Smirgel, J. (1964) 'Feminine guilt and the oedipus complex' in Chasseguet-Smirgel (ed.) (1970).

Chasseguet-Smirgel, J. (ed.) (1970) *Female Sexuality*, Ann Arbor, University of Michigan Press.

Deutsch, H. (1944, 1945) *Psychology of Women*, vols 1 and 2, New York, Grune & Stratton.

Deutsch, H. (1969 [1925]) 'The psychology of woman in relation to the functions of reproduction' in Fliess, R. (ed.) *The Psychoanalytic Reader: An Anthology of Essential Papers with Critical Introductions*, New York, International Universities Press.

Ferenczi, S. (1968 [1924]) *Thalassa: A Theory of Genitality*, New York, W.W. Norton.

Freud, S. (1931) *Female Sexuality*, Standard Edition, vol. 21, pp. 223–43.

Freud, S. (1933) *New Introductory Lectures on Psychoanalysis*, Standard Edition, vol. 22, pp. 3–182.

Gans, H. (1967) *The Levittowners*, New York, Vintage Books.

Goethals, G.W. (1973) 'Symbiosis and the life cycle', *British Journal of Medical Psychology*, vol. 46, pp. 91–6.

Grunberger, B. (1970 [1964]) 'Outline for a study of narcissism in female sexuality' in Chasseguet-Smirgel (ed.) (1970), pp. 68–83.

Hochschild, A.R. (1975) *Attending to, Codifying, and Managing Feelings: Sex Differences in Love*, paper presented to the American Sociological Association Meetings, San Francisco, 29 August.

Kephart, W.M. (1967) 'Some correlates of romantic love', *Journal of Marriage and the Family*, vol. 29, pp. 470–4.

Klein, M. (1964 [1937]) 'Love, guilt and reparation' in Klein, M. and Riciere, J. (eds) *Love, Hate and Reparation*, New York, W.W. Norton.

Komarovsky, M. (1967) *Blue-Collar Marriage*, New York, Vintage Books.

Komarovsky, M. (1974) 'Patterns of self-disclosure of male undergraduates', *Journal of Marriage and the Family*, vol. 36, no. 4, pp. 677–86.

Rich, A. (1976) *Of Woman Born: Motherhood as Experience and Institution*, New York, W. W. Norton.

Rosaldo, M.Z. and Lamphere, L. (eds) (1974) *Woman, Culture and Society*, Stanford, CA, Stanford University Press.

Rubin, G. (1975) 'The traffic in women: notes on the political economy of sex' in Reiter, R. (ed.) *Towards an Anthropology of Women*, New York, Monthly Review Press.

Rubin, Z. (1970) 'Measurement of romantic love', *Journal of Personality and Social Psychology*, vol. 6, pp. 265–73.

Stack, C.B. (1974) *All Our Kin*, New York, Harper and Row.

Wolff, C. (1971) *Love Between Women*, New York, Harper and Row.

Young, M. and Willmott, P. (1966 [1957]) *Family and Kinship in East London*, London, Penguin Books.

Zilboorg, G. (1973 [1944]) 'Masculine and feminine: some biological and cultural aspects' in Baker Miller, J. (ed.) *Psychoanalysis and Women*, New York, Penguin Books.

(Chodorow, 1999 [1978], pp. 191–209)

Conclusion

Chodorow tells us that our early relationships with significant others, particularly our parents, exert a determining influence on later relationships. This is because those early relationships continue to live on in our unconscious processes. In object relations theory (Hinshelwood, 1989, pp. 367–73; Laplanche and Pontalis, 1973, pp. 273–81), the psychological consequences of those early relationships are mediated by their internal representations – our 'object relations'. The fundamental insight of a psychoanalytic approach, and the basis of its critical potential, lies in its insistence that deep-set unconscious processes underlie all human activities, especially our intimate relationships.

Chodorow's work offers thus the possibility of a critical perspective on close relationships for four main reasons. First, it tells us that we cannot fully understand intimacy unless we are prepared to take on board the thorny issue of gender identities. Second, it challenges the individual/society dualism by showing how aspects of the social world take root in our internal worlds during development to become intra-psychic processes that are likely to operate, for good or ill, throughout our lives. Third, it challenges psychology's notion of the individual by highlighting the importance of the complex unconscious dynamics of subjectivity, processes that are brought into play in close relationships from the beginning of life. Finally, in this view, close relationships are much more than external relations between separately constituted individuals – they involve, instead, a kind of inter subjectivity, a meshing of the deepest needs, wishes and anxieties that have been repressed into the unconscious, a meeting of minds that has the potential fundamentally to change both participants.

Object relations theory departs from Freudian orthodoxy in its emphasis on the significance of pre-oedipal relationships. The emphasis is on the mental representations of our earliest significant relationships that we all carry around with us as psychological baggage throughout our lives. What is represented in unconscious fantasy is not the object (the significant person) itself, but a relationship between self and object, in which the object is invested with certain impulses relating to our drives as well as our perceptions of the responses of our significant others to those drives. Object relations theory talks about the ways in which significant others are taken into ourselves as internal objects and become fundamental parts of our unconscious selves.

The reason the pre-Oedipal period is so important in object relations theory is because it is the time of our earliest attachment (to the primary caregiver, most usually the mother) and it thus configures the particular way in which the subsequent Oedipus complex takes shape in our lives. Thus, Freud's emphasis on the ways in which the Oedipus complex inaugurates masculine and feminine development is mitigated, in object relations theory, by the identifications and attachments of the pre-Oedipal period. Thus the Oedipal crisis is not, as in Freud, simply about having or not having a penis (or, in Lacan (1977), the phallus), but marks instead the transition from a merged, narcissistic identity with the mother into a separate self. This is a process that involves a fundamental loss and, seen in this way, can cast the Freudian castration complex in rather a different light (Maguire, 1995; Mitchell, 1974; Wright, 1992, pp. 277–90).

Chodorow argues that males' and females' different psycho-sexual developmental experiences result in women developing a sense of self-in-relation while men acquire a sense of self that is less dependent on relationships and connection. She argues that chief among the outcomes of gendered development are the ways in which many women feel intuitively connected to others, and able to empathise, while many men assert independence and anxiety about intimacy if it signals dependence.

Chodorow gives an account of how women's (probably universal) responsibility for mothering creates asymmetrical relational capacities in males and females. As a result of being mothered by someone of the same gender, girls develop more fluid ego boundaries than boys and a sense of self that is continuous with (rather than separate from) others. This sense of self-in-relationship in turn underlies the desire to mother, and so the social organization of both gender and parenting are reproduced. By contrast, boys develop a sense of masculine self in opposition to the mother, through the establishment of more rigid ego boundaries and often a defensive denigration of that which is feminine. Chodorow identifies men's fear of the power of the pre-Oedipal mother, and hence of compromising their masculinity, as fuelling male dominance in society. Her thesis is that, if men could begin to 'mother' children like women do, boys and girls would grow up differently, and traditional gender categories would be disrupted, psychologically as well as socially. However, she does recognise that, in reality, social and cultural as well as psychological forces would militate against such a fundamental change.

Chodorow's application of psychoanalytic object relations theory to the development of gendered identities has major implications for how we think about close relationships. Her analysis shows that heterosexual intimacy has different meanings for men and women because it calls forth the different unconscious processes that were laid down during the development of their gendered identities.

Social psychologists have consistently found gender differences in patterns of both friendship and intimacy (Jamieson, 1998, pp. 93–100) Indeed, it is clear that gender-segregated patterns of friendship are firmly established in childhood (Jamieson, 1998). In adulthood, these systematic gender differences remain. Female friendships are characterised by emotional empathy, intimate 'disclosures' and reciprocal sharing of confidences, while friendships between men tend to be based around doing things together and sharing those experiences, though lacking an explicit deep emotional component (Jamieson, 1998). These gendered dimensions of friendship persist to a large extent in closer, intimate relationships, thereby lending support for the kind of reading of the stories of intimacy that psychoanalysis can offer (Benjamin, 1988).

However, it is important to acknowledge that there are considerable within-group variations that, to some extent at least, challenge any model of intimacy – whether psychoanalytically based or otherwise – which presupposes that either 'women' or 'men' are homogenous categories of being. For example, women as well as men 'do' things together with their friends and partners, and men as well as women have emotional undercurrents to their relationships, even when these are not always immediately visible on the surface.

Perhaps the most trenchant criticism that may be made of the mainstream psychological model of close relationships is that, in its focus on generalisation, quantification and objectivity, it cannot fully account for the unobservables in relationships – the deep emotional dimensions that connect one person to another below the surface. As we have seen, a psychoanalytic approach can address those hidden dimensions of intimacy. But, from the point of view of a mainstream psychologist, psychoanalysis as an interpretive enterprise can be seen as lacking the required validity and reliability that usually warrant psychological accounts in the experimental paradigm and make them generalisable across populations. Both mainstream psychology and psychoanalysis may be criticised for falling into the trap of assuming too much homogeneity within gender groups. While there may be dominant patterns that characterise gendered experiences of intimacy, it is also important to bear in mind that each woman and each man is an individual subject, with a multi-layered biography that structures and is structured by their own unique experience of close relationships throughout their lives.

References

Benjamin, J. (1988) *The Bonds of Love: Psychoanalysis, Feminism and the Problem of Domination*, New York, Pantheon.

Beck, U. and Beck-Gernsheim, E. (1995) *The Normal Chaos of Love*, Cambridge, Polity.

Berscheid, E. and Reis, H.T. (1998) 'Attraction and close relationships' in Gilbert, D.T., Fiske, S.T. and Lindzey, G. (eds) *The Handbook of Social Psychology* (4th edn), vol. 2, New York, McGraw Hill.

Buunk, B.P. (1996) 'Affiliation, attraction and close relationships' in Hewstone, M., Stroebe, W. and Stephenson, G.M. (eds) *Introduction to Social Psychology* (2nd edn), Oxford, Blackwell.

Chodorow, N. (1999 [1978]) 'The psychodynamics of the family' in Chodorow, N. (ed.) *The Reproduction of Mothering: Psychoanalysis and the Sociology of Gender*, Berkley, University of California Press.

Craib, I. (2001) *Psychoanalysis: A Critical Introduction*, Cambridge, Polity Press.

Duck, S. (1999) 'Developing a steady and exclusive partnership' in Duck, S. (ed.) *Relating to Others* (2nd edn), Buckingham, Open University Press.

Duck, S. (ed.) (1997) *Handbook of Personal Relationships* (2nd edn), Chichester, John Wiley and Sons.

Giddens, A. (1992) *The Transformation of Intimacy: Sexuality, Love and Eroticism in Modern Societies*, Cambridge, Polity Press.

Gray, J. (1993) *Men Are From Mars, Women Are From Venus: A Practical Guide for Improving Communications and Getting What You Want in Your Relationships*, London, Thorsons.

Haskey, J. (1996) 'Population review: families and households in Great Britain', *Population Trends*, vol. 85, pp. 7–24.

Henriques, J., Hollway, W., Urwin, C., Venn, C. and Walkerdine, V. (1988) *Changing the Subject: Psychology, Social Regulation and Subjectivity* (2nd edn), London, Routledge.

Hinshelwood, R.D. (1989) *A Dictionary of Kleinian Thought*, London, Free Association Books.

Hollway, W. and Jefferson, T. (2000a) *Doing Qualitative Research Differently: Free Association, Narrative and the Interview Method*, London, Sage.

Hollway, W. and Jefferson, J. (2000b) 'Narrative, discourse and the unconscious: the case of Tommy' in Andrews, M., Day Sclater, S., Squire, C. and Treacher, A. (eds) *Lines of Narrative: Psychosocial Perspectives*, London, Routledge.

Jamieson, L. (1998) *Intimacy: Personal Relationships in Modern Societies*, Cambridge, Polity Press.

Lacans, J. (1977) *Écrits: a Selection* (trans. A. Sheridan), London, Tavistock.

Laplanche, J. and Pontalis, J.B. (1973) *The Language of Psychoanalysis*, London, Karnac Books.

Lewis, J. (1999) 'Marriage, cohabitation and the nature of commitment', *Child and Family Law Quarterly*, vol. 11, no. 4.

Maguire, M. (1995) *Men, Women, Passion and Power: Gender Issues in Psychotherapy*, London, Routledge.

Malim, T. and Birch, A. (1998) *Introductory Psychology*, Basingstoke, Macmillan.

Minsky, R. (ed.) (1996) *Psychoanalysis and Gender: An Introductory Reader*, Cambridge, Polity Press.

Mitchell, J. (1974) *Psychoanalysis and Feminism*, London, Allen Lane.

Wright, E. (1992) *Feminism and Psychoanalysis: A Critical Dictionary*, Oxford, Blackwell.

Further reading

Baxter, L.A. and Montgomery, B.M. (1996) *Relating: Dialogues and Dialectics*, New York, Guilford Press.
This book sets out a 'dialogical' approach to close relationships based on the work of the philosopher Bakhtin, and represents an interdisciplinary study in the area between social psychology and communication studies.

Berscheid, E. and Reis, H.T. (1998) 'Attraction and close relationships' in Gilbert, D.T., Fiske, S.T. and Lindzey, G. (eds) *The Handbook of Social Psychology* (4th edn), vol. 2, New York, McGraw Hill.
This article describes the 'propinquity effect' in psychology, whereby the people who, by chance, are the ones you see and interact with the most often are the most likely to become your friends and lovers.

Chodorow, N. (1999 [1978]) *The Reproduction of Mothering: Psychoanalysis and the Sociology of Gender*, Berkley, University of California Press.
This book is a seminal text that was instrumental in inaugurating the debates about psychoanalysis, gender and feminism.

Duck, S. (ed.) (1988) *Handbook of Personal Relationships: Theory, Research and Interventions*, Chichester, John Wiley.
Comprehensive introductory handbook to the psychology of personal relationships, including chapters on intimacy and courtship in the section on 'social psychology'.

Duck, S. (1998) *Human Relationships* (3rd edn), London, Sage.
The central argument is that everyday, mundane communications between people are the basis of human relationships. The book explores meaning, communication, interactions and relationships within a psychological paradigm.

Chapter 3

Attitudes

by Stephanie Taylor, The Open University

Introduction

It is likely that the topic of this chapter – attitudes – will at first seem familiar. No doubt you understand the word 'attitude', at least in its ordinary uses, and you probably have experience of the kind of questionnaire research which records an attitude as a point on a graduated scale, perhaps from 'very much' to 'not at all' or 'completely disagree' to 'strongly agree'. Moreover, academic research on attitudes tends to address topics which are close to our everyday concerns. For example, since the 1930s social psychologists have tried to understand people's attitudes to others who seem different ('foreign-born' visitors, 'coloured immigrants') (e.g. LaPiere, 1967 [1934]; Triandis and Triandis, 1960) and the social and political relevance of this work has not diminished. Researchers have also studied attitudes to ordinary life practices: childcare (Manstead et al., 1983), donating blood (Giles and Cairns, 1995), the use of recreational drugs (Ajzen et al., 1982). Their research reflects a double interest, both in people's attitudes *to* something, generally called the 'object' (whether this is other people, a parenting practice, blood donation, a drug) and what people with a certain attitude will *do*: the attitude is interesting for its link to future behaviour. This is similar to the way that questionnaire research about products or political candidates is ultimately concerned with what people will buy or who they will vote for.

In this chapter you will read three extracts which in different ways consider how far an investigation of attitudes can predict behaviour. The readings discuss psychological research which employs different methodological approaches linked to different understandings and definitions of what an attitude is. They show some of the historical development and change in attitude research. However, as you will see, this is not a simple picture and there is no single contemporary position.

To understand some of the underlying assumptions of mainstream psychological research on attitudes, it is useful to look first at two definitions written sixty years apart. In 1935, Gordon Allport defined an attitude as 'a learned predisposition to respond to an object or a class of objects in a consistently favorable or unfavorable way' (Allport quoted in Fishbein, 1967, p. 477). Later, in 1993, Alice Eagly and Shelly Chaiken proposed that 'attitude is a psychological tendency that is expressed by evaluating a particular entity with some degree of favor or disfavor' (1993 p. 1). A starting point in both Allport's and Eagly and Chaiken's definitions is that attitudes are linked to an expression or response. The most straightforward way to find out about people's attitudes would therefore seem to be to ask them, for example by using a questionnaire. Reading 3.1 discusses the strengths and weaknesses of such an approach.

A second common point in these two definitions is that attitudes are evaluative, on a continuum from positive ('favour') to negative ('disfavour'). Most researchers make the further assumption that this evaluation can be measured, for example, by attributing a numerical value to each point on a scale of possible responses. Data can then be analysed using quantitative methods. In addition, both definitions, as already noted, link an attitude to an 'object' (Allport) or an 'entity' (Eagly and Chaiken) and to what someone does: they 'respond' or 'express by evaluating'. Allport's use of the term 'respond' invokes the kind of causal model associated with behaviourism, as if people can be explained in rather mechanical terms of cause and effect, stimulus and response. The wording of Eagly and Chaiken's definition is less restricted, allowing for the possibility that attitudes can be associated with forward-looking action, for example, towards goals or targets.

We can never predict with certainty what people will actually do. What if someone intended to act in a certain way but was strongly discouraged by other people's disapproval or threats of punishment, or even physically prevented? One way to allow for these contingencies is to make a further distinction between *behaviour* and *behavioural intentions*. This appears in these two definitions in the terms 'predisposition' (Allport) and 'tendency' (Eagly and Chaiken), which acknowledge the possibility of this kind of interference.

The terms 'tendency' and 'predisposition' carry the suggestion that an attitude might be a quality or aspect of a stable person. It endures beyond the moment: a person *already* holds an attitude, before encountering the relevant object or entity in a particular situation. But apart from this, the nature of an attitude is not very clear from the definitions. Many researchers employ a more complex three-part, or tripartite, model of attitude as involving cognition, affect and conation (for further discussion of this model see Chapter 8 of Hewstone et al., 1997). In other words, people's attitudes comprise thoughts, feelings and, as already noted, behaviour. However, these components are also assumed to be connected, in most situations anyway. (There are exceptions, such as when you think it's a good idea to do something, but don't actually feel positive about it, and hang back. You can probably think of some examples for yourself.) For this reason, research has often focused on behaviour (or behavioural intention) rather than the other two components of the model.

Allport says that an attitude is 'learned', while Eagly and Chaiken view it a '*psychological* tendency' and explain that this 'refers to a state that is internal to the person' (1997, p. 1). Does this mean an attitude is biological, or rooted in the unconscious? Is it a part of a person's identity? And what connection might there be between one person's attitude, for example, to people who are 'racially' different, and the attitudes shared by others within a society or culture? What could be the reason an attitude endures and, conversely, what could cause it to change? Attitude researchers have considered these questions and, where possible, addressed them through experiments which test particular hypotheses, but many of their answers remain speculative.

Psychologists have continually re-worked and re-defined the meaning of the term 'attitude' in response to previous studies and ongoing debates, and definitions exclude detail which has not been confirmed by research findings. Because an attitude cannot be observed directly, it is not described in ordinary physical or even emotional terms (as we might describe someone's brown eyes or allergy to cats or quick temper), but in terms of what *can* be observed and measured, such as a response or expression, or whatever else is theorised as connected to the attitude. In other words, for most researchers, the concern has been less with what (or where) an attitude is than how it functions in explanatory terms. The attitude itself, or its component parts, are often discussed as 'hypothetical, unobservable constructs' which are 'represented by observable measures' (Hewstone et al., 1997, p. 227). These constructs are elaborated to incorporate new findings. (For example, although researchers are interested in attitudes as a cause of behaviour they also note that attitudes can sometimes be affected *by* behaviour, such as a person's previous experience of doing something (e.g. Bem, 1970)). A famous model which attempts to connect attitudes to behaviours is the theory of reasoned action (TRA) which you will read about in Reading 3.2. A variation on this is the theory of planned behaviour (TPB), which was developed to improve the predictive power of the model.

Reading 3.1, 'Attitudes versus actions' by Richard LaPiere, is part of a long tradition of social psychological research into prejudice. From a paper originally published in 1934, it presents a two-part study of the attitudes of white Americans to Chinese visitors using an experiment, albeit one conducted relatively informally in the field, followed by a survey. LaPiere's main purpose, as already noted, is to challenge the connection between attitudes and actions and hence the usefulness of questionnaires in attitude research. Reading 3.2, 'From intentions to actions' by Icek Ajzen, can be read as an answer, at least in part, to this challenge. It presents the two models, TRA and TPB, which refine and elaborate on the link between attitudes and behaviour. It also presents a comparative study which investigated women's decisions to breast-feed or bottle-feed their babies. In this research a quantitative analysis of the participants' attitudes, measured on a graduated scale, confirms the connections between attitudes and behaviour predicted by the theory of reasoned action.

ACTIVITY 3.1

As you read the following extracts, consider these points:

■   How does each author define an attitude?

■   What connection between attitude and behaviour is assumed?

■   What was the purpose of the research study and how was it carried out?

Reading 3.1 is from a classic North American study of attitudes by Richard LaPiere, originally published in 1934.

'Attitudes versus actions'

Beginning in 1930 and continuing for two years thereafter, I had the good fortune to travel rather extensively with a young Chinese student and his wife. Both were personable, charming, and quick to win the admiration and respect of those they had the opportunity to become intimate with. But they were foreign-born Chinese, a fact that could not be disguised. Knowing the general 'attitude' of Americans towards the Chinese as indicated by the 'social distance' studies which have been made, it was with considerable trepidation that I first approached a hotel clerk in their company. Perhaps that clerk's eyebrows lifted slightly, but he accommodated us without a show of hesitation. And this in the 'best' hotel in a small town noted for its narrow and bigoted 'attitude' towards Orientals. Two months later I passed that way again, phoned the hotel and asked if they would accommodate 'an important Chinese gentleman.' The reply was an unequivocal 'No.' That aroused my curiosity and led to this study.

In something like ten thousand miles of motor travel, twice across the United States, up and down the Pacific Coast, we met definite rejection from those asked to serve us just once. We were received at 66 hotels, auto camps, and 'Tourist Homes,' refused at one. We were served in 184 restaurants and cafes scattered throughout the country and treated with what I judged to be more than ordinary consideration in 72 of them. Accurate and detailed records were kept of all these instances. An effort, necessarily subjective, was made to evaluate the overt response of hotel clerks, bell boys, elevator operators, and waitresses to the presence of my Chinese friends. The factors entering into the situations were varied as far and as often as possible. Control was not, of course, as exacting as that required by laboratory experimentation. But it was as rigid as is humanly possible in human situations. For example, I did not take the 'test' subjects into my confidence fearing that their behavior might become self-conscious and thus abnormally affect the response of others towards them. Whenever possible I let my Chinese friend negotiate for accommodations (while I concerned myself with the car or luggage) or sent them into a restaurant ahead of me. In this way I attempted to 'factor' myself out. We sometimes patronized high-class establishments after a hard and dusty day on the road and stopped at inferior auto camps when in our most presentable condition.

[...]

What I am trying to say is that in only one out of 251 instances in which we purchased goods or services necessitating intimate human relationships did the fact that my companions were Chinese adversely affect us. Factors entirely unassociated with race were, in the main, the determinant of significant variations in our reception. It would appear reasonable to conclude that the 'attitude' of the American people, as reflected in the behavior of those who are for pecuniary reasons presumably most sensitive to the antipathies of their white clientele, is anything but negative towards the Chinese. In terms of 'social distance' we might conclude that native Caucasians are not averse to residing in the same hotels, auto-camps, and 'Tourist Homes' as Chinese and will with complacency accept the presence of Chinese at an adjoining table in restaurant or cafe. It does not follow that there is revealed a distinctly 'positive' attitude towards the Chinese, that whites prefer the Chinese to other whites. But the facts as gathered certainly preclude the conclusion that there is an intense prejudice towards the Chinese.

Yet the existence of this prejudice, very intense, is proven by a conventional 'attitude' study. To provide a comparison of symbolic reaction to symbolic social situations with actual reaction to real social situations, I 'questionnaired' the establishments which we patronized during the two year period. Six months were permitted to lapse between the time I obtained the overt reaction and the symbolic. It was hoped that the effects of the actual experience with Chinese guests, adverse or otherwise, would have faded during the intervening time. To the hotel or restaurant a questionnaire was mailed with an accompanying letter purporting to be a special and personal plea for response. The questionnaires all asked the same question, 'Will you accept members of the Chinese race as guests in your establishment?' Two types of questionnaire were used. In one this question was inserted among similar queries concerning Germans, French, Japanese, Russians, Armenians, Jews, Negroes, Italians, and Indians. In the other the pertinent question was unencumbered. With persistence, completed replies were obtained from 128 of the establishments we had visited; 81 restaurants and cafes and 47 hotels, auto-camps, and 'Tourist Homes.' In response to the relevant question 92 per cent of the former and 91 per cent of the latter replied 'No.' The remainder replied 'Uncertain; depend upon circumstances.' From the woman proprietor of a small auto-camp I received the only 'Yes,' accompanied by a chatty letter describing the nice visit she had had with a Chinese gentleman and his sweet wife during the previous summer.

A rather unflattering interpretation might be put upon the fact that those establishments who had provided for our needs so graciously were, some months later, verbally antagonistic towards hypothetical Chinese. To factor this experience out responses were secured from 32 hotels and 96 restaurants located in approximately the same regions, but uninfluenced by this particular experience with Oriental clients. In this, as in the former case, both types of questionnaires were used. The results indicate that neither the type of questionnaire nor the fact of previous experience had important bearing upon the symbolic response to symbolic social situations.

It is impossible to make direct comparison between the reactions secured through questionnaires and from actual experience. On the basis of the above data [...] it would appear foolhardy for a Chinese to attempt to travel in the United States. And yet, as I have shown, actual experience [...] indicates that the American people, as represented by the personnel of hotels, restaurants, etc., are not at all averse to fraternizing with Chinese within the limitations which apply to social relationships between Americans themselves. The evaluations which follow are undoubtedly subject to the criticism which any human judgment must withstand. But the fact is that, although they began their travels in this country with considerable trepidation, my Chinese friends soon lost all fear that they might receive a rebuff. At first somewhat timid and considerably dependent upon me for guidance and support, they came in time to feel fully self-reliant and would approach new social situations without the slightest hesitation.

[...]

No doubt a considerable part of the data which the social scientist deals with can be obtained by the questionnaire method. The census reports are based upon verbal questionnaires and I do not doubt their basic integrity. If we wish to know how many children a man has, his income, the size of his home, his age, and the condition of his parents, we can reasonably ask him. These things he has frequently and conventionally converted into verbal responses. He is competent to report upon them, and will do so accurately, unless indeed he wishes to do otherwise. A careful investigator could no doubt even find out by verbal means whether the man fights with his wife (frequently, infrequently, or not at all), though the neighbors would be a more reliable source. But we should not expect to obtain by the questionnaire method his 'anticipatory set or tendency' to action should his wife pack up and go home to Mother, should Elder Son get into trouble with the neighbor's daughter, the President assume the status of a dictator, the Japanese take over the rest of China, or a Chinese gentleman come to pay a social call.

Only a verbal reaction to an entirely symbolic situation can be secured by the questionnaire. It may indicate what the responder would actually do when confronted with the situation symbolized in the question, but there is no assurance that it will. And so to call the response a reflection of a 'social attitude' is to entirely disregard the definition commonly given for the phrase 'attitude.' If social attitudes are to be conceptualized as partially integrated habit sets which will become operative under specific circumstances and lead to a particular pattern of adjustment they must, in the main, be derived from a study of humans behaving in actual social situations. They must not be imputed on the basis of questionnaire data.

The questionnaire is cheap, easy, and mechanical. The study of human behavior is time consuming, intellectually fatiguing, and depends for its success upon the ability of the investigator. The former method gives quantitative results, the latter mainly qualitative. Quantitative measurements are quantitatively accurate; qualitative evaluations are always subject to the errors of human judgment. Yet it would seem far more worth while to make a shrewd guess regarding that which is essential than to accurately measure that which is likely to prove quite irrelevant.

(LaPiere, 1967 [1934], pp. 26–31)

Reading 3.2 is from a chapter of a 1988 book, *Attitudes, Personality, and Behavior*, by one of the most famous 'names' in attitude theory and research, Icek Ajzen.

READING 3.2

'From intentions to actions'

Attitudes and subjective norms

According to the theory of reasoned action, intentions are a function of two basic determinants, one personal in nature and the other reflecting social influence. The personal factor is the individual's *attitude toward the behaviour* [...]. Unlike general attitudes toward institutions, people, or objects that have traditionally been studied by social psychologists, this attitude is the individual's positive or negative evaluation of performing the particular behavior of interest. The second determinant of intention is the person's perception of social pressure to perform or not to perform the behavior under consideration. Since it deals with perceived normative prescriptions, this factor is termed *subjective norm*. Generally speaking, people intend to perform a behavior when they evaluate it positively and when they believe that important others think they should perform it.

The theory assumes that the relative importance of attitude toward the behavior and subjective norm depends in part on the intention under investigation. For some intentions attitudinal considerations are more important than normative considerations, while for other intentions normative considerations predominate. Frequently, both factors are important determinants of the intention. In addition, the relative weights of the attitudinal and normative factors may vary from one person to another. Figure 1 is a graphic representation of the theory of reasoned action as described up to this point.

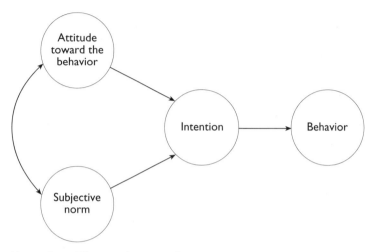

Figure 1   Theory of reasoned action

Many studies have provided strong support for the hypothesized links between intention as the dependent variable and attitude toward the behavior and subjective norm as the independent variables. [...]

For many practical purposes this level of explanation may be sufficient. We can to some extent account for the intentions people form by examining their attitudes toward the behavior, their subjective norms, and the relative importance of these two factors. However, for a more complete understanding of intentions it is necessary to explore why people hold certain attitudes and subjective norms.

[...]

[...] According to the theory of reasoned action, attitude toward a behavior is determined by salient beliefs about that behavior, termed *behavioral beliefs*. Each behavioral belief links the behavior to a certain outcome, or to some other attribute such as the cost incurred by performing the behavior. For example, a person may believe that 'going on a low sodium diet' (the behavior) 'reduces blood pressure,' 'leads to a change in life style,' 'severely restricts the range of approved foods,' and so forth (outcomes). The attitude toward the behavior is determined by the person's evaluation of the outcomes associated with the behavior and by the strength of these associations. [...]

[...]

[...] Subjective norms, the second major determinant of intentions in the theory of reasoned action, are also assumed to be a function of beliefs, but beliefs of a different kind, namely the person's beliefs that specific individuals or groups approve or disapprove of performing the behavior. Serving as a point of reference to guide behavior, these individuals and groups are known as *referents*.

For many behaviors, the important referents include a person's parents, spouse, close friends, coworkers, and, depending on the behavior involved, perhaps such experts as physicians or tax accountants. The beliefs that underlie subjective norms are termed *normative beliefs*. Generally speaking, people who believe that most referents with whom they are motivated to comply think they should perform the behavior will perceive social pressure to do so. Conversely, people who believe that most referents with whom they are motivated to comply would disapprove of their performing the behavior will have a subjective norm that puts pressure on them to avoid performing the behavior. [...]

[...]

The discussion up to this point shows how volitional behavior can be explained in terms of a limited number of concepts. Through a series of intervening steps the theory of reasoned action traces the causes of behavior to the person's salient beliefs. Each successive step in this sequence from behavior to beliefs provides a more comprehensive account of the factors that determine the behavior. At the initial level behavior is assumed to be determined by intention. At the next level these intentions are themselves explained in terms of attitudes toward the behavior and subjective norms. The third level accounts for attitudes and subjective norms in terms of beliefs about the consequences of performing the behavior and about the normative expectations of relevant referents. In the final analysis, then, a person's behavior is explained by considering his or her beliefs. Since people's beliefs represent the information (be it correct or incorrect) they have about themselves and about the world around them, it follows that their behavior is ultimately determined by this information.

[...]

A concrete example may help clarify the role of beliefs in determining the performance of a specific behavior. Manstead et al. (1983) compared the beliefs of mothers who breast-fed their babies with mothers who used the bottle-feeding method. Based on prior research in the field, the investigators selected the six reasons women cite most frequently for breast-feeding their babies and the six reasons they cite most frequently for bottle-feeding their babies. With respect to each of these 12 salient behavioral beliefs, women about to give birth were asked to provide two measures: their subjective probabilities that a given feeding method is associated with the cited consequence, and their evaluations of that consequence. The following are examples for each feeding method.

Behavioral beliefs

Breast-feeding protects a baby against infection

likely :__:__:__:__:__:__: unlikely

Bottle-feeding provides incomplete nourishment for a baby

likely :__:__:__:__:__:__: unlikely

Outcome evaluations

Using a feeding method that protects a baby against infection is

very important to me :__:__:__:__:__:__: completely unimportant to me

Using a feeding method that provides complete nourishment for my baby is

very important to me :__:__:__:__:__:__: completely unimportant to me

Table 1 shows the average likelihood rating (7 = likely, 1 = unlikely) provided by mothers who breast-fed their babies and mothers who bottle-fed their babies.

Statistical significance between the two groups is indicated. As can be seen, the two groups of mothers differed significantly on all six of the behavioral beliefs about breast-feeding. Examination of these differences reveals some of the reasons for choosing one or the other feeding method. Although all women tended to agree that breast-feeding establishes a close bond between mother and baby, the women who held this belief more strongly were more likely to choose the breast-feeding method. In a similar vein, the choice of breast-feeding increased with the perceived likelihood that this method is good for the mother's figure, provides the best nourishment for a baby, and protects a baby against infection. On the other hand, the more a woman believed that breast-feeding is embarrassing for the mother or limits her social life, the less likely she was to use this method.

Table 1   Mean behavioral belief ratings (after Manstead et al., 1983)

Behavioral beliefs	Mothers who breast-fed	Mothers who bottle-fed
About breast-feeding		
Establishes close bond between mother and baby	6.61	5.45[a]
Is embarrassing for mother	4.93	4.00[a]
Is good for mother's figure	5.98	4.45[a]
Limits mother's social life	3.90	3.13[a]
Provides best nourishment for baby	6.77	5.57[a]
Protects baby against infection	6.48	5.39[a]
About bottle-feeding		
Is a very convenient method of feeding baby	4.47	6.16[a]
Provides incomplete nourishment for baby	4.52	4.91
Makes it possible for baby's father to be involved in feeding	5.56	6.35[a]
Is an expensive feeding method	2.66	2.80
Is a trouble-free feeding method	3.29	4.80[a]
Allows one to see exactly how much milk baby has had	6.13	6.25

[a] Significant difference between breast- and bottle-feeding mothers ($P < 0.05$).

Table 2 Mean outcome evaluations (after Manstead et al., 1983)

Outcomes	Mothers who breast-fed	Mothers who bottle-fed
Allows me to go out socially	2.94	3.45
Is good for my figure	5.02	4.07[a]
Is convenient	4.69	5.22
Establishes a close bond between me and my baby	6.75	6.13[a]
Does not make me feel embarrassed	3.80	4.81[a]
Allows baby's father to be involved in feeding	4.32	6.15[a]
Provides complete nourishment for baby	6.94	6.72[a]
Is trouble-free	4.39	4.24
Is inexpensive	4.02	3.55
Allows one to see exactly how much milk baby has had	4.09	6.06[a]
Protects my baby against infection	6.86	6.56[a]

[a] Significant difference between breast- and bottle-feeding mothers ($P < 0.05$).

With respect to the bottle-feeding method, the two groups of mothers differed significantly on only three of the six behavioral beliefs. An examination of the significant differences shows that perceived outcomes of bottle-feeding which best explained the choice of this method were the beliefs that it is a very convenient method, that it enables the father to be involved in feeding, and that it is a trouble-free feeding method.

It is possible, in a similar fashion, to compare the outcome evaluations of mothers who breast-fed their babies with those of mothers who chose the bottle-feeding method. Such a comparison provides additional information about the reasons for choosing one method over the other. Table 2 presents the average outcome evaluations for the two groups (1 = completely unimportant, 7 = very important). Examining the six evaluations that distinguished significantly between the two groups, it can be seen that mothers tended to choose the breast-feeding method if, in comparison to mothers who chose the bottle-feeding method, they judged as relatively important the following outcomes: having a good figure, establishing a close bond with their babies, providing complete nourishment for their babies, and protecting their babies against infection. In addition, these mothers also rated as relatively unimportant the outcomes of feeling embarrassed, allowing the baby's father to be involved in the feeding, and being able to see exactly how much milk baby has had.

The study by Manstead et al. (1983) also reported interesting data concerning the effects of normative beliefs on the choice of breast- versus bottle-feeding.

The salient normative referents identified in this context were the baby's father, the mother's own mother, her closest female friend, and her medical adviser (usually a gynecologist). With respect to each referent, normative beliefs about breast-feeding and about bottle-feeding were assessed, as was motivation to comply with each referent. The following scales illustrate the procedures used.

Normative beliefs

The baby's father thinks that I

definitely should breast-feed :__:__:__:__:__:__:__: definitely should not
                                                        breast-feed

Motivation to comply

In general, how much do you care what the baby's father thinks you should do?

Do not care at all :__:__:__:__:__:__:__: Care very much

Table 3 shows the average normative beliefs for the two groups of mothers. The differences between mothers who breast-fed their babies and mothers who used the bottle are statistically significant for each normative belief. Inspection of the normative beliefs for mothers who used the breast-feeding method reveals that, in their opinions, important referents strongly preferred this method over the alternative bottle-feeding method. In contrast, women who believed that their referents had no strong preferences for either method were more likely to feed their babies by means of a bottle.

Finally, the mothers' average motivations to comply with each of the four salient referent individuals are presented in Table 4. Both groups of mothers were highly motivated to comply with the baby's father, and they had moderately strong motivations to comply with their own mothers and closest female friends. The only significant difference emerged with respect to the women's medical advisers. Mothers who eventually decided to breast-feed their babies were more highly motivated to comply with their medical advisers than were mothers who eventually decided to use the bottle. This is consistent with the finding that the former mothers perceived their medical advisers to be strong advocates of the breast-feeding method (see Table 3).

To summarize briefly, research on the theory of reasoned action describes how people tend to proceed on a course of action in quite a deliberate manner. The initial considerations deal with the likely consequences of performing a certain behavior and expectations of important referent individuals or groups. Depending on the evaluation of the behavior's likely consequences and motivation to comply with referent sources, attitudes and subjective norms emerge that guide the formation of behavioral intentions. Barring unforeseen events that might change the intentions, and contingent on the behavior being under volitional control, the intentions are carried out under appropriate circumstances.

Table 3   Mean normative beliefs (after Manstead et al., 1983)

Normative beliefs	Mothers who breast-fed	Mothers who bottle-fed
About breast-feeding		
Baby's father	6.21	4.45
Own mother	5.57	4.45

Normative beliefs	Mothers who breast-fed	Mothers who bottle-fed
Closest female friend	5.39	4.47
Medical adviser	6.20	5.25
About bottle-feeding		
Baby's father	2.89	4.16
Own mother	3.24	3.99
Closet female friend	3.43	3.98
Medical adviser	2.96	3.55

Note: All differences between breast-feeding and bottle-feeding mothers are statistically significant ($P < 0.05$).

Table 4   Mean motivations to comply (after Manstead et al., 1983)

Referent	Mothers who breast-fed	Mothers who bottle-fed
Baby's father	6.07	5.61
Own mother	4.84	4.60
Closest female friend	3.38	3.52
Medical adviser	5.36	4.52 [a]

[a] Significant difference between breast- and bottle-feeding mothers ($P < 0.05$).

The case of incomplete volitional control

The theory of reasoned action was developed explicitly to deal with purely volitional behaviors. In this context it has proved quite successful. Complications are encountered, however, when we try to apply the theory to behaviors that are not fully under volitional control. A well-known example is that many smokers intend to quit but, when they try, fail to attain their goal. In the theory of reasoned action, intentions are the prime motivating force and they mediate the effects of other factors, i.e. of attitude toward the behavior and of subjective norm. The stronger are people's intentions to engage in a behavior or to achieve their behavioral goals, the more successful they are expected to be. However, the degree of success will depend not only on one's desire or intention, but also on such partly nonmotivational factors as availability of requisite opportunities and resources. To the extent that people have the required opportunities and resources, and intend to perform the behavior, they should succeed in doing so.

At first glance, the problem of behavioral control may appear to apply to a limited range of actions only. Closer scrutiny reveals, however, that even very mundane activities, which can usually be executed (or not executed) at will, are sometimes subject to the influence of factors beyond one's control. Such a simple behavior as driving to the supermarket may be thwarted by mechanical trouble with the car. Control over behavior can thus best be viewed as a continuum. On one extreme are behaviors that encounter few if any problems of control. A good case in point is voting choice: once the voter has entered the voting booth, selection among the candidates can be done at will. At the other extreme are events, such as sneezing or lowering one's blood pressure, over which we have very little or no control. Most behaviors, of course, fall somewhere in between these extremes. People usually encounter few problems of control when trying to attend lectures or read a book, but problems of control are more readily apparent when they try to overcome such powerful habits as smoking or drinking or when they set their sights on such difficult-to-attain goals as becoming a movie star. Viewed in this light it becomes clear that, strictly speaking, most intended behaviors are best considered *goals* whose attainment is subject to some degree of uncertainty. We can thus speak of behavior-goal units, and of intentions as plans of action in pursuit of behavioral goals (Ajzen, 1985).

[...]

As is true of time and opportunity, the inability to behave in accordance with intention because of dependence on others need not affect the underlying motivation. Often an individual who encounters difficulties related to interpersonal dependence may be able to perform the desired behavior in cooperation with a different partner. Sometimes, however, this may not be a viable course of action. A wife's adamant refusal to have more children will usually cause the husband eventually to abandon his plan to enlarge the family, rather than shift his effort to a different partner.

In short, lack of opportunity and dependence on others often lead only to temporary changes in intentions. When circumstances prevent the performance of a behavior, the person may wait for a better opportunity and, when another person fails to cooperate, a more compliant partner may be sought. However, when repeated efforts to perform the behavior result in failure, more fundamental changes in intentions can be expected.

[...] many factors can disrupt the intention-behavior relation. Although volitional control is more likely to present a problem for some behaviors than for others, personal deficiencies and external obstacles can interfere with the performance of any behavior. Collectively, these factors represent people's *actual* control or lack of control over the behavior. [...]

A recent attempt to provide a conceptual framework that addresses the problem of incomplete volitional control is Ajzen's *theory of planned behavior* (Ajzen, 1985; Ajzen and Madden, 1986; Schifter and Ajzen, 1985). This conceptual framework is an extension of the theory of reasoned action. As in the original model, a central factor in the theory of planned behavior is an individual's intention to perform the behavior of interest. In contrast to the original version, however, the theory of planned behavior postulates three, rather than two, conceptually independent determinants of intentions. The first two – attitude toward the behavior and the subjective norm – are the same as before. The third and novel antecedent of intention is the degree of *perceived behavioral control*. This factor [...] refers to the perceived ease or difficulty of performing the behavior and it is assumed to reflect past experience as well as anticipated impediments and obstacles. As a general rule, the more favorable the attitude and subjective norm with respect to a behavior, and the greater the perceived behavioral control, the stronger should be the individual's intention to perform the behavior under consideration.

[...]

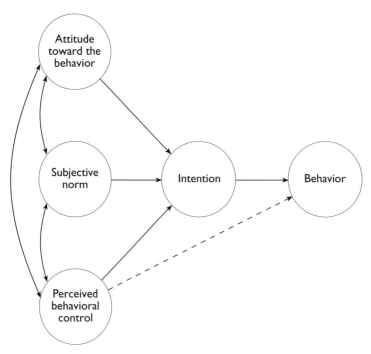

Figure 2   Theory of planned behaviour

References

Ajzen, I. (1985) 'From intentions to actions: a theory of planned behavior' in Kuhl, J. and Beckmann, J. (eds) *Action Control: From Cognition to Behavior*, New York, Springer-Verlag, pp. 11–39.

Ajzen, I. and Madden, T. (1986) 'Prediction of goal-directed behavior: attitudes, intentions, and perceived behavioral control', *Journal of Experimental Social Psychology*, vol. 22, pp. 453–74.

Manstead, A., Proffitt, C. and Smart, J. (1983) 'Predicting and understanding mothers' infant-feeding intentions and behavior: testing the theory of reasoned action', *Journal of Personality and Social Psychology*, vol. 44, pp. 657–71.

Schifter, D. and Ajzen, I. (1985) 'Intention, perceived control, and weight loss: an application of the theory of planned behavior', *Journal of Personality and Social Psychology*, vol. 49, pp. 843–51.

(Ajzen, 1988, pp. 112–33)

Commentary

The author of Reading 3.1, LaPiere, is interested in attitudes as predictors or determinants of behaviour and in the limitations of questionnaires as a means of investigating them. The original published date of the article (1934) is reflected in some details and also, perhaps, in the author's own attitudes (in the ordinary sense of the term), for example, towards women. The style is dense and quite formal but there is a journalistic tone which is personal, even jokey: this is not conventionally 'objective' writing. Nonetheless, LaPiere is making a serious and still relevant point. He is challenging the effectiveness of questionnaires, which were widely used even in the 1930s. He suggests that a questionnaire is appropriate for some purposes, including (he says elsewhere) 'the measurement of "political attitudes"' (LaPiere, 1967[1934], p. 29) but he suggests that their findings are a poor predictor of certain behaviours.

Reading 3.2, from Ajzen (1988), is more recognisably 'scientific' in style. The extract summarises a study (Manstead et al., 1983) in which the researchers used a questionnaire approach to investigate the beliefs which could affect mothers' decisions to breast-feed or bottle-feed babies. The form of the questionnaire was far more elaborate than LaPiere's request for a 'yes', 'no' or 'undecided' answer to a question about future actions. Manstead et al. asked their participants to indicate on a graduated scale the strength of their belief about what each method of feeding could do, such as protect against infection or improve the mother's body shape ('behavioural beliefs') and also how much the mother valued each effect ('outcome evaluations'). The responses were given a numerical value and the beliefs of breast-feeding and non-breast-feeding mothers averaged and compared. The findings were that 'the two groups of mothers differed significantly on all six of the behavioral beliefs about breast-feeding' and also in their evaluations of particular outcomes. The researchers used a similar analysis to investigate the impact of other people's opinions on the mothers' decisions about feeding.

Using a highly influential model, Fishbein and Ajzen's TRA (Ajzen and Fishbein, 1980; Fishbein, 1980; Fishbein and Ajzen, 1975), this research assumes that a person's intention to perform a behaviour (in this case, breast-feeding) depends partly on her attitude towards that behaviour, based on 'belief strength' and 'outcome evaluation', and partly on 'subjective norms', which are her beliefs about other people's approval or disapproval. For Manstead et al. (1983), an attitude is not indicated by a declared intention to behave in a certain way (as in LaPiere's study): it is a construct which has a numerical value calculated on the basis of the participants' responses which are themselves given numerical values. The research produced statistically significant findings and has clear potential applications. It can be seen to confirm the predictive power and the usefulness of the TRA model.

LaPiere was interested in racial prejudice and Reading 3.1 gives some indications of the social values which prevailed at the time of his research. For example, it seems clear that he did not expect the people who answered his questionnaire to refrain from exhibiting prejudice, and also that it was commonplace for businesses openly to reject customers on the grounds of race or nationality. Nonetheless, his definition of attitudes focuses on individual behaviour (he defines them as 'partially integrated habit sets which will become operative under specific circumstances and lead to a particular pattern of adjustment'). Although he calls for attitude researchers to study people 'in actual social situations' as an alternative to questionnaires, and refers to 'social attitudes' and 'the general "attitude" of Americans towards the Chinese', we get little sense of the larger social context or why, at this period, he expected to find prejudice against Chinese visitors. Reading 3.2 similarly gives little sense of attitudes as the product of the larger society or participants' wider circumstances. An answer to that question might require a different kind of research, into contemporary political issues, the media and US culture more generally for the first study, and, for the second, into the social acceptability of breast-feeding in different societies and also the availability and affordability of alternative baby foods for different mothers.

The TRA model presented in Reading 3.2 suggests that an intention to act in a certain way is based on both the person's attitude and a 'subjective norm'. This norm is not a reference to (what the participant believes to be) general public opinion but the opinions of specific others ('referents'). In Manstead et al.'s study (1983), the referents included each participant's own mother or her medical adviser. The participant was also asked how important this person's opinion was to her. It was found that the mothers in the study who chose to breast-feed believed that 'important referents strongly preferred this method'. The picture, therefore, is of an individual who holds a certain attitude in interaction with other individuals who have their own attitudes.

In contrast, Reading 3.3, by Jonathan Potter and Margaret Wetherell (1987), presents a very different study of attitudes. Their research makes the wider social context a central concern. The reading begins with a critique of 'traditional attitude theory' in psychology and then moves on to present an alternative qualitative data analysis. This qualitative study is an example of discourse analysis, a theoretical and methodological approach now established as part of discursive psychology. (You will explore discourse analysis again in Chapter 6.) Potter and Wetherell are presenting a theoretical and a methodological challenge to research which uses participants' responses as evidence of attitudes. They question the whole concept of an attitude being held by a person as some kind of assessable 'mental state' towards 'an object of thought', and, like LaPiere, they question any straightforward link between attitudes and behaviour. In doing so, they are proposing a radically different approach to psychology – one which moves beyond the individual and, as the term 'discourse' indicates, one which foregrounds language, and specifically talk.

ACTIVITY 3.2

As you read the following extract, consider these points:

- What criticisms are made of the evidence used by 'traditional' attitude researchers?
- What criticisms are made of their concept of an attitude?

■   How does Potter and Wetherell's research study differ from those described in
    Readings 3.1 and 3.2?

Reading 3.3 is from the 1987 book by Jonathan Potter and Margaret Wetherell
that helped establish discourse analysis and discursive work as a separate area
of theory and research within social psychology.

READING 3.3

'Unfolding discourse analysis'

Attitudes in discourse

[...]

McGuire claims that empirical studies of attitudes work with, at least implicitly,
the following basic definition. When people are expressing attitudes they are
giving responses which 'locate "objects of thought"' on "dimensions of
judgment"' (McGuire, 1985, p. 239). That is, when they are speaking or acting,
people are taking some idea or object of interest and giving it a position in an
evaluative hierarchy. We will describe a concrete example to make this concept
sharper.

[...]

In 1976 a British researcher, Alan Marsh, asked a random sample of 1,785
people to express their attitude to 'coloured immigrants' by placing a mark on a
scale which ran from 'completely sympathetic', through to, 'no feelings about
them either way', to 'completely unsympathetic'. In McGuire's terms the object of
thought would be the 'coloured immigrants', while the dimension of judgement
would consist of the 'sympathy' which the respondent can offer or refuse.
Marsh's survey resembles myriads of other surveys, the techniques he used are
extremely common in attitude research. Having collected his responses, Marsh
went on to split his scale up 'logically' into categories. These are labelled 'very
hostile', 'hostile', 'neutral' and so on (see Table 1).

From the point of view of a discourse analyst, there are a number of interesting
points to be made, both about McGuire's minimal definition of attitudes and the
kind of practical research procedures illustrated by Marsh's scale; we will
concentrate on three issues.

Table 1   Distribution of sympathetic and unsympathetic feelings
towards coloured immigrants

Completely unsympathetic		No feelings about them either way				Completely sympathetic
0	1–20	21–45	46–55	56–79	80–99	100
12%	13%	17%	25%	20%	10%	3%
Very hostile	Hostile	Unsympathetic	Neutral	Sympathetic	Positive	Very positive

No. in sample: unweighted = 1,785, weighted = 1,482; 'don't know' (excluded = 4%).

Source: Marsh, 1976

First, there are obvious problems with the status of 'coloured immigrants' as an object of thought. One way of looking at the term 'coloured immigrants' would be as a simple category label for a group of people, in fact those people who fit the descriptions 'coloured' and 'immigrant'. However, things are a lot more complex than this. For example, there is no clear-cut neutral way of deciding how to apply the category 'coloured immigrant'. That is, there are no objective criteria for category membership [...].

The proper application of 'coloured' is dependent on unstated theories of race and biology. But modern theories of genetics and population give no support to the idea that 'races' of people can be distinguished in terms of unambiguous, underlying physical, and ultimately genetic, differences (Husband, 1982). In addition, 'immigrant' means (in the dictionary sense) a person who comes into a foreign country as a settler. Yet Marsh (1976) does not address the problem of splitting 'coloured immigrants' from 'coloured residents', and it is clear that he takes the term 'coloured immigrant' as a bland descriptive category covering both these groups. In fact this is reflected in the very title of his article, which is called 'Who hates the Blacks' not 'Who hates those people who are both recent settlers in Britain and black defined'. His terminology is not neutral. If you have lived in a country for the whole of your life you might be concerned if people start calling you an immigrant – a term often used to connote aliens or outsiders (Reeves, 1983; Sykes, 1985).

A second problem arises when we examine the transformations which Marsh makes to his subjects' responses. If we look at Table 1 we can see that Marsh has transformed one dimension, running from 'completely unsympathetic' to 'completely sympathetic', into a more complex set of labels: 'very hostile', 'hostile', 'unsympathetic' etc. There is no coherent justification for making transformations of this kind. For example, it is probably wrong to suggest respondents mean the same thing by the words 'very hostile' and 'completely unsympathetic'. For one thing, the term hostility is often used to imply an *active* disposition, while if someone lacks sympathy, they are *without* a certain kind of active disposition. By making this transformation the analyst is riding roughshod over subtle distinctions that may play a crucial role in the participants' discourse, and certainly in their methods of making sense of the survey questions.

A third problem also concerns translation: in this case the researchers' translation of participants' responses into the underlying theoretical category of attitude. The aim of attitude scales is not merely to show how people fill in these scales, but to identify attitudes. That is, in McGuire's terms, to identify where on a specific dimension a person locates an object of thought; in the current example, where the respondents locate 'coloured immigrants' on the dimension of 'sympathy'. The crucial assumption of attitude researchers is that there is something enduring within people which the scale is measuring – the attitude.

Discourse analysis points to many difficulties with this. We need to ask, for instance, whether people filling in an attitude scale are performing a neutral act of describing or expressing an internal mental state, their attitude or whether they are engaged in producing a specific linguistic formulation tuned to the context at hand. From the discourse analytic perspective, given different purposes or a different context a very different 'attitude' may be espoused. Put another way, if a certain attitude is expressed on one occasion it should not necessarily lead us to expect that the same attitude will be expressed on another. Instead there may be systematic variations in what is said, which cast doubt on the enduring homogeneous nature of the supposed internal mental attitude.

How, then, should we deal with these three problems which are by no means unique to Marsh: first, the meaning of interpretation given to the terms in the attitude scale; second, the translation between participants' discourse and analysts' categories; and third, the treatment of linguistic products as transparent indicators of underlying objects or dispositions. More generally, what might a study of participants' discourse tell us about phenomena traditionally understood in terms of attitudes? The time has come to get down to the nitty-gritty of accounts and perform our own analysis.

Discourses of immigration

[...] we will indicate how a discourse analyst might go about researching attitudes to constructed categories such as 'coloured immigrants'. We will closely examine some accounts produced in a less organized environment than Marsh's survey, but which, nonetheless, are easily recognizable as evaluative expressions concerning race and immigration. All the accounts we shall analyze have been extracted from open-ended interviews with white, middle-class New Zealanders. These interviews discussed generally 'controversial' issues in New Zealand society.

The goals of our analysis will obviously differ from those determining traditional attitude research. Broadly speaking, discourse analysts are interested in the different ways in which texts are organized, and the consequences of using some organizations rather than others. So our aim will be to look at the different forms taken by evaluative discourse about minority groups, and the effects of these forms. At the same time, the analysis will try to avoid the three problems we identified as endemic in traditional attitude research, namely presupposing the existence of the 'attitudinal object', making translations from unexplicated participants' discourse to unexplicated analysts' discourse, and treating utterances as indicators of the presence of enduring, underlying attitudes. We shall try to show why the concept of an enduring attitude is theoretically redundant.

Context

Perhaps the first thing which becomes apparent when embarking on this task is the sheer complexity of working with extended sequences of talk rather than the brief isolated utterances which make up responses to attitude questionnaires. Take the following interview extract for example.

1   *Respondent.* I'm not anti them at all you know (Benton [...]).

We do not have any trouble in reading this as a relatively positive statement of the speaker's position on 'them' – in this case, in the New Zealand context, 'Polynesian immigrants'. In attitude terms, the 'object of thought' is 'Polynesian immigrants', the 'dimension of judgment' lies from pro to anti, and the position espoused is pro. Following standard attitude theory, we would treat this speaker as possessing a specific attitude. If they had to fill in Marsh's questionnaire they might endorse the 'sympathetic' end of the scale – or so the traditional account would have it.

Yet, when we look at more of this sequence, the simplicity starts to fall away. Here is the entire turn of talk from which Extract One was taken.

2   *Respondent.* I'm not anti them at all you know, I, if they're willing to get on and be like us; but if they're just going to come here, just to be able to use our social welfares and stuff like that, then why don't they stay home? (Benton [...])

There are a number of interesting features here which immediately question our first interpretation. To begin with, the 'pro immigrants' claim is made contingent on immigrants exhibiting a willingness 'to be like us'. Thus we can no longer read it as an unqualified expression of sympathy. Moreover, the whole statement is organized within a complex linguistic structure of conditionals and contrasts. This can be shown clearly if we rearrange the extract.

2b   A1 If [they're willing to get on and be like us]

A2 then [I'm not anti them]

but

B1 if [they're just going... .to use our social welfares]

B2 then [why don't they stay home]

In technical terms, contrast structures are now revealed. Taken in isolation, the consequences of these kinds of contrast structures are not easy to ascertain. However, it is notable that studies of the way public speakers, such as Margaret Thatcher and other politicians, elicit applause have found that constructions of this sort are very effective in producing audience appreciation (Atkinson, 1984; Heritage and Greatbach, 1986). And it may well be that this kind of construction is commonplace in everyday discourse because it helps package the message to make it more convincing.

A further feature of Extract Two also highlights its persuasive orientation. It draws upon what Pomerantz (1986) has called the *extreme case* formulation. For example, if someone is asked why they carry a gun and they respond, '*everybody* carries a gun', they are providing an effective warrant. Gun-toting is depicted not as a notable or restricted activity but as normative, something shared by everybody. Extreme case formulations take whatever evaluative dimension is being adopted to its extreme limits. Thus if it is a question of numbers, then it is 'everybody' or 'only one', things are 'very' or 'terribly' bad etc. In the second part of Extract Two the speaker produces an extreme case formulation of this type: 'if they are *just* going to come here *just* to be able to use our social security and stuff'. The repeated use of the word 'just' paints a picture of people whose *sole* purpose in coming to New Zealand is the collection of social security, a selfish motive much more blameworthy than, say, coming to provide essential labour but being laid off due to economic recession. By representing it in this extreme way the criticisms are made to appear more justifiable.

Finally, if we look back to the first part of Extract Two – 'I am not anti them at all' – we can see that this operates as a *disclaimer*. Hewitt and Stokes (1975) define a disclaimer as a verbal device which is used to ward off potentially obnoxious attributions. Thus, if someone says 'I am no sexist but ...' they are aware that what they are about to say may sound sexist, but are trying to head off such an attribution. In this case, the speaker is disclaiming possible attributions of racism consequent on the suggestion that immigrants should 'stay home'.

Now, these interpretations of Extract Two are tentative. They are not based on a systematic study of many instances but on a detailed reading of a single one. But they suggest two things. First, that even a small amount of additional information about context can throw into question what, at first, appears to be a reasonable interpretation of a person's utterance. Second, that discourse has an action orientation; it is constructed in such a way that particular tasks – in this case blaming and disclaiming responsibility for the obnoxious effects of this blaming – are facilitated. [...]

These points have important implications for attitude scale research. If the person filling in the scale is viewed as merely *describing* or *expressing* their attitude, things seem quite clear-cut. Yet, if we start to view their response as a discursive act, which it always is, things become murkier, because there is a great deal of scope to perform different kinds of acts when filling in the scale. For example, a person might fill in the scale to perform the task of disclaiming by marking the 'sympathetic' pole; or they might perform the task of blaming by marking the 'unsympathetic' pole. They might hesitate because they see themselves as sympathetic and unsympathetic at the same time – 'I'm not anti but ...'. Two people putting the same mark on the scale could well be doing very different things with their discourse. If the opinion pollster is coordinating an interview, rather than requiring paper and pen responses the person might offer the whole utterance to the pollster and how it emerges, in terms of the category scales, will depend on the pollsters' current method of scaling.

One way we could proceed, given this line of argument, is to suggest that attitude measurement might survive in its present form if it became a more subtle business, more sensitive to the different acts performed. We should note, however, that this continues to assume that there is such a thing as 'an attitude' or an enduring, underlying state expressed in talk and behaviour. This position becomes extremely difficult to maintain when we look at the variations which appear in participants' accounts.

Variability

The following example is typical of the sort of variation in accounts which has now been documented in a wide swathe of different kinds of discourse. These two extracts are taken from subsequent pages of the interview transcript.

3   *Respondent.* What I would li ... rather see is that, sure, bring them
    ['Polynesian immigrants'] into New Zealand, right, try and train them in a skill,
    and encourage them to go back again (Pond [...])

4   *Respondent.* I think that if we encouraged more Polynesians and Maoris to be skilled people they would want to stay here, they're not um as uh nomadic as New Zealanders are (*Interviewer.* Haha.) so I think that would be better (Pond [...])

The contradiction is stark. In Extract Three the respondent states that they would like Polynesian immigrants to be trained in New Zealand and then to return to the Pacific Islands. In Extract Four the respondent claims it would be better if Polynesians were encouraged to become skilled and then stay in New Zealand. What are we to make of this variability? The problem is particularly acute for the attitude researcher because of the conflict between versions. An attempt to recover the person's 'underlying attitude' is not going to get very far.

The discourse analyst's response is rather different from the attitude researcher. We do not intend to use the discourse as a pathway to entities or phenomena lying 'beyond' the text. Discourse analysis does not take for granted that accounts reflect underlying attitudes or dispositions and therefore we do not expect that an individual's discourse will be consistent and coherent. Rather, the focus is on the discourse *itself*: how it is organized and what it is doing. Orderliness in discourse will be viewed as a product of the orderly *functions* to which discourse is put.

If we return to the accounts quoted above, and provide a bit more of the context, we can illustrate how a functional analysis might begin.

5   *Interviewer.* [Do] you think that, say, immigration from the Pacific Islands should be encouraged [ ] to a much larger extent than it is? It's fairly restricted at the moment.

     Respondent. Yes. Um, I think there's some problems in, in encouraging that too much, is that they come in uneducated about our ways, and I think it's important they understand what they're coming to. I, what I would li ... rather see is that, sure, bring them into New Zealand, right, try and train them in a skill, and encourage them to go back again because their dependence on us will be lesser. I mean [ ] while the people back there are dependent on the people being here earning money to send it back, I mean, that's a very very negative way of looking at something. [ ] people really should be trying, they should be trying to help their own nation first (Pond [...])

6   Polynesians, they are doing jobs now that white people wouldn't do. So in many sectors of of the community or or life, um, we would be very much at a loss without them, I think. Um, what I would like to see is more effort being made to train them into skills, skilled jobs, because we are without skilled people and a lot of our skilled people, white people, have left the country to go to other places. I think that if we encouraged more Polynesians and Maoris to be skilled people they would want to stay here, they're not as, uh, nomadic as New Zealanders are (*Interviewer.* Haha.) so I think that would be better (Pond [...])

Now we have a bit more of the context available we can see that the question of Polynesians returning to the Islands is related to a different issue in each extract. In Extract Five returning is related to the problem of 'dependence'. The speaker expresses concern that if Polynesians stay in New Zealand they will become dependent upon their incomes to support people in the Pacific Islands. The speaker suggests it would be better if they returned with skills to contribute to their 'own nation'.

In Extract Six, on the other hand, returning is related to problems with the New Zealand workforce. The speaker suggests that Polynesians are doing dirty jobs disliked by 'whites', so their leaving would precipitate economic problems. Moreover, she goes on to claim, the emigration of skilled whites has left a hole in the labour market which Polynesians should be trained to fill. So the speaker's two different versions of whether Polynesians ought to stay or not can be seen to flow logically and naturally from the formulations in the surrounding text. It is, of course, only sensible to adjust one's response to a topic according to the context. However, this kind of adjustment tends to be overlooked by the attitude researcher who would expect the speaker to be able to articulate on a decontextualized scale a static constant attitude regarding whether Polynesians should stay or return. If it is not static and constant then much of the point of this kind of measurement technology disappears.

Constitution

In traditional attitude theory, the attitude is considered to be separate from the 'object of thought'. The entire logic of attitude measurement, where a scale is used to compare different people's attitudes to the same object, is based upon this. If the object is not the same for different people there is no sense in comparing attitudes and the notion ceases to have utility. However, when we come to look at the detail of people's accounts this separation becomes virtually impossible to sustain. Far from the object of thought being a simple already present entity, the object is formulated and constructed in discourse in the course of doing evaluation.

Take the following extract, for example, which is part of an answer to a question about Polynesian crime.

7   *Respondent.* Then again, it's a problem of their racial integration. They've got a big racial minority coming in now and so they've got to get used to the way of life and, er, perhaps rape is accepted over in Samoa and Polynesia, but not in Auckland. They've got to learn that. And the problem's that a lot of people coming in with mental disease I think it is, because there is a lot of interbreeding in those islan ... islands. And that brings a big, high increase of retards and then people who come over here, retards perhaps and they//

Interviewer. // and that causes problems?

Respondent. And that's pretty general I know (Johnston [...])

In this passage the speaker is not just giving his views *about* 'Polynesian immigrants', he is formulating the very nature of the Polynesian immigrant. That is, he is not working with a neutral description of an object and then saying how he feels about it; he is constructing a *version* of the object. It is in this way evaluation is displayed. His version of the object carries off his evaluation. Polynesian immigrants are floridly depicted as a group who are involved in rapes and are carriers of 'mental disease'. It is implied they are from a culture which cannot control its desires properly, something they will have to learn to do before settling in New Zealand.

A central feature in this speaker's construction of 'Polynesian immigrants' is his use of broad explanatory principles. He does not rest at merely describing phenomena, he explains them too. Specifically he accounts for the prevalence of mental disease in terms of simple farmyard genetics; it is a consequence of 'interbreeding'. This drawing together of description, evaluation and broad systems of explanation is dramatically illustrated in the next extract from another speaker.

8   *Interviewer.* Yeah, so [crime] is partly sort of immig., it's related to immigration?

Respondent. Yeah, we don't, seeing them coming through, off the aircraft at night, half of them can't speak English. Um, if they can't speak English they're not going to be able to get a job, they're going to go and be in their little communities and they're not going to be able to contribute anything. And they're going to get frustrated because they're going to get bored. And they're going to, you know, there's nothing for them to do so the kids are going to start hanging around in the streets. At home Mum and Dad can't speak English and so the kids can't speak English. They go to school and suddenly they are confronted with English – 'we can't speak that, and what do we do?' – nothing. And so by the time they get to fifteen they just drop out. They have had it up to here with school and it's not the school's fault. They have brilliant lives, they have brilliant lives back in, family lives, back in the Islands and that is where they should be (Jones [...])

There are many fascinating features of this passage as a rhetorical construction. But the central thing to note is the way the final claim – that potential immigrants should stay in the Islands – is warranted through the use of an elaborate psychological and sociological story starting with a charged image of Polynesians slipping off the plane at night, going through language difficulties encountered by immigrants, which is taken to cause unemployment, and, eventually, the children's alienation from school. All this is contrasted with the 'brilliant family lives' available if they had not come to New Zealand. Throughout the passage we see a complex intertwining of description, explanation and evaluation.

Crucially, what we find when we examine naturally occurring discourse in detail is that the distinction between 'object of thought' and position on a 'dimension of judgment' becomes virtually impossible to make. It seems this distinction is an *artifact* of the way attitude scales are put together: all respondents are supposedly reacting to the same object of thought. Yet, as we can see from the extracts discussed in this chapter, sameness of wording does not necessarily mean that respondents will understand the terms or formulate the object of thought in an identical way. We have seen how different respondents formulate 'Polynesian immigrants', and how the *same* respondent might reformulate this notion on different occasions. If a researcher really wishes to get to grips with racism then a vital part of their activity must be the investigation of how description and explanation are meshed together and how different kinds of explanations assume different kinds of objects or supply the social world with varying objects.

[...]

In summary, a brief analysis of some extracts from interviews has highlighted the importance of a number of phenomena which have been relatively neglected in traditional attitude research. We stressed first the importance of examining context. Contextual information gives the researcher a much fuller understanding of the detailed and delicate organization of accounts. In addition, an understanding of this organization clarifies the action orientation of talk and its involvement in acts such as blaming and disclaiming.

The second phenomenon we illustrated was variability. A high degree of variation in accounts is a central prediction of the discourse approach: widely different kinds of accounts will be produced to do different things. On the other hand, considerable consistency must be predicted if participants are producing their language in the light of sets of attitudes which are stable across different contexts. Variability of the kind seen in detailed studies of discourse is thus a considerable embarrassment to traditional attitude theories.

The third phenomena we noted was the construction of the attitudinal object in discourse. The customary view is that attitudes are about distinct entities. Attitudes to immigrants, for instance, should concern an existing out–there-in-the-world group of people. Yet when we examined actual discourse this simple 'word and object' view of attitudes became unworkable. It is clear that the attitudinal object can be constituted in alternative ways, and the person's evaluation is directed at these *specific* formulations rather than some abstract and idealized object.

In response to these difficulties, the discourse approach shifts the focus from a search for underlying entities – attitudes – which generate talk and behaviour to a detailed examination of how evaluative expressions are produced in discourse. Two central and novel questions become dramatized. How is participants' language constructed, and what are the consequences of different types of construction? Whether at the end of this examination space is found for some modified notion of attitudes is, as yet, unclear (cf. Lalljee et al., 1984). [...]

References

Atkinson, J.M. (1984) *Our Master's Voices: The Language and Body Language of Politics*, London, Methuen.

Heritage, J. and Greatbach, D. (1986) 'Generating applause: a study of rhetoric and response at party political conferences', *American Sociological Review*, vol. 92, pp. 110–57.

Hewitt, J.P. and Stokes, R. (1975) 'Disclaimers', *American Sociological Review*, vol. 40, pp. 1–11.

Husband, C. (1982) 'Introduction: "race", the continuity of a concept' in Husband, C. (ed.) *'Race' in Britain: Continuity and Change*, London, Hutchinson.

Lalljee, M., Brown, L.B. and Ginsberg, G.P. (1984) 'Attitudes: disposition, behaviour or evaluation', *British Journal of Social Psychology*, vol. 23, pp. 233–44.

McGuire, W.J. (1985) 'Attitudes and attitude change' in Lindzey, G. and Aronson E. (eds) *Handbook of Social Psychology* (3rd edn), vol. 2, New York, Random House.

Marsh, A. (1976) 'Who hates the blacks?', *New Society*, 23 September, pp. 649–52.

Pomerantz, A. (1986) 'Extreme case formulations: a new way of legitimating claims' in Button, G., Drew, P. and Heritage, J. (eds) *Human Studies*, Interaction and language use special issue, vol. 9, pp. 219–30.

Reeves, W. (1983) *British Racial Discourse: A Study of British Political Discourse about Race and Race-Related Matters*, Cambridge, Cambridge University Press.

Sykes, M. (1985) 'Discrimination in discourse' in van Dijk, T.A. (ed.) *Handbook of Discourse Analysis*, vol. 4, London, Academic Press.

(Potter and Wetherell, 1987, pp. 32–55)

Conclusion

Reading 3.3 is another example of research about prejudice. It begins with a critique of Marsh's (1976) British research about 'coloured immigrants'. It then goes on to analyse accounts of Polynesian immigrants to New Zealand, taken not from questionnaire responses but from interviews. The extract can be read as a direct criticism of the kind of predictive model outlined in Reading 3.2, as is also indicated by Potter and Wetherell's book sub-title 'Beyond attitudes and behaviour'. They present a double challenge to the main tradition of attitude research. The first is methodological. They suggest that research which uses a graduated scale to record an attitude is flawed because it takes responses out of context; it ignores the inconsistencies in what people say and also the ways that meanings are constructed in ordinary talk. There are some similarities here with LaPiere's much earlier criticisms of questionnaire research. Potter and Wetherell also question the assumption that an evaluation can be translated into a numerical value to enable quantitative data analysis. In contrast, their own analysis is qualitative and interpretive; the 'attitudes' of their participants are situated within the larger context of Polynesian immigration to New Zealand and the then-current debates about it.

Their second challenge is theoretical and relates to the concept of an attitude as 'an enduring, underlying state expressed in talk and behaviour'. Potter and Wetherell approach both an attitude and its object as fluid, their meanings constantly redefined according to the context and purpose of the talk. They also question the assumption that either an attitude or its object is the same for different people. Their analysis of the attitudes 'in' people's talk focuses on how the talk, or account, is constructed and what functions it fulfils (such as warding off negative attributions). They note that the same person will say things which, they suggest, a conventional attitude researcher might interpret as the expression of different underlying attitudes. However, Potter and Wetherell are not interested in the individual speaker as a holder of attitudes. They have a very different conception which derives from their theorisation of talk and the person. They do not approach talk as an expression of something inside the speaker (a 'mental state'). Instead, they are interested in what people *do* in talk, although this is different to the behaviour discussed in the earlier extracts. They are not looking at causes but at talk as a kind of action in itself.

This is because of a larger assumption – that talk is social. Potter and Wetherell see the interaction between speakers (including an interview interaction) as the context in which meanings, like attitudes, are constructed. Beyond this, we might see all the talk of a society as a kind of huge collective activity through which meanings are circulated, debated and modified. Rather than producing wholly new talk from inside themselves, individual speakers join in the ongoing debates and take up ideas and arguments (for instance, about immigrants). In this sense, talk *is* the social context and an analysis of talk becomes an analysis of meanings and values which prevail within that society.

Potter and Wetherell's use of the term 'discourse' carries double associations. One is of discourse as speaking or interaction. The other, derived from the work of Michel Foucault (see Gordon, 1980, for more on this), is of the interconnected meanings which are established within a society and make sense of what is said and done within it, including the relationships of the powerful and powerless. As an example, immigration can only be understood through reference to the meanings of nation-state, national territory and citizenship, passport control and visas, and all the accepted ideas of 'us' and 'them' in terms of race and culture which are linked to national identity, as well as all the social and personal meanings and practices which flow on from these. Potter and Wetherell's analysis approaches context in these complex terms.

There are several possible responses to these challenges. A relatively minor one is that attitude researchers have not always used the kind of graduated response scale which Potter and Wetherell discuss, although the analyses have generally been statistical. More important points relate, first, to the nature of attitudes, and second, to the larger project of psychology. One of the claims made in Reading 3.3 is that 'The *crucial* assumption of attitude researchers is that there is something enduring within people which the scale is measuring – the attitude' (emphasis added). This statement indicates a major concern of discourse analysis and, later, discursive psychology, and Wetherell's work is part of a challenge to the theorisation of the person assumed to underlie conventional psychological research, including attitude research. This is the model of a contained, rational and stable individual who exists within and is governed by chains of cause-and-effect processes, which themselves can be analysed in terms of discrete variables and, ultimately, predicted and manipulated (Hollway, 2006). In contrast to this, discourse analysts, discursive psychologists and others understand a person as a complicated composite of the different selves which are brought into being by the multiple circumstances of a life. Different writers offer different interpretations of these ideas (e.g. Harré and Gillett, 1994; Wetherell, 1998) and the theoretical debates continue (see, for instance, Smith, 2000; Hollway and Jefferson, 2000; Wetherell, 2003).

You might be tempted to consider the extracts in this chapter as a critical sequence – LaPiere questions the link between expressions of attitude and future action, Ajzen elaborates on it, and Potter and Wetherell criticise the kind of approach used by Ajzen. However, this would be an oversimplification. Readings 3.2 and 3.3 are better taken as an indication of the breadth of the concerns of contemporary social psychology. Although there has been recent discursive psychological work on attitudes (e.g. Wiggins and Potter, 2003; Durrheim and Dixon, 2004), the majority of attitude researchers do not follow Potter and Wetherell's methodological approach. Nor are they part of the project of discursive psychologists, and others, to explain the nature of the person. The mainstream of attitude research in psychology follows from the kind of theorising and empirical research presented in Reading 3.2. Its concern is *not* with an attitude as something inside a person but, as noted in the Introduction, as a hypothetical, unobservable construct. And this is not assumed to be enduring but to change because of intervening variables. This tradition of work is critical in a different way, in the progressive refinement of theories to facilitate their practical application (a point which has been noted as a weakness of discursive research; see Willig, 1999). Its priority is indicated in a final quotation, from Eagly and Chaiken (1993): 'Understanding how people's attitudes cause them to behave is [...] an essential part of the shared mission of all psychologists, *which is understanding the causes of behaviour*' (p. 216, emphasis added).

References

Ajzen, I. (1988) *Attitudes, Personality, and Behavior*, Milton Keynes, Open University Press.

Ajzen, I. and Fishbein, M. (1980) *Understanding Attitudes and Predicting Behavior*, Englewood Cliffs, NJ, Prentice-Hall.

Ajzen, I. Timko, C. and White, J. (1982) 'Self-monitoring and the attitude behavior-relation', *Journal of Personality and Social Psychology*, vol. 42, pp. 426–35.

Bem, D.J. (1970) *Beliefs, Attitudes and Human Affairs*, Belmont, Brooks/Cole.

Durrheim, K. and Dixon, J. (2004) 'Attitudes in the fibre of everyday life: the discourse of racial evaluation and the lived experience of desegregation', *American Psychologist*, vol. 59 pp. 626–36.

Eagly, A. and Chaiken, S. (1993) *The Psychology of Attitudes*, Fort Worth, TX, Harcourt Brace College Publishers.

Fishbein, M. (1967) *Readings in Attitude Theory and Measurement*, London, Wiley.

Fishbein, M. (1980) 'A theory of reasoned action: some applications and implications' in Howe, H. and Page, M. (eds) *Nebraska Symposium on Motivation*, vol. 27, pp. 65–116, Lincoln, NB, University of Nebraska Press.

Fishbein, M. and Ajzen, I. (1975) *Belief, Attitude, Intention, and Behavior: An Introduction to Theory and Research*, Reading, MA, Addison-Wesley.

Giles, M. and Cairns, E. (1995) 'Blood donation and Ajzen's theory of planned behaviour: an examination of perceived behavioural control', *British Journal of Social Psychology*, vol. 34, pp. 173–88.

Gordon, C. (1980) *Power/Knowledge: Selected Interviews and Other Writings 1972–1977, Michel Foucault*, Hemel Hempstead, Harvester Wheatsheaf.

Harré, R. and Gillett, G. (1994) *The Discursive Mind*, London, Sage.

Hewstone, M., Manstead, A. and Stroebe, W. (1997) *The Blackwell Reader in Social Psychology*, Oxford, Blackwell.

Hollway, W. (2006) 'Methods and knowledge in social psychology' in Hollway, W., Lucey, H. and Phoenix, A. (eds) *Social Psychology Matters*, Maidenhead, Open University Press/Milton Keynes, The Open University.

Hollway, W. and Jefferson, T. (2000) *Doing Qualitative Research Differently: Free Association, Narrative and the Interview Method*, London, Sage.

LaPiere, R.T. (1967 [1934]) 'Attitudes versus actions' in Fishbein (ed.) (1967).

Manstead, A., Proffitt, C. and Smart, J. (1983) 'Predicting and understanding mothers' infant-feeding intentions and behavior: testing the theory of reasoned action', *Journal of Personality and Social Psychology*, vol. 44, pp. 657–71.

Marsh, A. (1976) 'Who hates the blacks?', *New Society*, 23 September, pp. 649–52.

Potter, J. and Wetherell, M. (1987) 'Unfolding discourse analysis' in Potter, J. and Wetherell, M. (eds) *Discourse and Social Psychology: Beyond Attitudes and Behaviour*, London, Sage.

Smith, J. (2000) *The Psychology of Action*, Basingstoke, Macmillan.

Triandis, H. and Triandis, L. (1960) 'Race, social class, religion and nationality as determinants of social distance', *Journal of Abnormal and Social Psychology*, vol. 61, pp. 110–18.

Wetherell, M. (1998) 'Positioning and interpretative repertoires: conversation analysis and post-structuralism in dialogue', *Discourse and Society*, vol. 9, pp.387–412.

Wetherell, M. (2003) 'Paranoia, ambivalence and discursive practices: concepts of position and positioning in psychoanalysis and discursive psychology' in Harré, R. and Moghaddam, F. (eds) *The Self and Others: Positioning Individuals and Groups in Personal, Political and Cultural Contexts*, Westport, CT, Praegar.

Wiggins, S. and Potter, J. (2003) 'Attitudes and evaluative practices: category vs. item and subjective vs. objective constructions in everyday food assessments', *British Journal of Social Psychology*, vol. 42, pp. 513–31.

Willig, C. (1999) 'Introduction: making a difference' in Willig, C. (ed.) *Applied Discourse Analysis: Social and Psychological Interventions*, Buckingham, The Open University Press.

Further reading

Bohner, G. and Wänke, M. (2002) *Attitudes and Attitude Change*, Hove, Psychology Press.
A recent book that provides an overview.

Fishbein, M. (1967) *Readings in Attitude Theory and Measurement*, London, Wiley.
A collection of classic texts and discussions.

Look also at the list of researchers and publications on the website for Social Psychological Attitude Researchers (SPAR) based at the University of Leeds, UK: www.psyc.leeds.ac.uk/research/spar (Accessed 7 August 2006).

Chapter 4

The fundamental attribution error

by Darren Langdridge, The Open University

Introduction

Attribution theory is the study of how we explain people's behaviour. It emerged with the work of Fritz Heider in the late 1950s and remains a central topic in contemporary social psychology (Vaughan and Hogg, 2004). Heider (1958) noted that people appeared to attribute the behaviour of other people either to internal dispositions or external circumstances. For example, imagine you are driving your car and another driver cuts in front of you. What is likely to be your first reaction? You might think that the other driver is incompetent or crazy and thereby make a dispositional attribution. Alternatively, you might see that the road is busy and wonder whether the driver is unfamiliar with this particular road: a situational attribution. Either way, Heider (1958) noted that people tend to look for causes for events, and these tend to be attributed either to internal dispositions or the external situation.

But why does this matter? Well, whether we attribute causes to people or the environment can have important consequences for our attitudes, beliefs and behaviour. Think again of our driving scenario and whether you attribute the cause of the bad driving to the person or the situation. If you attribute the cause to the person you are more likely to react negatively, perhaps shouting and waving your fist or even speeding up and chasing after the other driver. Whereas if you think the poor driving was caused by their unfamiliarity with the road and the difficult traffic conditions you may well proceed with caution, giving them more space and time to deal with the conditions. The practical point then is that our attributions have real and important consequences. And the attribution of causality does not just matter with driving behaviour. If you were on a jury and having to decide whether a defendant acted in self-defence or with malicious intent, or if you were having an argument with your partner, deciding whether the cruel remarks were due to the stressful situation or them being a nasty person, you would need to attribute causality and witness the consequences of your decision. On a more macro level, who do you think is responsible for unemployment: the unemployed person for being too feckless to get a job or the national situation for failing to provide the necessary opportunities and support to enable a person to get a job? All of these situations involve the attribution of cause. So, attribution theory really does matter because it can and does have practical consequences for the way we live our lives.

We attribute the causes of behaviour on a routine basis in our everyday lives. When we meet a new person who says very little we may think that they are shy, while someone else who is very talkative may be thought an extrovert. In both cases we are attributing their different behaviours to some aspect of their 'personality'. It may well be the case that we are right and that the people we have met are generally shy or extroverted, but this is not necessarily so. They may have been having an 'off day', been in an odd situation or found us difficult (or easy) to talk to; the possible explanations for such behaviours are almost endless. None the less, a great deal of research has shown that we still tend to attribute the cause of other people's behaviour more to personal characteristics and less to the situation. This attributional bias or tendency is known as the *fundamental attribution error* (FAE) (Ross, 1977) and forms the focus of this chapter.

Attributional biases (or errors) have been a central concern of attribution researchers since Heider (1958) first proposed an attribution theory, and the FAE in particular has been the most intensively researched bias in social perception (Fiske and Taylor, 1991; Jones, 1990). However, in spite of the considerable interest in the fundamental attribution error, its causes remain a mystery. The extensive research on the FAE has led to the proliferation of findings showing ever more subtle differences in the way in which the FAE operates, with numerous theories designed to make sense of all the variations, some of which will be mentioned in this chapter. There is still a sense, in spite of all this attention, that the FAE is yet to be explained. Why do people appear, according to existing research at least, to attribute the cause of events more to the person than the situation? Why do children demonstrate this bias in late adolescence rather than early childhood? Why is this perceptual bias predominantly found in Western cultures? And why is a supposedly fundamental perceptual bias affected by individual differences?

In this chapter, I take the FAE as my focus and contrast two very different ways of understanding this simple and seemingly pervasive phenomenon. First, I will provide some more background to attribution theory; in particular, I will highlight the way in which the early work of Heider (1944, 1958), which has often been ignored or forgotten, has left a lasting legacy in this area and most importantly provided vital clues for understanding the fundamental attribution error. I then move on to introduce Reading 4.1, by Lee Ross (1977), in which he provides a comprehensive overview of attribution research in the late 1970s. While you may wonder if this is still relevant, given the years that have passed since it was written, this summary statement not only provides comprehensive coverage of a very great deal of early research but also will enable you to see how the majority of work on attribution theory, and especially on the fundamental attribution error, since Heider, has been increasingly focused on the accumulation of ever smaller pieces of information gleaned predominantly through the experimental method.

Reading 4.2, written in 2004 by Trevor Butt and myself, aims to provide an alternative understanding of the fundamental attribution error, grounded in phenomenology, which in many ways represents a return to the original work of Heider. In the final section of this chapter, I attempt to explore further how we might more fruitfully understand attribution theory by approaching it from a phenomenological perspective, in which people's experience is prioritised and the attribution of causality understood as an intrinsic part of the way in which we intuitively try to make sense of the world.

As mentioned above, it was Heider (1944, 1958), within social psychology at least, who first noted that a person attribution was more likely than a situation attribution, arguing that this was due to persons being understood as the 'prototype of origins', that is, the source of a change which brought about some effect, such as behaviour (Heider, 1944, p. 359). Hewstone (1989) points out that this was probably influenced by the legal philosophy of Fauconnet, who identified the person as 'first cause' and therefore culpable for their actions. The tendency to view the person as the 'prototype of origins' in turn leads to the underestimation of situational factors, and the normal interrelationship between person and situation, as we think of people being responsible for all their behaviour.

Heider left a lasting legacy for social psychology, and in particular attribution theory, but the nature of his contribution is often forgotten. Hewstone (1989), following Ross and Fletcher (1985), highlights four central ideas that remain important in social psychology that can be directly traced to Heider and his early work. First, Heider thought the process of attributing causality for events was similar, in many respects, to the perceptual process. What Heider stressed was that, while an object might consist of very many 'objective' properties (such as length or mass), what was most important, psychologically speaking, was the way in which it was perceived. Consequently, the tendency to perceive dispositional properties as central in the attribution of causality was in part due to the need that we have to make our world stable, predictable and controllable. This understanding led Heider (1958) to make the distinction between person (dispositional) and situation (environmental) attributions, which was his second central contribution to the field. Heider's third contribution is an elaboration of this point, with his suggestion that person attributions were more readily made for intentional than unintentional events. Finally, Heider (1958) suggested that three pieces of information were central to understanding why we attribute effects to the person, the object or mediating conditions: 'factors within the perceiver', 'properties of the object' and 'mediating conditions'. A number of these ideas were the inspiration for later developments in the field.

Heider's approach to social psychology was thought by some to be phenomenological (e.g. Shaver, 1975), particularly influenced by Gestalt psychology, even though he himself rejected that label, preferring to focus his work on explanatory causal analysis – an anathema to phenomenology, which is concerned with description rather than explanation. It is clear, however, that his first two contributions, the focus on perception as a model and people's need to gain control over their world, are phenomenological concepts, present in early phenomenological philosophy and exemplified in the work of Merleau-Ponty (1962). This point is picked up and employed as a key analytic strategy in Langdridge and Butt (2004), and we shall return to it in the discussion.

While Heider laid the foundations of attribution theory, and particularly raised the question of the fundamental attribution error, his work was to be superseded by later theorists, notably Jones and Davis (1965) and Kelley

(1967), who began to change attribution theory, theoretically and methodologically, in quite a profound way. With their work, attribution theory became ever more focused on the micro level, with studies concerned with unpicking the detail of phenomena like the fundamental attribution error, and also on the individual, rather than the social, with research grounded in the cognitive tradition that has come to dominate contemporary social psychology. Perhaps this was the necessary consequence of the desire to produce theories which were more formal and therefore more testable, a central aim of the scientific project of which much social psychology has been a part. There is no doubt that there has been a considerable amount of useful work done because of the increasing formalisation and sophistication of research, with findings feeding into important aspects of our everyday lives. Reading 4.1, by Ross, presents an overview of contemporary work on attributional errors (or biases) in 1977, including some particularly insightful conceptual discussion by one of the leading figures in the field. You will read about a number of now classic experiments and the ingenious designs that have been used to unpick the intricacies of the fundamental attribution error.

ACTIVITY 4.1

As you read the following extract, consider these points:

- What assumptions about the person underpin the methods that Ross describes?
- Ross talks of the advances that have come as a result of psychologists starting to understand the person as an intuitive psychologist. What do you think are the advantages and disadvantages of this model of human nature?

Reading 4.1 was written in 1977 by Lee Ross, a leading attribution theorist in the experimental tradition. It provides a summary of work on attribution theory and, in particular, the FAE.

READING 4.1

'The intuitive psychologist and his shortcomings: distortions in the attribution process'

I   Introduction to attribution theory and attribution error

A   Attribution theory and intuitive psychology

Attribution theory, in its broadest sense, is concerned with the attempts of ordinary people to understand the causes and implications of the events they witness. It deals with the 'naive psychology' of the 'man in the street' as he interprets his own behaviors and the actions of others. The current ascendancy of attribution theory in social psychology culminates a long struggle to upgrade that discipline's conception of man. No longer the stimulus–response (S–R) automaton of radical behaviorism, promoted beyond the rank of information processor and cognitive consistency seeker, psychological man has at last been awarded a status equal to that of the scientist who investigates him. For man, in the perspective of attribution theory, is an intuitive psychologist who seeks to explain behavior and to draw inferences about actors and their environments.

To better understand the perceptions and actions of this intuitive scientist we must explore his methods. First, like the academic psychologist, he is guided by a number of implicit assumptions about human nature and human behavior, for example, that the pursuit of pleasure and the avoidance of pain are ubiquitous and powerful human motives, or that conformity to the wishes and expectations of one's peers is less exceptional and less demanding of further interpretation than is nonconformity. The amateur psychologist, like the professional one, also relies heavily upon data. Sometimes these data result from first-hand experience; more often, they are the product of informal social communication, mass media, or other indirect sources. Moreover, the representativeness or randomness of the available data is rarely guaranteed by formal sampling procedures. The intuitive psychologist must further adopt or develop techniques for coding, storing, and retrieving such data. Finally, he must resort to methods for summarizing, analyzing, and interpreting his data, that is, rules, formulas, or schemata that permit him to extract meaning and form inferences. The intuitive scientist's ability to master his social environment depends in large measure upon the accuracy and adequacy of his hypotheses, evidence, and methods of analysis and inference. Conversely, sources of oversight, error, or bias in his assumptions and procedures may have serious consequences, both for the lay psychologist himself and for the society that he builds and perpetuates. These shortcomings, explored from the vantage point of contemporary attribution theory, provide the focus of the present chapter.

While the label 'attribution theory' and some of the jargon of its proponents may be relatively new and unfamiliar, its broad concerns – naive epistemology and the social inference process – have a long and honorable history in social psychology. The Gestalt tradition, defying the forces of radical behaviorism, has consistently emphasized the *subject's* assignment of meaning to the events that unfold in the psychological laboratory and in everyday experience (cf. Asch, 1952). Icheiser (1949) explicitly discussed some fundamental social perception biases and their origins almost 30 years ago. Long before attribution theory's current vogue, Kelly (1955, 1958) brought an attributional perspective to the study of psychopathology and, in fact, explicitly suggested the analogy between the tasks of the intuitive observer and those of the behavioral scientist. Schachter and Singer (1962) and Bem (1965, 1967, 1972) further anticipated current attributional approaches in their respective analyses of emotional labelling and self-perception phenomena.

The broad outlines of contemporary attribution theory, however, were first sketched by Heider (1944, 1958) and developed in greater detail by Jones and Davis (1965), Kelley (1967), and their associates (e.g., Jones, Kanouse, Kelley, Nisbett, Valins, & Weiner, [1971]; Weiner, 1974). These theorists emphasized two closely related tasks confronting the social observer. The first task is causal judgment: the observer seeks to identify the cause, or set of causes, to which some particular effect (i.e., some action or outcome) may most reasonably be *attributed*. The second task is social inference: the observer of an episode forms inferences about the *attributes* of relevant entities, that is, either the dispositions of actors or the properties of situations to which those actors have responded.

Causal judgment and social inference tasks have both been the subject of intensive theoretical and empirical inquiry and, until recently, had constituted virtually the entire domain of attribution theory. Lately, however, a third task of the intuitive psychologist has begun to receive some attention; that task is the *prediction* of outcomes and behavior. Episodes characteristically lead the intuitive psychologist not only to seek explanations and to make social inferences but also to form expectations and make predictions about the future actions and outcomes. Thus, when a presidential candidate promises to 'ease the burden of the average taxpayer,' we do attempt to judge whether the promise might have resulted from and reflected the demands of political expediency rather than the candidate's true convictions. However, we are likely also to speculate about and try to anticipate this candidate's and other candidates' future political actions. The psychology of intuitive prediction is thus a natural extension of attribution theory's domain.

The three attribution tasks are, of course, by no means independent. Explanations for and inferences from an event are obviously and intimately related, and together they form an important basis for speculation about unknown and future events. Each task, moreover, can reveal much about the assumptions, strategies, and failings of the intuitive psychologist. Each, however, provides some unique problems of interpretation and methodology that we should explore before proceeding.

In describing causal judgments, researchers from the time of Heider's early contributions to the present have relied heavily upon a simple internal–external or disposition–situation dichotomy. That is, they have tried to identify those configurations of possible causes and observed effects that lead the observer to attribute an event to 'internal' dispositions of the actor (e.g., abilities, traits, or motives) or to aspects of the 'external' situation (e.g., task difficulties, incentives, or peer pressures). While this seemingly simple dichotomy has undeniable intuitive appeal, it creates a host of conceptual problems and methodological pitfalls (see also Kruglanski, 1975). For instance, attribution researchers (e.g., Nisbett, Caputo, Legant, & Maracek, 1973) frequently require subjects to explain why a particular actor has chosen a particular course of behavior. These attributions are then coded as 'situational' or 'dispositional' on the basis of the *form* of the subject's response. Thus the statement 'Jack bought the house because it was so secluded' is coded as an external or situational attribution, whereas 'Jill bought the house because she wanted privacy' is coded as an internal or dispositional attribution. The rationale for such coding seems straightforward: The former statement cites something about the object or situation to which the actor responded while the latter statement cites something about the actor. However, when one attends not to the *form* of the attributer's statement but to its *content*, the legitimacy of many such situation–disposition distinctions becomes more dubious. First, it is apparent that causal statements which explicitly cite situational causes implicitly convey something about the actor's dispositions; conversely, statements which cite dispositional causes invariably imply the existence and controlling influence of situational factors. For instance, in accounting for Jack's purchase of a house the 'situational' explanation (i.e., 'because *it* was so secluded') implies a disposition on the part of this particular actor to favor seclusion. Indeed, the explanation provided is no explanation at all unless one *does* assume that such a disposition controlled Jack's response. Conversely, the dispositional explanation for Jill's purchase (i. e., because *she* likes privacy) clearly implies something about the house (i.e., its capacity to provide such privacy) that, in turn, governed Jill's behavior. Thus the content of both sentences, notwithstanding their differences in form, communicates the information that a particular feature of the house exists and that the purchaser was disposed to respond positively to that feature. In fact, the form of the sentences could have been reversed without altering their content to read 'Jack bought the house because he wanted seclusion' and 'Jill bought the house because it provided privacy.'

Is there a more meaningful basis for a distinction between situational and dispositional causes? One possibility merits consideration. One could ignore the form of subjects' causal statements and, by attending to content, distinguish between (1) explanations that do not state or imply any dispositions on the part of the actor beyond those typical of actors in general, and (2) explanations that do state or imply unique relatively atypical or distinguishing personal dispositions. Thus the causal statements 'I was initially attracted to Sally because she is so beautiful' and 'I was initially attracted to Sally because her astrological sign is Libra' should be coded differently in terms of the proposed distinction despite their similar form. Specifically, while the former explanation conveys that I, *like* most men, am particularly attracted to beautiful women, the latter implies that I, *unlike* most men, am particularly attracted to women of one specific astrological sign. In a sense, the former statement constitutes a situational explanation because it invokes a widely accepted and generally applicable S–R law; the latter explanation, by contrast, is dispositional because it resorts to an individual difference or distinguishing personality variable.

The interpretation of causal statements in the manner just described is obviously a difficult undertaking and many investigators may favor the second attribution task, i.e., the formation of social inferences. This task, at first glance, seems to offer a far less forbidding but no less rewarding research target. For instance, the subject who learns that Joan has donated money to a particular charity may infer that the relevant act reflected (or, in Jones and Davis' (1965) terms, 'corresponded' to) some personal disposition of Joan. Alternatively, the subject may infer that Joan's actions reflected not her personal characteristics but the influence of social pressures, incentives, or other environmental factors. The attribution researcher, accordingly, can measure the subject's willingness to assert something about Joan's traits, motives, abilities, beliefs, or other personal dispositions on the basis of the behavioral evidence provided. Specifically, the subject could be required to characterize Joan by checking a Likert-type scale anchored at 'very generous' and 'not at all generous' with a midpoint of 'average in generosity.' An alternative version of the scale might deal with the degree of confidence the rater is willing to express in his social inferences.

Such measures of social inference are, indeed, simple to contrive and simple to score. Nevertheless, nontrivial problems of interpretation do arise. Most obvious is the fact that the meaning of a given point on these scales differs for different subjects. More importantly, that meaning may depend upon subtle features of research context and instruction, features often beyond the experimenter's knowledge or control.

Even subtler problems of interpretation may arise. One common format, for instance, asks subjects to indicate whether the specified person is 'generous' or 'ungenerous,' or that they 'can't say, depends upon circumstances.' Superficially, the first two options indicate willingness to infer the existence or influence of a personal disposition, whereas the third option suggests unwillingness to do so. But a more careful examination of the rater's perceptions may reveal that the third option reflects the rejection only of a *broad* or *general* dispositional label. Thus, further interrogation might reveal that the rater judged the relevant actor to be unexceptional with respect to the behavioral domain in question, that is, like most actors behaving generously or not as situational pressures and constraints dictate. In such a case it seems that no disposition has been inferred (and that the rater has made a situational rather than a dispositional attribution of relevant behavior). On the other hand, the rater's reluctance to choose either trait label may convey his judgment that the actor is relatively more generous than his fellows in some specific circumstances but less generous in others, i.e., that his generosity is inconsistent or idiosyncratic [...]. In the latter case a disposition *has* been inferred, albeit a relatively specific one, for example, a tendency to be unusually generous to one's employees but not to one's family, or vice versa. In fact, several important papers in the attribution area (e.g., Jones & Nisbett, 1971; Nisbett et al., 1973), have failed to distinguish adequately between the absence of trait inferences and the rejection of broad trait labels in favor of narrow or situation-specified ones. Inevitably, confusion and unwarranted conclusions have been the product of this failure.

The third type of attribution task, prediction of behavior [...], permits simple unambiguous questions and produces responses that can be scored objectively. Thus the witness to an ostensibly generous act by Joan might be required to predict Joan's behavior in a series of other episodes that seemingly test an actor's generosity or lack of it. Alternatively, the question put to the social observer might be: 'What percentage of students (or of people, or of women, or of Joan's socioeconomic peers, etc.) would have behaved as generously as Joan did?' The logical relationship of the prediction task to the tasks of causal judgment and social inference is worth reemphasizing [...]. To the extent that a given action or outcome is attributed to the actor rather than his situation and that some stable disposition is inferred, the attributer should prove willing to make confident and distinguishing predictions about the actor's subsequent behaviors or outcomes. Conversely, to the extent that an act is attributed to situational pressures that would dispose all actors to behave similarly, and to the extent that no inferences are made about the actor's dispositions, the observer should eschew such 'distinguishing' predictions; instead, he should invoke the 'null hypothesis' and rely upon his baseline information or estimates about how 'people in general' respond in the specified situation.

Prediction measures of attribution processes have a crucial advantage (beyond their simplicity and seeming objectivity). Unlike causal judgments or social inferences, predictions can often be evaluated with respect to their *accuracy*. That is, whenever authentic information is available about the behavior of various actors in more than one situation, the success of the intuitive psychologist's attribution strategy can be measured and the direction of biases can be determined. [...]

[...] Motivational and nonmotivational sources of bias

The central concern of the present chapter, and an increasingly important goal of contemporary research and theory, is not the logical schemata which promote understanding, consensus, and effective social control; instead, it is the sources of systematic bias or distortion in judgment that lead the intuitive psychologist to misinterpret events and hence to behave in ways that are personally maladaptive, socially pernicious, and often puzzling to the social scientist who seeks to understand such behavior.

In speculating about possible distortions in an otherwise logical attribution system, theorists were quick to postulate 'ego-defensive' biases through which attributers maintained or enhanced their general self-esteem or positive opinion of their specific dispositions and abilities (Heider, 1958; Jones & Davis, 1965; Kelley, 1967). Attempts to prove the existence of such a motivational bias have generally involved demonstrations of asymmetry in the attribution of positive and negative outcomes – specifically, a tendency for actors to attribute 'successes' to their own efforts, abilities, or dispositions while attributing 'failure' to luck, task difficulty, or other external factors. Achievement tasks (e.g., Davis & Davis, 1972; Feather, 1969; Fitch, 1970; Wolosin, Sherman, & Till, 1973) and teaching performances (e.g., Beckman, 1970; Freize & Weiner, 1971; Johnson, Feigenbaum, & Weiby, 1964) have provided most of the evidence for this asymmetry. It has also been shown that actors may give themselves more credit for success and less blame for failure than do observers evaluating the same outcomes (Beckman, 1970; Gross, 1966; Polefka, 1965).

Critics, skeptical of broad motivational biases, however, have experienced little difficulty in challenging such research. [...] First, it is obvious that subjects' private perceptions and interpretations may not correspond to (and may be either less or more 'defensive' than) their overt judgments. Second, asymmetries in the attributions of success and failure or differences in the judgments of actors and observers need not reflect motivational influences. As several researchers have noted, success, at least in test situations, is likely to be anticipated and congruent with the actor's past experience, whereas failure may be unanticipated and unusual. Similarly, successful outcomes are intended and are the object of plans and actions by the actor, whereas failures are unintended events which occur in spite of the actor's plans and efforts. Observers, furthermore, rarely are fully aware of the past experiences or present expectations and intentions of the actors whose outcomes they witness.

Challenges to the existence of pervasive ego-defensive biases have been empirical as well as conceptual. Thus, in some studies subjects seem to show 'counterdefensive' or esteem-attenuating biases. For example, Ross, Bierbrauer, and Polly (1974), using an unusually authentic instructor–learner paradigm, found that instructors rated their own performances and abilities as more important determinants of failure than of success. Conversely, the instructors rated their learner's efforts and abilities as less critical determinants of failure than success. In the same study these seemingly counterdefensive attributional tendencies proved to be even more pronounced among professional teachers than among inexperienced undergraduates, a result which contradicted the obvious derivation from ego-defensiveness theory that those most directly threatened by the failure experience would be most defensive.

Researchers who insist that self-serving motivational biases exist can, of course, provide alternative interpretations of studies that seem to show no motivational biases or counterdefensive biases. Indeed, in many respects the debate between proponents and skeptics has become reminiscent of earlier and broader debates in learning theory and basic perception in which the fruitlessness of the search for a 'decisive' experiment on the issue of motivational influences (i.e., one that could not be interpreted by the 'other side') became ever more apparent as data multiplied and conceptual analysis sharpened. One approach favored by many researchers has been an attempt to specify relevant moderator variables that might determine when ego defensiveness will distort the attribution process and when it will not do so. An alternate and perhaps more fruitful strategy, however, may be to temporarily abandon motivational constructs and to concentrate upon those informational, perceptual, and cognitive factors that mediate and potentially distort attributional judgments 'in general.' A fuller understanding of such factors, in turn, might well allow us, ultimately, to understand and anticipate the particular circumstances in which attributions of responsibility will unduly enhance or attenuate an attributer's self-esteem [...].

Unfortunately the existing attribution literature provides relatively little conceptual analysis or evidence pertaining to nonmotivational biases. The first identified (Heider, 1958) and most frequently cited bias or error, one which we shall term the *fundamental* attribution error, is the tendency for attributers to underestimate the impact of situational factors and to overestimate the role of dispositional factors in controlling behavior. [...]

Our consideration of other previously cited nonmotivational biases shall be brief. Perhaps the most provocative contribution concerning nonmotivational biases has been Jones and Nisbett's (1971) generalization regarding the 'divergent' perceptions of actors and observers [...]. Essentially, it was proposed that actors and observers differ in their susceptibility to the fundamental attribution error; that is, in situations where actors attribute their own behavioral choices to situational forces and constraints, observers are likely to attribute the same choices to the actors' stable abilities, attitudes, and personality traits. An interesting and unusual feature of the Jones and Nisbett paper is its careful consideration of underlying processes – informational, cognitive, and perceptual in nature – which might *account for* these divergent perceptions of actors and observers [...]. Another interesting line of investigation (one, incidentally, which promises to subsume Jones and Nisbett's actor–observer generalization) involves 'perceptual focusing' (Duncker, 1938; Wallach, 1959). It appears that whatever or whomever we 'focus our attention on' becomes more apt to be cited as a causal agent (Arkin & Duval, 1975; Duval & Wicklund, 1972; Regan & Totten, 1975; Storms, 1973; Taylor & Fiske, 1975).

Other attributional biases that have been proposed in the literature have been less systematically investigated. Our list, although incomplete, is perhaps representative. Jones and Davis (1965), for instance, proposed that actions directed towards the attributer, or having consequences for him, are more likely to be attributed to dispositions of the actor than are acts which do not personally involve or affect the attributer. Walster (1966) reported a questionnaire study suggesting that actors are held more responsible (and 'chance' or 'luck' less responsible) for acts that have serious consequences than for acts with trivial consequences. Finally Kelley (1971), summarizing the results of several prior questionnaire studies, observed that the actor is also held more responsible for acts which lead to reward than for acts which prevent loss or punishment.

II   Attributional biases: instances, causes, and consequences

A   The fundamental attribution error

Our exploration of the intuitive psychologist's shortcomings must start with his general tendency to overestimate the importance of personal or dispositional factors relative to environmental influences. As a psychologist he seems too often to be a nativist, or proponent of individual differences, and too seldom an S–R behaviourist. He too readily infers broad personal dispositions and expects consistency in behavior or outcomes across widely disparate situations and contexts. He jumps to hasty conclusions upon witnessing the behavior of his peers, overlooking the impact of relevant environmental forces and constraints. Beyond anecdotes and appeals to experience, the evidence most frequently cited for this general bias (e.g., Jones & Nisbett, 1971; Kelley, 1971) involves the attributer's apparent willingness to draw 'correspondent' personal inferences about actors who have responded to very obvious situational pressures. For instance, Jones and Harris (1967) found that listeners assumed some correspondence between communicators' pro-Castro remarks and their private opinions even when these listeners *knew* that the communicators were obeying the experimenter's explicit request under 'no choice' conditions. A more direct type of evidence that observers may ignore or underestimate situational forces has been provided by Bierbrauer (1973), who studied subjects' impressions of the forces operating in the classic Milgram (1963) situation. In Bierbrauer's study, participants witnessed a faithful verbatim reenactment of one subject's 'obedience' to the point of delivering the maximum shock to the supposed victim. Regardless of the type and amount of delay before judging [...], regardless of whether they actually played the role of a subject in the reenactment or merely observed, and regardless of their perceptual or cognitive 'set,' Bierbrauer's participants showed the fundamental attribution error; that is, they consistently and dramatically underestimated the degree to which subjects in general would yield to those situational forces which compelled obedience in Milgram's situation. In other words, they assumed that the particular subject's obedience reflected his distinguishing personal dispositions rather than the potency of situational pressures and constraints acting upon all subjects. The susceptibility of observers to the fundamental attribution error has been noted by many theorists (e.g., Heider, 1944, 1958; Icheiser, 1949) and disputed by few. The relevance of this error to the phenomena and research strategies of contemporary social psychology, however, has been less widely recognized. [...]

References

Arkin, R.M. and Duval, S. (1975) 'Focus of attention and causal attributions of actors and observers', *Journal of Experimental Social Psychology*, vol. 11, pp. 427–38.

Asch, S. (1952) *Social Psychology*, Englewood Cliffs, NJ, Prentice-Hall.

Beckman, L. (1970) 'Effects of students' performance on teachers' and observers' attributions of causality', *Journal of Educational Psychology*, vol. 61, pp. 75–82.

Bem, D.J. (1965) 'An experimental analysis of self-persuasion', *Journal of Experimental Social Psychology*, vol. 1, pp. 199–218.

Bem, D.J. (1967) 'Self-perception: an alternative interpretation of cognitive dissonance phenomena', *Psychological Review*, vol. 74, pp. 183–200.

Bem, D.J. (1972) 'Self-perception theory' in Berkowitz, L. (ed.) *Advances in Experimental Social Psychology*, vol. 6, New York, Academic Press.

Bierbrauer, G. (1973) 'Effects of set, perspective, and temporal factors in attribution', unpublished doctoral dissertation, Stanford University.

Davis, W.L. and Davis, D. E. (1972) 'Internal–external control and attribution of responsibility for success and failure', *Journal of Personality*, vol. 40, pp. 123–36.

Duncker, K. (1938) 'Induced motion' in Ellis, W. (ed.) *A Sourcebook of Gestalt Psychology*, New York, Harcourt, pp. 161–72.

Duval, S. and Wicklund, R.A. (1972) *A Theory of Objective Self-Awareness*, New York, Academic Press.

Feather, N.T. (1969) 'Attribution of responsibility and valence of success and failure in relation to initial confidence and task performance', *Journal of Personality and Social Psychology*, vol. 13, pp. 129–44.

Fitch, G. (1970) 'Effects of self-esteem, perceived performance, and chance on causal attributions', *Journal of Personality and Social Psychology*, vol. 16, pp. 311–15.

Freize, I. and Weiner, B. (1971) 'Cue utilization and attributional judgments for success and failure', *Journal of Personality*, vol. 39, pp. 591–606.

Gross, A. (1966) 'Evaluation of the target person in a social influence situation', unpublished doctoral dissertation, Stanford University.

Heider, F. (1944) 'Social perception and phenomenal causality', *Psychological Review*, vol. 51, pp. 358–73.

Heider, F. (1958) *The Psychology of Interpersonal Relations*, New York, Wiley.

Icheiser, G. (1949) 'Misunderstandings in human relations: a study in false social perception', *American Journal of Sociology*, vol. 55, Part 2, pp. 1–70.

Johnson, T.J., Feigenbaum, R. and Weiby, M. (1964) 'Some determinants and consequences of the teacher's perception of causation', *Journal of Experimental Psychology*, vol. 55, pp. 237–46.

Jones, E.E. and Davis, K.E. (1965) 'From acts to dispositions: the attribution process in person perceptions' in Berkowitz, L. (ed.) *Advances in Experimental Social Psychology*, vol. 2, New York, Academic Press.

Jones, E.E. and Harris, V.A. (1967) 'The attribution of attitudes', *Journal of Experimental Social Psychology*, vol. 3, pp. 1–24.

Jones, E.E., Kanouse, D.E., Kelley, H.H., Nisbett, R.E., Valins, S. and Weiner, B. (1971) *Attribution: Perceiving the Causes of Behavior*, Morristown, NJ, General Learning Press.

Jones, E.E. and Nisbett, R.E. (1971) 'The actor and the observer: divergent perceptions of the causes of behavior' in Jones, E.E. et al. (eds) (1971).

Kelley, H.H. (1967) 'Attribution theory in social psychology' in Levine, D. (ed.) *Nebraska Symposium on Motivation*, vol. 15, Lincoln, University of Nebraska Press.

Kelley, H.H. (1971) 'Attribution in social interaction' in Jones, E.E. et al. (eds) (1971).

Kelly, G. (1955) *The Psychology of Personal Constructs*, New York, Norton, 2 vols.

Kelly, G. (1958) 'Man's construction of his alternatives' in Lindzey, G. (ed.) *Assessment of Human Motives*, New York, Holt.

Kruglanski, A. (1975) 'The endogenous-exogenous partition in attribution theory', *Psychological Review*, vol. 82, pp. 387–406.

Milgram, S. (1963) 'Behavioral study of obedience', *Journal of Abnormal and Social Psychology*, vol. 67, pp. 371–8.

Nisbett, R.E., Caputo, C.G., Legant, P. and Maracek, J. (1973) 'Behavior as seen by the actor and as seen by the observer', *Journal of Personality and Social Psychology*, vol. 27, pp. 154–64.

Polefka, J. (1965) 'The perception and evaluation of responses to social influences', unpublished doctoral dissertation, Stanford University.

Regan, D.T. and Totten, J. (1975) 'Empathy and attribution: turning observers into actors', *Journal of Personality and Social Psychology*, vol. 32, pp. 850–6.

Ross, L., Bierbrauer, G. and Polly, S. (1974) 'Attribution of educational outcomes by professional and non-professional instructors', *Journal of Personality and Social Psychology*, vol. 29, pp. 609–18.

Schachter, S. and Singer, J.E. (1962) 'Cognitive, social and physiological determinants of emotional state', *Psychological Review*, vol. 69, pp. 379–99.

Storms, M. (1973) 'Videotape and the attribution process: reversing actors' and observers' points of view', *Journal of Personality and Social Psychology*, vol. 27, pp. 165–75.

Taylor, S.E. and Fiske, S.T. (1975) 'Point of view and perceptions of causality', *Journal of Personality and Social Psychology*, vol. 32, pp. 439–45.

Wallach, H. (1959) 'The perception of motion', *Scientific American*, vol. 201, pp. 56–60.

Walster, E. (1966) 'Assignment of responsibility for an accident', *Journal of Personality and Social Psychology*, vol. 3, pp. 73–9.

Weiner, B. (1974) *Achievement Motivation and Attribution Theory*, Morristown, NJ, General Learning Press.

Wolosin, R.J., Sherman, S.J. and Till, A. (1973) 'Effects of cooperation and competition on responsibility attribution after success and failure', *Journal of Experimental Social Psychology*, vol. 9, pp. 220–35.

(Ross, 1977, pp. 173–220)

Commentary

In Reading 4.1 by Ross (1977) it is clear that social psychologists have become focused on the minutiae of attribution theory. Researchers since Ross continue to use experimental methods to unpick the detail of the phenomena being studied. The work has to a very great extent become even more micro: increasingly focused on the individual, and conducted in the laboratory with considerably less consideration of the broader social context in which the FAE operates. This has led to some very interesting findings and a greater understanding of the way in which the FAE operates in different conditions. However, it has also generated calls (e.g. Sabini, Siepmann and Stein, 2001) for an adequate theoretical understanding that is able to account for the findings we now have.

Why is this kind of incremental addition to understanding, in response to more and more detailed questions, a problem? Is not increasing knowledge to be found in ever more detailed questioning and hence ever more micro-level findings? Several psychologists, and many philosophers (such as Kuhn and Feyerabend), think this faith in the gradual accumulation of facts is misguided. Kelly (1955), the founder of personal construct theory (see Chapter 8), termed this 'accumulative fragmentalism' and argued instead that scientific knowledge emerges from the adoption of new theoretical perspectives.

Ross is not uncritical of work on attribution theory, however, and it is possible to identify some early indicators here of the conceptual problems with the FAE which are taken further in Reading 4.2. In particular, Ross questions the simple internal–external distinction that forms the very basis of psychological work on the fundamental attribution error. It is of course possible for attributions coded as internal to be coded as external and vice versa. The example given in Ross of Jack and Jill buying houses demonstrates the point well. Ross is also critical of Likert-type scales used to measure attributions, recognising that 'meaning may depend upon subtle features of research context and instruction, features often beyond the experimenter's knowledge or control'. Ross does not offer solutions to these problems but at least recognises the potential for these and other difficulties to lead to confused and even unwarranted conclusions.

Reading 4.2 (Langdridge and Butt, 2004) seeks to address these problems by proposing a new perspective, which, we argue, better enables us to understand the myriad findings we have about the fundamental attribution error. But, unlike many other attempts to make the case for new theoretical frameworks, we do not invent a new framework but instead return to one –

phenomenological social psychology – that has to some extent been forgotten with the continuing rise of the cognitive perspective in social psychology. A phenomenological perspective is now becoming increasingly recognised among qualitative social psychologists. The first section of Reading 4.2 is a concise overview of the latest research on the FAE with discussion of the way in which age, culture, individual differences, mood and method may affect the fundamental attribution error. We then review existing attempts to theorise the fundamental attribution error, including the cognitive stage theories of Trope (1986) and Quattrone (1982), which have proven to be particularly popular among 'mainstream' attribution theory researchers.

Reading 4.2, then, introduces existential phenomenology and in particular the work of the French phenomenological philosopher and psychologist, Maurice Merleau-Ponty. Merleau-Ponty, like Heider, focused on perception arguing against 'objective thought', the belief that the world consists of separate objects – including psychological phenomena like beliefs and attitudes – whose dimensions can be defined and measured. He argued instead for a focus on the 'lived world' (Merleau-Ponty, 1962), based on our, always ambiguous, *experience* of the world. This argument has been adopted by a growing number of phenomenological social psychologists who focus on people's lived experience (e.g. Ashworth, 2003; Finlay, 2004; Smith, 1996, 2004). Finally, in this reading, Langdridge and Butt use the arguments of Merleau-Ponty to attempt to provide an overarching framework to understand better the existing findings about the fundamental attribution error.

ACTIVITY 4.2

As you read the following extract, consider these points:

■   What do you think are the strengths and weaknesses of the phenomenological approach advocated in Reading 4.2 in contrast with a cognitive social approach?

■   The authors argue that 'the job of social psychology becomes not one of discovering lawful relationships, but instead of understanding experience'. What do you think of this claim and how would the discipline change if it were adopted as the norm?

Reading 4.2 is from a 2004 article by Darren Langdridge and Trevor Butt which was published in the British Journal of Social Psychology. The article considers attribution using a phenomenological approach.

READING 4.2

'The fundamental attribution error: a phenomenological critique'

The fundamental attribution error (FAE)

The FAE (or 'correspondent bias' – Fleming and Darley, 1989; Gilbert and Jones, 1986) is the tendency to attribute another person's behaviour to their dispositional qualities, rather than situational factors (Heider, 1958; Ross, 1977). Almost 50 years of research have established the fundamental attribution error as a seemingly fundamental phenomenon whereby people systematically underestimate the degree to which behaviour is externally caused (Fiske and Taylor, 1991). It is important to note, however, that the phenomenon is not as concrete or simple as this definition suggests. We will address work which has questioned the fundamental nature of this perceptual bias below. However, we begin with a brief overview of explanations for this 'bias'.

One of the earliest explanations for why people consistently make this perceptual error is the argument, drawing on principles from Gestalt psychology, that behaviour engulfs the field (Heider, 1958). When we are engaged in interaction with another person it is that person's behaviour which becomes dominant in our perception (the 'figure' is dominant against the situational 'ground'). Accordingly, the observer will underestimate the effect of the situation (or 'ground') because of their focus on the person (or 'figure').

Later theorists have taken the idea that the behaviour engulfs the field further and argued that the FAE is an automatic outcome of certain perceptual experiences (McArthur and Baron, 1983). They argue that certain stimulus configurations will always produce this perceptual bias because the structure is in the stimulus itself. There are, however, a number of problems with this explanation. Firstly, the FAE is almost certainly learned. Young children do not make dispositional attributions, instead focusing on the situation. It is only when children reach late childhood that they begin to make dispositional attributions for events (Kassin and Pryor, 1985; White, 1988). Secondly, the FAE is *arguably* not universal across all cultures. It is undoubtedly a fundamental feature of the attribution of causality in the West but not as dominant in non-Western cultures (Norenzayan and Nisbett, 2000). However, this is arguable, as some recent research points to its prevalence in Western individualist cultures *and* non-Western collectivist cultures (e.g. China, India, Taiwan) (Krull et al. 1999). Thirdly, there is evidence of individual differences in the expression of the FAE (Block and Funder, 1986) and evidence that the FAE can be affected by experimental manipulation (Tetlock, 1985). Fourthly, recent evidence has demonstrated the effect of mood on the FAE, with happy moods enhancing dispositional attributions and sad moods reducing them (Forgas, 1998). Finally, the FAE is demonstrated when pencil and paper (rather than face-to-face) descriptions of behaviour are used (Winter and Uleman, 1984).

Trope's (1986) two-stage model provides a more elaborate (and widely supported) explanation for the FAE. This model breaks the attribution process down into two stages: (1) spontaneous identification and (2) a deliberate inferential process. Trope argues that the observer firstly identifies informational cues about the person from the actor's immediate behaviour, the situation, and any prior information the observer may have about the actor. These identifications are then used as the data for inferences about the actor's disposition. Situational expectancies are subtracted from the disposition implied by the behaviour. The observer's inferences about the immediate behaviour is then combined with prior information about the actor in order to make an attribution about the cause of the behaviour. Quattrone (1982), using a similar model, argued that the FAE consisted of three stages (categorization, characterization and correction). These cognitive stage models have received support from experimental research (Gilbert and Krull, 1988; Gilbert, Pelham, and Krull, 1988) which, for instance, demonstrates that the FAE increases when observers are cognitively busy with a competing task.

Vonk (1999) distinguishes between cognitive and motivational explanations for the FAE. Cognitive explanations include those outlined above, which have built and elaborated upon the initial idea of Heider that the behaviour engulfs the field. Motivational explanations, however, argue that perception is goal-directed with people wishing to predict and control others' behaviour. Vonk (1999) argues that people tend to make dispositional attributions because stable traits and attitudes are useful heuristics for predicting and controlling future behaviour. Building on earlier work from a motivational perspective (Berscheid, Graziano, Monson, and Dermer, 1976; Gilbert and Malone, 1995; Miller and Norman, 1975; Miller, Norman, and Wright, 1978), Vonk (1999) showed that salient outcome dependency produces a reduction in the FAE, most particularly in conditions in which the potential costs of an error were higher.

Most recently, Sabini et al. (2001) have argued, on the basis of a re-examination of classic social influence and attribution studies, that traditional notions of internal (dispositional) versus external (situational) causality are misguided. They argue convincingly that this distinction is problematic because what we have traditionally defined as situational in attribution studies may very easily be re-cast as dispositional and vice versa. Behaviour should instead be understood as the product of both person and environment. Sabini et al. (2001) give a number of examples, including 'the addict' who is generally understood to be driven by an 'internal' need (an internal craving resulting in intolerable pain if it is left unfulfilled) but who can also be understood to be under 'external' control from the drug they crave. They argue that people do not 'have a general tendency to attribute one way or another, but that they underestimate the importance of certain specific factors' (p. 2). These specific factors include, for instance, the motivation to save face and avoid embarrassment. Fein (2001) concurs with this and expands their argument with his own work on suspicion. He argues that 'the internal–external distinction does not map onto their [his participants] phenomenology...' (p. 17). Furthermore, Fein (2001) noted that the context in which participants are asked to make attributions is critical. He found that suspicious observers (that is, where cues have been used to alert them to the possible presence of ulterior motives on the part of the actor) were less likely to make the FAE, and instead recognize appropriate contextual information. Unlike Sabini et al. (2001), Fein (2001) does not believe that problematizing the internal–external distinction necessarily marks the end of research on the fundamental attribution error. He also argues that the ego–syntonic/ego–dystonic distinction (the distinction between causes of behaviour congruent or incongruent with a person's view of their self) proposed by Sabini et al. (2001) does not improve our understanding of the problem. Not surprisingly, Ross (2001) also argues that Sabini et al. have not undermined the classic findings of research on the fundamental attribution error. However, whilst there are limitations to Sabini et al.'s proposals, they have made telling points about the distinction between internal and external factors that attribution theory must deal with. We also intend to address this important issue and, we hope, provide a more convincing and more radical solution.

However, despite the extensive work conducted on this pervasive perceptual bias, there is still no unifying theory which can account for the myriad findings and address the limitations of the current dominant theoretical perspective. Attempts have been made but they do not provide the (appropriate) perspectival shift necessary for the debate to develop. Lipe (1991) effectively maintained a social cognitive perspective, arguing that attribution theories in general are based on the use of counterfactual information. In brief, she argued that all the major attribution theories (and also the fundamental attribution error) can be re-cast within a counterfactual information framework. This approach is based on the belief that people engage in a complicated process of causal logic (that is, analysis of substitute information – covariation and information about alternative explanations for Lipe (1991) – about whether the event would have occurred if the proposed cause had not occurred) when attributing causality for events. Indeed, even Lipe (1991) concedes, when discussing the psychological plausibility of the model and more specifically whether people naturally and spontaneously reason counterfactually, that 'The evidence is admittedly meager' (p. 467). This model may be parsimonious and theoretically able to account for attributional findings but lacks face validity and adequate empirical support. Andrews (2001) moves away from social cognitive decision-making models, towards a reductionist perspective that does not appear fruitful for social psychological research. Drawing on evolutionary psychology, he argues that the FAE is one element of the 'theory of mind' necessary for detecting deception and therefore increasing one's fitness (Andrews, 2001). We agree with Miller, Ashton, and Mishal (1990), admittedly writing before Lipe (1991) and Andrews (2001), when they state that '...the search for a more general, unifying conceptualization continues' (p. 635). In this paper, we propose an understanding drawing principally on the existential phenomenology of Merleau-Ponty.

Existential phenomenology

Phenomenology focuses on what appears to consciousness, and the way in which it appears. Husserl (see Moran, 2000), who initiated the phenomenological movement, saw it as a radical way of doing philosophy, one that bracketed our preconceptions in an attempt to arrive at a pure description of phenomena. This set of preconceptions, or 'the natural attitude' is drawn from cultural assumptions that predispose us to certain explanations and thus contaminate our appreciation of phenomena. Husserl recommended a process he termed phenomenological reduction in order to stand back from the natural attitude. The existential phenomenologists (Heidegger, Sartre, Merleau-Ponty) all emphasized the impossibility of ever achieving a 'God's eye' and value-free perspective, stressing the embodied and intersubjective nature of our perception. Merleau-Ponty's (1962) most valuable contribution to phenomenological thought was his elaboration of the lived body, a concept that was profoundly anti-dualist and emphasized the importance of perception as our direct contact with the world (cf. Gibson, 1979). Consciousness was primarily a practical matter: one of 'I can' rather than 'I think'. For Merleau-Ponty (1962), the natural attitude towards the body was particularly hampered by psychology's importing of the 'objective thought' prevalent in the natural sciences. This both promotes and is promoted by the dualism that has been inherited from folk psychology.

Objective thought and the lived world

In *Phenomenology of perception* (1962), Merleau-Ponty constructed a powerful argument against the use of objective thought in psychology. Objective thought is the position that the world consists of separate objects whose dimensions and properties can ultimately be defined and measured. Because these objects exist independently of each other, 'external', or causal relations exist between them. Social psychologists, then, investigate the relationships between beliefs, attitudes and behaviour as though they were separate entities inside the individual. The naïve realism of objective thought also maintains a clear separation of subject and object, between the world as it really is, and the world as it appears to us through perception. When this separation is assumed, perception becomes problematic; psychologists ask how it is that we come to have internal representations of the real world. Merleau-Ponty (1962) identified two contrasting strategies that psychologists have adopted in the light of this thinking: empiricism and intellectualism. Empiricism privileges the objective realm, beginning its analyses with stimuli that impinge on the receptors of a relatively 'empty' organism. Behaviourist approaches clearly fall into this category, underrating the person's ability to confer a meaning on events. However, intellectualism overemphasizes the power of the subject to render meaningful the 'buzzing, booming confusion' of sensation, and project idiosyncratic meanings on the world. Intellectualism begins its analyses with Descartes' *cogito*, the rational centre of gravity of the person through which he or she comes to know the world. Cognitive social psychology, with its stress on the constitutive power of attitudes and the projective force of attributions, is a good example of the intellectualist approach (Ashworth, 1980).

Merleau-Ponty's (1962) objections to objective thought stem from a phenomenological analysis of the lived world, identifying various ways in which experience is misrepresented in objective thought. He drew on the Gestaltists' perceptual demonstrations to emphasize that our perception cannot be deconstructed into its constituent parts, as the empiricists claimed, but neither can an individual choose to see things as they wish, as intellectualism implies. Instead, the perception is a joint enterprise *between* the person and the world; the sole property of neither, but a dialectical relationship in which each unfolds in relation to the other. So the lived world is always ambiguous, open to more than one interpretation. Ihde (1984) uses multi-stable figures like the Necker Cube to demonstrate this, together with the fact that we can train ourselves to overcome the natural attitude and see many more inversions than the two normally described in texts on perception. Using a similar strategy, Merleau-Ponty (1962) showed that the lived world is always ambiguous and that it does not comprise discrete objects with definite limits. Everything is contextualized, and figure/ ground relationships can change to produce new perceptions. From this perspective, it is not surprising, for example, that people hold 'contradictory' attitudes. Merleau-Ponty (1962) claimed that there are no attitudes 'inside' us that then manifest themselves in overt behaviour. 'There is no inner man ... man is in the world, and only in the world does he know himself' (Merleau-Ponty, 1962; p. xi). An attitude is a term that properly refers to a stance we take up in the social world, one that must always be understood in terms of the context in which it arises. We frequently simultaneously experience supposedly incompatible feelings and hold apparently contradictory beliefs.

Dualism and intersubjectivity

Cartesian dualism pervades intellectualism, and cognitive social psychology has inherited the faculties of the *cogito*. It conceives of cognition, emotion and behaviour in external relation to each other. Objective thought has been usefully applied in the natural sciences (although, even in this field, the Einsteinian revolution showed it not to be universally applicable). But when we turn its focus upon people, it fails to capture their experience. Psychological entities such as thought, emotion and behaviour cannot be thought of as separate from and causally related to each other. Instead 'internal relations' apply, where one feature of the lived world cannot be specified without implying the others. A person's attitude to war does not cause her to think it unacceptable, go on demonstrations and feel angry; this whole configuration constitutes the stance we call an attitude. Intellectualism involves what Ryle (1949) saw as a typical Cartesian category error. Here, we make the mistake of thinking we have identified two categories of events: mental and material. In fact, we are using two alternative constructions of the same set of events or, as Crossley (2001) puts it, talking in two different discursive registers. The cognitive functioning of the mind is thought of as separate to and in interaction with the material realm in which the body operates.

When we assume that people are minds inside bodies, we have to explain the mediating process through which one mind communicates with another. One mind views another body, and tries to work out what the mind inside it is signalling. But Merleau-Ponty proposed that embodied subjects naturally and directly read each others' intentions. From this perspective, the perception of others is not problematic, and does not involve any cognitive judgement, inference or attribution. The natural attitude of dualism is acquired. Referring to studies in child development, Merleau-Ponty (1962) contended that at Piaget's pre-operational level, children have the uncritical expectation that others will experience things as they do. The de-centring involved in achieving an understanding of different perspectives is seen as part of the maturation process, but Merleau-Ponty (1962) points out that the primitive position of humankind is one that assumes that we are all participants in the same world (and hence not as vulnerable to the FAE). Our relationship to our own body pre-figures our relation to that of the other:

> Between my consciousness and my body as I experience it, between this phenomenal body of mine and that of the other as I see it from the outside, there exists an internal relation which causes the other to appear as the completion of the system. The other can be evident to me because I am not transparent to myself and because my subjectivity draws its body in its wake.

> (Merleau-Ponty, 1962, p. 352)

For Merleau-Ponty, it is what goes on *between* two people, rather than inside either of them, that is paramount. Our pre-reflective action and connection to the world out-runs us, and is ahead of what we can say about it. Subjectivity is primarily the result of interaction with the physical and the social world, and consequently 'draws its body in its wake'. We can see that in the existential phenomenology of Merleau-Ponty, we have the basis of a truly social psychology. As Madison (1981) comments, his phenomenological analysis leads us not to an individual that precedes and constitutes the social world, but 'with a reflective subject ... that discovers itself to be (socially) derived' (p. 44). From this theoretical perspective, many of the problems of cognitive social psychology recede in importance, being seen to be the result of dualistic assumptions [author note: see also Hollway, 2006a and 2006b].

[...]

A phenomenological understanding of the FAE

It has been argued above that our connection with the world is first and foremost practical. We ask what elements in the world, including other people, can do for us or to us. We wish to know what we can use for tools, protection, to entertain us and capture our imagination, and who will help, harm or interest us. This engagement is pre-reflective – we do not have to spell things out in an internal dialogue. The nature of our embodiment is such that we quickly and pre-reflectively read other people's intentions, the way they connect to the world. We are equipped to do this, without conscious thought, although we may reflect on this engagement, being able to capture the process to the extent that we have available the necessary vocabulary and syntax. We read the other's intentionality directly – it is an intersubjective understanding, and not due to a process of cognitive inference, for which, quite literally, there would be no time. When assessing another's intentionality we are less concerned about the reasons or causes for their behaviour than with their *project* (Sartre, 1969) or *care* (Heidegger, 1962), that is, their principal concerns or objectives in the world.

In spite of the facts concerning the effect of situations on behaviour, in everyday life, people apparently find the attribution of dispositions and traits useful. This is surely because in day-to-day transactions we need to anticipate others' actions. Vonk (1999) recognized this when he made clear the distinction between cognitive and motivational explanations for the FAE. However, whilst Vonk (1999) makes this distinction, his conceptualization of motivational explanations is still based on an elaborate process of information-processing. From a phenomenological perspective, when we label someone aggressive, we are not concerned that this is merely a description masquerading as an explanation. It furnishes us with a rule: 'avoid/don't annoy/placate this person'. When I see a child-minder smack a child, it does not concern me that she is under intolerable pressure and that the child was naughty. The fact is that not *everybody* in the same situation would smack, and this is enough for me to resolve that I will not leave my child in her care. It may be that I witnessed a unique event, but I am prepared to make a Type 1 FAE. So assessment in terms of traits and dispositions is based on the need for a rule to guide action, and need not have the quality of a once-and-for-all belief. A discussion that focused me on the historical, cultural and situational factors operating might lead to my making a less harsh judgement of the person, though it still might have little bearing on my decisions about my own child. The research that shows that people forewarned of the error might take steps to avoid it demonstrates the importance of reflection and the power of taking up alternative perspectives. The studies by van Boven, Kamada, and Gilovich (1999) further emphasize ability. People recognize how an observer will perceive them. The 'spotlight effect' (Gilovich, Medvec, and Savitsky, 2000) testifies to our ability to de-centre and take up the perspective of another. Piaget (1959) saw this as an achievement of maturity, an acquisition that is evidence of reaching the formal operational stage. As we have seen above, Merleau-Ponty (1962) noted that this overlays a developmental position on which it builds and relies:

> Piaget brings the child to a mature outlook as if the thoughts of the adult were self-sufficient and disposed of all contradictions. But in reality, it must be the case that the child's outlook is in some way vindicated against the adult's and against Piaget, and that the unsophisticated thinking of our earliest years remains an indispensable acquisition underlying that of maturity, if there is to be for the adult one single intersubjective world.
>
> (Merleau-Ponty, 1962, p. 355)

Objective thought assumes the existence of a shared lived world, the properties of human embodiment that are the ground on which all our psychological abstractions as well as those more fundamental theories about time and space are built. As a child develops, objective thought develops and we witness a move from a shared lived world to a world differentiated into subjects and objects. This, of course, is why the child is not as vulnerable to the FAE (Kassin and Pryor, 1985; White, 1988):

> The child lives in a world which he unhesitatingly believes accessible to all around him. He has no awareness of himself or of others as private subjectivities, nor does he

> suspect that all of us, himself included, are limited to one certain point of view of the world
> ... He has no knowledge of points of view. For him, men are empty heads turned towards
> one single, self-evident world.
>
> (Merleau-Ponty, 1962, p. 355)

The FAE rests on an assumption of dualism: that there is a clear division between what is inside and outside the person. That there exists a 'ghost in the machine', a very special spectral motor with its own laws (Ryle, 1949) is part of the natural attitude in modern societies. It is a cultural assumption that is held to be natural and self-evident. Nevertheless, it is an acquired attitude, and one that is evidently not shared by young children (Kassin and Pryor, 1985; White, 1988) and people in different cultural contexts (Norenzayan and Nisbett, 2000). This dualism is re-cycled by cognitive social psychology, which has validated and authorized the search for internal cognitive entities and their interaction with the material body.

Explanations of the FAE have tended to focus on a debate about the viability of a two-stage (or three-stage) process (Quattrone, 1982; Trope, 1986). These models essentially build on the initial proposition of Heider that the behaviour engulfs the field with the addition of further information processing mechanisms. Heider's (1958) original proposition about attribution was made in the context of the influence of Gestalt psychology. He wanted to emphasize that we do not just see a series of meaningless 'behaviours' in another person. Instead we assume we are faced with another intentional being like ourselves. We immediately see sense in their action, and attribute intentionality to them. We assume we are not meeting a different person the next time we meet them. This is a case of perceptual constancy – an aspect of perception that Merleau-Ponty developed (1962, p. 7). There can be no point-to-point correspondence between objective stimuli and our perception of them; perception cannot be reduced to sensation that is subsequently interpreted by a homunculus in the occipital lobes of the cortex. Two objectively equal lines look unequal with the addition of subsidiary lines, as in the Müller-Lyer illusion, and a grey spot changes shade when it is placed against a white rather than a black background. In the lived world, we do not abstract one property like colour or length – we see it always in a context. There is no external relation – no linear causality. Instead there is a circular, internal relationship between object and subject. When we see a person, as Heider (1958) proposed, we see the person not their behaviour – he or she becomes the figure and the situation is the ground against which they stand out.

However, figure/ground relationships can and do change. It is not the case that one particular type of stimulus, a person, 'naturally' fills the field. The studies demonstrating the prevalence of the phenomenon are evidence that the configuration with the person as figure is a strong default position. Reversal of figure/ground may occur as a result of changes in the field itself or in the way in which it is perceived. Asking people to beware of a possible FAE is one way of bringing about such a reversal. The use of hermeneutic devices like story lines to open perception to new possibilities afforded by the field have been demonstrated by Ihde (1984). But to see this as a two-stage (or three-stage) process (Quattrone, 1982; Trope, 1986) is to misrepresent the nature of perception. Our experience tells us that it is difficult, if not impossible, to bring about perceptual change through will-power. It is not that there is a 'natural' sensation-led perception, followed sometimes by a 'learned' reason-led appraisal. Even with the Necker Cube, we cannot change the inversions at will. What we can do is to coax ourselves, as Ihde (1984) suggests, taking up imaginary positions in space above and below the cube, or telling ourselves that we are looking down on a pyramid with the top removed, in order to bring about change in the way we perceive.

The problem with orthodox analyses of the FAE is that they take us into the person's interiority, and away from the patterning that occurs in the perceptual field between people. Intellectualism takes us away from the possibility of a truly social psychology, restricting itself to individual interpretations of the social world. Its conclusions are therefore necessarily provisional and local. More research is always the answer, until we can piece together a census of how everybody will act in every circumstance. It focuses on individual information-processing, assuming a separation between reality and representing, and seeks cognitive strategies to modify interpretation. But interpretation occurs instantaneously, in the perceptual field. We see this person as dangerous, that one as sexually attractive. The configuration presents itself as such, and we do not weigh up evidence first and then reach a quasi-rational decision. Gestalt psychology has been squeezed into a cognitive approach because a focus on individual 'meaning making' seemed like the only alternative to the unreconstructed behaviourism of the 1950s. Intellectualism presented a contrast to empiricism. However, this ignores an excluded middle that both the Gestaltists and Merleau-Ponty tried to promote.

Concluding remarks

We have argued that the FAE is an interesting phenomenon, one worthy of investigation. It is indeed important to recognize the bias, to note under what conditions it is most salient, and to guard against it in various arenas in social life. But from the perspective of existential phenomenology, it is not a mystery in need of explanation in cognitive terms. We have suggested that it is the maintenance of dualism that is responsible for the status of mystery. Half a century after Ryle's refutation of dualism, the ghost in the machine has not been exorcised. Psychology was invented as a parallel Newtonian enterprise, one that would discover the laws governing mental life in the same way that physics had done in the physical world. Academic and folk psychology both still interact to reproduce the myth of dualism, along with the belief in external causal relations in the internal sphere. This natural attitude pervades research in social psychology and the FAE, attempting to produce cognitive explanations for perceptual phenomena despite criticism, from within and without, of many of its central conceptual assumptions (e.g. Edwards and Potter, 1992; Fein, 2001; Sabini et al., 2001).

A phenomenological social psychology would focus on the way in which people construct meaning in the social world as part of their *project*. Phenomenological psychologists claim that we are primarily social beings, and that the social world and our experience of it precede the individual. We find ourselves already immersed in it, and the phenomenological project attempts to capture this experience. There are many social phenomena from this point of view that need description and analysis, but not explanation. The job of social psychology becomes not one of discovering lawful causal relationships, but instead of understanding experience. The way we should do this is not by trying to look inside people, but by making sense of experience through an appreciation of its social context.

[...]

References

Andrews, P.W. (2001) 'The psychology of social chess and the evolution of attribution mechanisms: explaining the fundamental attribution error', *Evolution and Human Behavior*, vol. 22, pp. 11–29.

Ashworth, P.D. (1980) 'Attitude, action and the concept of structure', *Journal of Phenomenological Psychology*, vol. 11, pp. 39–66.

Berscheid, E., Graziano, W., Monson, T. and Dermer, M. (1976) 'Outcome dependency: attention, attribution, and attraction', *Journal of Personality and Social Psychology*, vol. 34, pp. 978–89.

Block, J. and Funder, D.C. (1986) 'Social roles and social perception: individual differences in attribution and error', *Journal of Personality and Social Psychology*, vol. 51, pp. 1200–97.

Crossley, N. (2001) *The Social Body: Habit, Identity and Desire*, London, Sage.

Edwards, D. and Potter, J. (1992) *Discursive Psychology*, London, Sage.

Fein, S. (2001) 'Beyond the fundamental attribution era?', *Psychological Inquiry*, vol. 12, pp. 16–21.

Fiske, S.T. and Taylor, S.E. (1991) *Social Cognition* (2nd edn), New York, McGraw-Hill.

Fleming, J. and Darley, J.M. (1989) 'Perceiving choice and constraint: the effects of contextual and behavioral cues on attitude attribution', *Journal of Personality and Social Psychology*, vol. 56, pp. 27–40.

Forgas, J.P. (1998) 'On being happy and mistaken: mood effects on the fundamental attribution error', *Journal of Personality and Social Psychology*, vol. 75, pp. 318–31.

Gibson, J. (1979) *The Ecological Approach to Visual Perception*, Boston, Houghton Mifflin.

Gilbert, D.T. and Jones, E.E. (1986) 'Exemplification: the self-presentation of moral character', *Journal of Personality*, vol. 54, pp. 593–615.

Gilbert, D.T., and Krull, D.S. (1988) 'Seeing less and knowing more: the benefits of perceptual ignorance', *Journal of Personality and Social Psychology*, vol. 54, pp. 193–202.

Gilbert, D.T. and Malone, P.S. (1995) 'The correspondence bias', *Psychological Bulletin*, vol. 117, pp. 21–38.

Gilbert, D.T., Pelham, B.W. and Krull, D.S. (1988) 'On cognitive busyness: when person perceivers meet persons perceived', *Journal of Personality and Social Psychology*, vol. 54, pp. 733–9.

Gilovich, T., Medvec, V., and Savitsky, K. (2000) 'The spotlight effect in social judgement: an egocentric bias in estimates of the salience of one's own actions and appearance', *Journal of Personality and Social Psychology*, vol. 78, pp. 211–22.

Heidegger, M. (1962) *Being and Time* (trans. J. Macquarrie and E. Robinson), Oxford, Blackwell.

Heider, F. (1958) *The Psychology of Interpersonal Relations*, New York, Wiley.

Hollway, W. (2006a) 'Methods and knowledge in social psychology' in Hollway, Lucey and Phoenix (eds) *Social Psychology Matters*, Maidenhead, Open University Press/Milton Keynes, The Open University.

Hollway, W. (2006b) 'Self' in Hollway, Lucey and Phoenix (eds) *Social Psychology Matters*, Maidenhead, Open University Press/Milton Keynes, The Open University.

Ihde, D. (1984) *Experimental Phenomenology*, Albany, SUNY Press.

Kassin, S.M., and Pryor, J.B. (1985) 'The development of attribution processes' in Pryor, J. and Day, J. (eds) *The Development of Social Cognition*, pp. 3–34. New York, Springer.

Krull, D.S., Hui-Min Loy, M., Lin, J., Wang, C., Chen, S. and Zhao, X. (1999) 'The fundamental fundamental attribution error: correspondence bias in individualist and collectivist cultures', *Personality and Social Psychology Bulletin*, vol. 25, pp. 1208–19.

Lipe, M.G. (1991) 'Counterfactual reasoning as a framework for attribution theories', *Psychological Bulletin*, vol. 109, pp. 456–71.

Madison, G. (1981) *The Phenomenology of Merleau-Ponty*, Athens, Ohio, Ohio University Press.

McArthur, L.Z. and Baron, R. (1983) 'Toward an ecological theory of social perception', *Psychological Review*, vol. 90, pp. 215–38.

Merleau-Ponty, M. (1962) *Phenomenology of Perception* (trans. C. Smith), London, Routledge.

Miller, A.G., Ashton, W. and Mishal, M. (1990) 'Beliefs concerning the features of constrained behavior: a basis for the fundamental attribution error', *Journal of Personality and Social Psychology*, vol. 59, pp. 635–50.

Miller, D.T., and Norman, S.A. (1975) 'Actor-observer differences in perceptions of effective control', *Journal of Personality and Social Psychology*, vol. 31, pp. 503–15.

Miller, D.T., Norman, S.A. and Wright, E. (1978) 'Distortion in person perception as a consequence of the need for effective control', *Journal of Personality and Social Psychology*, vol. 36, pp. 598–602.

Moran, D. (2000) *Introduction to Phenomenology*, London, Routledge.

Norenzayan, A. and Nisbett, R.E. (2000) 'Culture and causal cognition', *Current Directions in Psychological Science*, vol. 9, pp. 132–5.

Piaget, J. (1959) *The Language and Thought of the Child*, London, Routledge.

Quattrone, G.A. (1982) 'Overattribution and unit formation: when behaviour engulfs the person', *Journal of Personality and Social Psychology*, vol. 42, pp. 593–607.

Ross, L.D. (1977) 'The intuitive psychologist and his shortcomings: distortions in the attribution process' in Berkowitz, L. (ed.) *Advances in Experimental Social Psychology*, vol. 10, pp. 174–221, New York, Academic Press.

Ross, L.D. (2001) 'Getting down to fundamentals: lay dispositionism and the attributions of psychologists', *Psychological Inquiry*, vol. 12, pp. 37–40.

Ryle, G. (1949) *The Concept of Mind*, London, Hutchinson.

Sabini, J., Siepmann, M. and Stein, J. (2001) 'The really fundamental attribution error in social psychological research', *Psychological Inquiry*, vol. 12, pp. 1–15.

Sartre, J.P. (1969) *Being and Nothingness: an Essay on Phenomenological Ontology* (trans. H.E. Barnes), London, Routledge.

Tetlock, P.E. (1985) 'Accountability: a social check on the fundamental attribution error', *Social Psychology Quarterly*, vol. 48, pp. 227–36.

Trope, Y. (1986) 'Identification and inferential processes in dispositional attribution', *Psychological Review*, vol. 93, pp. 239–57.

Van Boven, L., Kamada, A., and Gilovich, T. (1999) 'The perceiver as perceived: everyday intuitions about the correspondence bias', *Journal of Personality and Social Psychology*, vol. 77, pp. 1188–99.

Vonk, R. (1999) 'Effects of outcome dependency on correspondence bias', *Personality and Social Psychology Bulletin*, vol. 25, pp. 382–9.

White, P.A. (1988) 'Causal processing: origins and development', *Psychological Bulletin*, vol. 104, pp. 36–52.

Winter, L. and Uleman, J.S. (1984) 'When are social judgements made? Evidence for the spontaneousness of trait inferences', *Journal of Personality and Social Psychology*, vol. 47, pp. 237–52.

(Langdridge and Butt, 2004, pp. 357–69)

Conclusion

Langdridge and Butt (2004) are not the first psychologists to have questioned theoretical understandings of the fundamental attribution error. Steiner (1974) argued strongly that a very great deal of attributional research was too individualistic and not social enough. But this is only part of the problem, and Langdridge and Butt, through the use of ideas from the phenomenology of Merleau-Ponty, seek to do more than simply suggest that work on attribution theory needs to be more social. Indeed, they are calling for nothing less than a fundamental shift in understanding, for researchers to move away from a cognitive social psychology, which remains the dominant approach, and towards a phenomenological social psychology. There are two important theoretical points being made in this regard in Reading 4.2, both of which are key concepts in phenomenological psychology. The first concerns what Merleau-Ponty termed 'objective thought', and the second 'individual–social dualism', both of which continue to haunt cognitive social psychology.

As Langdridge and Butt (2004) explain, objective thought is the belief that the world consists of separate objects whose properties can be defined and measured. Understanding objects as separate, as we do in objective thought, means that causal relationships can be determined between them. So, for instance, in social psychology the norm for many researchers, especially cognitive social psychologists, is to define precisely the objects of study, such as attributional processes or attitudes, and then look for causal relationships within or between them. In attribution theory, this might entail a researcher bringing their participants into the laboratory in order to have them engage in a variety of tasks designed to unpick the processes involved in making attributional judgements, with the aim of explaining the phenomenon through identification of causal pathways.

The problem with this, identified by Langdridge and Butt (2004), is that we are always in relation with the world. Therefore, all perception, which is after all what attribution theory is all about, involves a relationship between the person and the world, which cannot be broken down into its component parts. Everything must be seen in context, and this includes psychological phenomena as much as physical objects. This is a key idea in phenomenological social psychology, and because of this researchers from this particular perspective focus on people's experience rather than cognitive processes thought to be operating inside people's heads. It does not matter whether a person is right or wrong in their perception; the focus is always on their perception of the world 'in its appearing': nothing more, nothing less. All reference to reality is set aside, not because phenomenologists do not believe in a real world but rather because phenomenological social psychologists believe that all we have to work with is people's experience. That is, all knowledge claims centre on the primacy of perception and the way in which the world appears to people, rather than on any objective notion of the world. Phenomenological social psychologists argue that the distinction between person and situation (or individual and social world) is a false division since we can never separate subject and object, individual and environment or indeed mind and body.

Sabini et al. (2001) make a similar point, albeit from a different perspective, about the FAE and the distinction between internal (dispositional) and external (situational) attributions. As Reading 4.2 explains, Sabini et al. problematise the distinction between internal and external that is basic to the fundamental attribution error. Using the example of a drug addict, Sabini et al. show how internal attributions can be recast as external and vice versa; the distinction is anything but clear-cut. Langdridge and Butt (2004) go a stage further, however, arguing that all social psychological phenomena must be understood in context, being inseparable from the persons situated in a particular culture, time and place. The focus on perception that is central to phenomenological social psychology in many ways represents a return to the naïve psychology of Heider (1944, 1958). With a phenomenological perspective to social psychology, the model of the person becomes the consciously experiencing embodied individual always in relation with the social world, rather than the information-processing individual in a social context, as we see in cognitive social psychology. Appropriate methods of inquiry also follow and involve a focus on first-person accounts and rich description of social experience derived through the senses, rather than experimental control and identification of cognitive processes.

The suggestions for further reading below should enable you to follow up these issues and read more about this debate. But for now what is important is that these issues are foregrounded and made salient for contemporary social psychology. To this end, this chapter has sought to highlight a number of issues as they relate to one simple but pervasive phenomenon: the fundamental attribution error. This is not the end of the story, however. While a phenomenological approach has been offered here as an alternative, there are a number of criticisms that could also be levelled at this perspective. A contemporary social psychoanalytic psychologist might wonder about the place of unconscious processes in the attribution of causality, while a discursive psychologist may question the way in which language is thought to represent the lived world of the participant and instead focus on the conversational context of the phenomenon. These are important debates but beyond the scope of this chapter. Nonetheless, I hope you have seen how different understandings of this phenomenon are possible, from the earliest naïve psychology of Heider, through the cognitive perspective of the researchers that followed and continue to dominate the field, to a phenomenological perspective, which in many ways represents a return to the foundations and perceptual work of Heider in the late 1950s. This speaks most directly, of course, to the way in which social psychological knowledge, whether of the FAE or any other phenomenon, is not ahistorical and universal, as some might claim, but deeply embedded in the history and culture of the discipline in which the knowledge was produced.

References

Ashworth, P.D. (2003) 'An approach to phenomenological psychology: the primacy of the lifeworld', *Journal of Phenomenological Psychology*, vol. 34, no. 2, pp. 145–56.

Finlay, L. (2004) 'The intertwining of body, self and world: a phenomenological study of living with recently diagnosed multiple sclerosis', *Journal of Phenomenological Psychology*, vol. 34, no. 2, pp. 157–78.

Fiske, S.T. and Taylor, S.E. (1991) *Social Cognition* (2nd edn), New York, McGraw-Hill.

Heider, F. (1944) 'Social perception and phenomenal causality', *Psychological Review*, vol. 51, pp. 358–74.

Heider, F. (1958) *The Psychology of Interpersonal Relations*, New York, John Wiley & Sons.

Hewstone, M. (1989) *Causal Attribution: From Cognitive Processes to Collective Beliefs*, Oxford, Basil Blackwell.

Jones, E.E. (1990) *Interpersonal Perception*, New York, Freeman.

Jones, E.E. and Davis, K.E. (1965) 'From acts to dispositions: the attribution process in person perception' in Berkowitz, L. (ed.) *Advances in Experimental Social Psychology*, vol. 2, New York, Academic Press.

Kelley, H.H. (1967) 'Attribution theory in social psychology' in Levine, D. (ed.) *Nebraska Symposium on Motivation*, vol. 15, Lincoln, University of Nebraska Press.

Kelly, G. (1955) *The Psychology of Personal Constructs*, New York, Norton.

Langdridge, D. and Butt, T.W. (2004) 'The fundamental attribution error: a phenomenological critique', *British Journal of Social Psychology*, vol. 43, no. 3, pp. 357–69.

Merleau-Ponty, M. (1962) *Phenomenology of Perception* (trans. C. Smith), London, Routledge.

Quattrone, G.A. (1982) 'Overattribution and unit formation: when behaviour engulfs the person', *Journal of Personality and Social Psychology*, vol. 42, pp. 593–607.

Ross, L. (1977) 'The intuitive psychologist and his shortcomings: distortions in the attribution process' in Berkowitz, L. (ed.) *Advances in Experimental Social Psychology*, New York, Academic Press.

Ross, M. and Fletcher, G.J.O. (1985) 'Attribution and social perception' in Lindzey, G. and Aronson, E. (eds) *Handbook of Social Psychology* (3rd edn), vol. 2, New York, Random House.

Sabini, J., Siepmann, M., and Stein, J. (2001) 'The really fundamental attribution error in social psychological research', *Psychological Inquiry*, vol. 12, no. 1, pp. 1–15.

Shaver, K. G. (1975) *An Introduction to Attribution Processes*, Cambridge, MA, Winthrop.

Smith, J.A. (1996) 'Beyond the divide between cognition and discourse: using interpretative phenomenological analysis in health psychology', *Psychology & Health*, vol. 11, pp. 261–71.

Smith, J.A. (2004) 'Reflecting on the development of interpretative phenomenological analysis and its contribution to qualitative research in psychology', *Qualitative Research in Psychology*, vol. 1, pp. 39–54.

Steiner, I.D. (1974) 'Whatever happened to the group in social psychology?' *Journal of Experimental Social Psychology*, vol. 10, pp. 94–108.

Trope, Y. (1986) 'Identification and inferential processes in dispositional attribution', *Psychological Review*, vol. 93, pp. 239–57.

Vaughan, G. and Hogg, M.A. (2004) *Social Psychology*, Harlow, Pearson Education.

Further reading

Hewstone, M. (1989) *Causal Attribution: From Cognitive Processes to Collective Beliefs*, Oxford, Basil Blackwell.
A classic state-of-the-art discussion of attribution theory. Now a little dated but still one of the most intelligent books written on the subject.

Ihde, D. (1986) *Experimental Phenomenology: An Introduction*, Albany, SUNY Press.
An excellent introduction to phenomenology, which, through the medium of visual perception, introduces many of the fundamentals of this difficult philosophical perspective.

Langdridge, D. (2007) *Phenomenological Psychology: Theory, Research and Method*, Harlow, Pearson Education.
A comprehensive and practical introduction to the latest theory, research and methods employed by phenomenological psychologists.

Sabini, J., Siepmann, M., and Stein, J. (2001) 'The really fundamental attribution error in social psychological research', *Psychological Inquiry*, vol. 12, no. 1, pp. 1–15 plus commentaries (pp. 14 –16) and authors' response (pp. 41–8) that make up this special issue.
An up-to-date account of the FAE and the debates surrounding this phenomenon.

Chapter 5

Intragroup processes: entitativity

by Ann Phoenix, The Open University

Introduction

Collectives are at the heart of human social life and so have received attention in all the human sciences. There is, however, no clear definition of what constitutes a 'group'. Wendy Stainton-Rogers (2003, p. 264) notes that 'social psychology takes a very broad sweep when it comes to groups – from collections of, say, four or five people brought together to do an experiment, to viewing, say, "Chinese" as a group to which people belong, have allegiance to and from which they derive their social identity.' Not surprisingly then, many social psychologists have tried to devise ways of classifying groups. The following five types are commonly identified:

1   Reference groups are based on identification and provide a frame of reference for understanding our identities. They may include friends, families, colleagues, nationalities and communities.

2   Membership groups are task oriented – for example, juries, tutorial groups, work groups, clubs or committees – and members may have minimal involvement with each other outside the task context.

3   Social category groups are based on categories such as gender, religion, ethnicity etc. that have social meaning, but are so large that most members will never meet.

4   Cultural groups are also large, but generally share common beliefs, values, often language and understandings of their origins.

5   Crowds are large numbers of people who come together for a common purpose, for example, a football match or a political demonstration.

While this typology makes useful distinctions that would be recognised by many social psychologists, it is not the only typology you will find and social psychology publications may not use exactly these terms. However, it is accepted that groups:

■   are of varied sizes and structures

■   come together in different places for different purposes

■   comprise diverse kinds of people

■   last for different periods

- have different levels of commitment to membership

- vary in how tightly bounded, cohesive and emotionally involved they are and how much they support each other.

With all this variety, does it make social psychological sense to include all these collectives under the umbrella term 'groups'? Stangor (2004) argues that there are basic principles that can be used to understand all social groups. He suggests that 'we can define the group as a collection of individuals who are seen as being entitative' (p. 28) – i.e. that insiders and/or outsiders feel that a collection of individuals constitute a group or entity. The term 'entitativity' was coined by Campbell (1958) and popularised by Hamilton and Sherman (1996).

The types of groups identified by psychologists are not mutually exclusive. For example, a group identified as a reference group could also belong to one of the other four types, and social categories and cultures may overlap. Everybody belongs to social category groups and cultural groups as well as having reference groups. Many people belong to membership groups and are sometimes part of crowds. All groups can be said to be social categories. Is it, therefore, worth drawing distinctions between them? In practice these different groups have often raised different social psychological issues and are associated with different social psychological processes, theories and methods (Stainton-Rogers, 2003). For example, in relation to the definitions above, reference groups are associated with identity processes while social 'loafing' and social facilitation have been studied in membership groups.

Groups can also produce contrary effects. On the one hand, they can provide support, make achievements through collective action and allow opportunities for development (Kelly and Breinlinger, 1996). Group membership is related to social identity in that it helps us to understand what sort of people we are and what kind of people we differentiate ourselves from (Mead, 1934; Tajfel, 1982). In consequence, group membership has implications for dynamics both within and between groups. On the other hand, much concern is expressed about groups. For example, young people's friendship groups are sometimes feared as 'bad influences'; football crowds are feared as dangerous mobs; and fundamentalist religious groups are feared for their potential to produce extreme behaviour. Central to these concerns are assumptions that individuals lose their individuality and suspend critical thought in groups, becoming capable of doing undesirable things they would not do when alone (e.g. Erikson, 1968). As you will see in Readings 5.1 and 5.2, crowds are particularly vilified as potential mobs. Social psychologists have identified several negative aspects of group membership, such as de-individuation, 'groupmind', outgroup hostility, social loafing, 'risky shift' and 'groupthink', a concept you will explore in more detail in Reading 5.1 (Brown, 2000; Stangor, 2004). This negative focus led one social psychologist to entitle a paper 'Humans would do better without groups' (Buys, 1978).

The negative focus on groups raises ontological questions (questions about the nature of being and existence – in this case, of groups). For instance, when individuals come together in groups, do their individual characteristics become submerged – to the detriment of both group and individual? This dichotomising of individual and group behaviour has been much debated.

Allport (1962), for example, argued that there was no psychology of groups that was separate from the psychology of individuals. In other words, groups had no independent minds. Other social psychologists (Asch, 1952; Sherif, 1966) also eschewed the notion that groups had a mind independent of the individuals who compose them, but considered that group processes are psychologically important in their own right and that individual and group processes are equally important to the understanding of groups.

This chapter focuses on two concerns relevant to the study of groups: the impact of intragroup processes on group behaviour and outcomes; and the complexity of defining some groups, i.e. ontological issues of group entitativity. Entitativity is relevant to intragroup processes in that who is included and who is excluded from a group influences what groups can do. This chapter uses two readings that are of theoretical and practical importance: Reading 5.1 by Irving Janis (1972) looks at the concept of 'groupthink'; Reading 5.2 from Jonathan Potter and Stephen Reicher (1987) examines discourses of community and conflict. Each reading provides innovative understandings of how definitions of groups affect what is considered appropriate behaviour.

Janis (1918–1990), was a prolific social psychologist at Yale University, USA (from 1947 to 1985). He researched a variety of theoretically linked social psychological issues which were influential because they had immediate practical relevance (e.g. on psychological stress and decision-making processes). In this, Janis was in concert with Kurt Lewin (1948) who coined the term 'action research' because he was committed to doing research relevant to ordinary people. Janis's work has been summed up as 'theory-guided "positivist" research' (Smith, 1992, p. 813). However, he believed that different research problems required different methods and he was methodologically eclectic, doing both laboratory experiments (which took a positivist approach) and field research (which did not). He was also trained in research-oriented psychoanalysis.

Janis is best known for his research on 'groupthink' (1972). This describes a process by which a group makes catastrophic decisions *because* it is concerned to maintain itself as a cohesive ingroup while being under pressure to make important decisions. Janis, who used historical records to test his theories about psychological stress and decision making, was inspired by his own puzzlement about why 'brilliant, conscientious men' sometimes made disastrous decisions. As you will see, he argued that in a groupthink situation, each member of the group conforms to what they understand to be the group consensus and does not consider all the available alternatives, with the result that the group agrees upon a course of action which none of them might take individually.

As you read the extract, think about the following points.

1   Why do you think Janis talks of 'symptoms' of groupthink?

2   What effect does entitativity (the feeling that they constitute a social group) have on groups' decision-making processes?

Note that Janis was writing at a time when there were not clear conventions about using non-sexist language.

Reading 5.1 is taken from the 1972 book *Victims of Groupthink: A Psychological Study of Foreign-Policy Decisions and Fiascoes* by the American psychologist Irving Janis, which presents his classic concept of 'groupthink'.

READING 5.1

'Victims of groupthink: A psychological study of foreign-policy decisions and fiascos'

What is groupthink?

The group dynamics approach is based on the working assumption that the members of policy-making groups, no matter how mindful they may be of their exalted national status and of their heavy responsibilities, are subjected to the pressures widely observed in groups of ordinary citizens. In my earlier research on group dynamics, I was impressed by repeated manifestations of the effects – both unfavorable and favorable – of the social pressures that typically develop in cohesive groups – in infantry platoons, air crews, therapy groups, seminars, and self-study or encounter groups of executives receiving leadership training. In all these groups, just as in the industrial work groups described by other investigators, members tend to evolve informal objectives to preserve friendly intragroup relations and this becomes part of the hidden agenda at their meetings. When conducting research on groups of heavy smokers at a clinic set up to help people stop smoking, I noticed a seemingly irrational tendency for the members to exert pressure on each other to increase their smoking as the time for the final meeting approached. This appeared to be a collusive effort to display mutual dependence and resistance to the termination of the group sessions.

Sometimes, even long before members become concerned about the final separation, clear-cut signs of pressures toward uniformity subvert the fundamental purpose of group meetings. At the second meeting of one group of smokers, consisting of twelve middle-class American men and women, two of the most dominant members took the position that heavy smoking was an almost incurable addiction. The majority of the others soon agreed that no one could be expected to cut down drastically. One heavy smoker, a middle-aged business executive, took issue with this consensus, arguing that by using will power he had stopped smoking since joining the group and that everyone else could do the same. His declaration was followed by a heated discussion, which continued in the halls of the building after the formal meeting adjourned. Most of the others ganged up against the man who was deviating from the group consensus. Then, at the beginning of the next meeting, the deviant announced that he had made an important decision. 'When I joined,' he said, 'I agreed to follow the two main rules required by the clinic – to make a conscientious effort to stop smoking and to attend every meeting. But I have learned from experience in this group that you can only follow one of the rules, you can't follow both. And so, I have decided that I will continue to attend every meeting but I have gone back to smoking two packs a day and I will not make any effort to stop smoking again until after the last meeting.' Whereupon, the other members beamed at him and applauded enthusiastically, welcoming him back to the fold. No one commented on the fact that the whole point of the meetings was to help each individual to cut down on smoking as rapidly as possible. As a psychological consultant to the group, I tried to call this to the members' attention, and so did my collaborator, Dr. Michael Kahn. But during that meeting the members managed to ignore our comments and reiterated their consensus that heavy smoking was an addiction from which no-one would be cured except by cutting down very gradually over a long period of time.

This episode – an extreme form of groupthink – was only one manifestation of a general pattern that the group displayed. At every meeting, the members were amiable, reasserted their warm feelings of solidarity, and sought complete concurrence on every important topic, with no reappearance of the unpleasant bickering that would spoil the cozy atmosphere. The concurrence-seeking tendency could be maintained, however, only at the expense of ignoring realistic challenges (like those posed by the psychological consultants) and distorting members' observations of individual differences that would call into question the shared assumption that everyone in the group had the same type of addiction problem. It seemed that in this smoking group I was observing another instance of the groupthink pattern I had encountered in observations of widely contrasting groups whose members came from diverse sectors of society and were meeting together for social, educational, vocational, or other purposes. Just like the group in the smoking clinic, all these different types of groups had shown signs of high cohesiveness and of an accompanying concurrence-seeking tendency that interfered with critical thinking – the central features of groupthink.

[...]

Selection of the fiascoes

When I began to investigate the Bay of Pigs invasion, the decision to escalate the Korean War, and other fiascoes, for purposes of studying sources of error in foreign policy decision-making, I was initially surprised to discover the pervasiveness of symptoms of groupthink [...] signs of poor decision–making as a result of concurrence-seeking were unmistakable.

[...]

I was looking for instances in which a defective decision was made in a series of meetings by a few policy-makers who constituted a cohesive group. By a defective decision, I mean one that results from decision-making practices of extremely poor quality. In other words, the fiascoes that I selected for analysis deserved to be fiascoes because of the grossly inadequate way the policy-makers carried out their decision-making tasks.

At least six major defects in decision-making contribute to failures to solve problems adequately. First, the group's discussions are limited to a few alternative courses of action (often only two) without a survey of the full range of alternatives. Second, the group fails to reexamine the course of action initially preferred by the majority of members from the standpoint of nonobvious risks and drawbacks that had not been considered when it was originally evaluated.

Third, the members neglect courses of action initially evaluated as unsatisfactory by the majority of the group: They spend little or no time discussing whether they have overlooked nonobvious gains or whether there are ways of reducing the seemingly prohibitive costs that had made the alternatives seem undesirable. Fourth, members make little or no attempt to obtain information from experts who can supply sound estimates of losses and gains to be expected from alternative courses of actions. Fifth, selective bias is shown in the way the group reacts to factual information and relevant judgments from experts, the mass media, and outside critics. The members show interest in facts and opinions that support their initially preferred policy and take up time in their meetings to discuss them, but they tend to ignore facts and opinions that do not support their initially preferred policy. Sixth, the members spend little time deliberating about how the chosen policy might be hindered by bureaucratic inertia, sabotaged by political opponents, or temporarily derailed by the common accidents that happen to the best of well-laid plans. Consequently, they fail to work out contingency plans to cope with foreseeable setbacks that could endanger the overall success of the chosen course of action.

I assume that these six defects and some related features of inadequate decision-making result from groupthink. But, of course, each of the six can arise from other common causes of human stupidity as well – erroneous intelligence, information overload, fatigue, blinding prejudice, and ignorance. Whether produced by groupthink or by other causes, a decision suffering from most of these defects has relatively little chance of success.

[...]

The imperfect link between groupthink and fiascoes

Simply because the outcome of a group decision has turned out to be a fiasco, I do not assume that it must have been the result of groupthink or even that it was the result of defective decision-making. Nor do I expect that every defective decision, whether arising from groupthink or from other causes, will produce a fiasco. Defective decisions based on misinformation and poor judgment sometimes lead to successful outcomes.

[...]

Groupthink is conducive to errors in decision-making, and such errors increase the likelihood of a poor outcome. Often the result is a fiasco, but not always. Suppose that because of lucky accidents fostered by absurd command decisions by the Cuban military leaders, the Kennedy administration's Bay of Pigs invasion had been successful in provoking a civil war in Cuba and led to the overthrow of the Castro regime. Analysis of the decision to invade Cuba would still support the groupthink hypothesis, for the evidence shows that Kennedy's White House group was highly cohesive, clearly displayed symptoms of defective decision-making, and exhibited all the major symptoms of groupthink. Thus, even if the Bay of Pigs decision had produced a triumph rather than a defeat, it would still be an example of the potentially adverse effects of groupthink (even though the invasion would not, in that case, be classified as a fiasco).

Hardhearted actions by softheaded groups

At first I was surprised by the extent to which the groups in the fiascoes I have examined adhered to group norms and pressures toward uniformity. Just as in groups of ordinary citizens, a dominant characteristic appears to be remaining loyal to the group by sticking with the decisions to which the group has committed itself, even when the policy is working badly and has unintended consequences that disturb the conscience of the members. In a sense, members consider loyalty to the group the highest form of morality. That loyalty requires each member to avoid raising controversial issues, questioning weak arguments, or calling a halt to softheaded thinking.

Paradoxically, softheaded groups are likely to be extremely hardhearted toward out-groups and enemies. In dealing with a rival nation, policy-makers comprising an amiable group find it relatively easy to authorize dehumanizing solutions such as large-scale bombings. An affable group of government officials is unlikely to pursue the difficult and controversial issues that arise when alternatives to a harsh military solution come up for discussion. Nor are the members inclined to raise ethical issues that imply that this 'fine group of ours, with its humanitarianism and its high-minded principles, might be capable of adopting a course of action that is inhumane and immoral.'

Many other sources of human error can prevent government leaders from arriving at well worked out decisions, resulting in failures to achieve their practical objectives and violations of their own standards of ethical conduct. But, unlike groupthink, these other sources of error do not typically entail increases in hardheartedness along with soft headedness. Some errors involve blind spots that stem from the personality of the decision-makers. Special circumstances produce unusual fatigue and emotional stresses that interfere with efficient decision-making. Numerous institutional features of the social structure in which the group is located may also cause inefficiency and prevent adequate communication with experts. In addition, well-known interferences with sound thinking arise when the decision-makers comprise a noncohesive group. For example, when the members have no sense of loyalty to the group and regard themselves merely as representatives of different departments, with clashing interests, the meetings may become bitter power struggles, at the expense of effective decision-making.

The concept of groupthink pinpoints an entirely different source of trouble, residing neither in the individual nor in the organizational setting. Over and beyond all the familiar sources of human error is a powerful source of defective-judgment that arises in cohesive groups – the concurrence-seeking tendency, which fosters overoptimism, lack of vigilance, and sloganistic thinking about the weakness and immorality of out-groups. This tendency can take its toll even when the decision-makers are conscientious statesmen trying to make the best possible decisions for their country and for all mankind.

I do not mean to imply that all cohesive groups suffer from groupthink, though all may display its symptoms from time to time. Nor should we infer from the term 'groupthink' that group decisions are typically inefficient or harmful. On the contrary, a group whose members have properly defined roles, with traditions and standard operating procedures that facilitate critical inquiry, is probably capable of making better decisions than any individual in the group who works on the problem alone. And yet the advantages of having decisions made by groups are often lost because of psychological pressures that arise when the members work closely together, share the same value and above all face a crisis situation in which everyone is subjected to stresses that generate a strong need for affiliation. In these circumstances, as conformity pressures begin to dominate, groupthink and the attendant deterioration of decision-making set in.

The central theme of my analysis can be summarized in this generalization, which I offer in the spirit of Parkinson's laws: *The more amiability and esprit de*

*corps among the members of a policy-making in-group, the greater is the danger
that independent critical thinking will be replaced by groupthink, which is likely to
result in irrational and dehumanizing actions directed against out-groups.*

[...]

A working assumption about who is susceptible

Who is susceptible to groupthink pertains not only to the nationality of the policy-
makers but also to their personality predispositions. Some chief executives, for
example, probably become more dependent than others on an inner circle of
advisers and set up group norms that encourage unanimity. Psychological
studies have shown marked individual differences in responsiveness to social
pressure. Some individuals consistently yield to the views of the majority, and
others consistently adhere to their own independent judgments. Recent research
suggests that conformity tendencies may be strongest in persons who are most
fearful of disapproval and rejection. People with strong affiliative needs prefer
their work colleagues to be good friends, even if those friends are not very
competent. Such people give priority to preserving friendly relationships, at the
expense of achieving success in the group's work tasks.

Most of the systematic research from which these findings are derived, however,
has dealt with superficial conformity in groups made up of strangers who meet
together once and do not expect to see one another again. To understand the
predispositions conducive to groupthink, we need studies of groups that meet
together for many weeks and work on decisions to which each member will be
committed. Such studies are also essential to find out whether other
characteristics of group members in addition to personality factors give rise to
individual differences in susceptibility to groupthink – for example, social class,
ethnic origin, occupational training, prior experience in group decision-making.
Richard Barnet, in *The Economy of Death*, emphasizes the homogeneous social
and educational backgrounds of the officials who man the top posts in
Washington. This type of homogeneity may also be an important factor that
increases the chances of groupthink.

Groups of individuals showing a preponderance of certain personality and social
attributes may prove to be the ones that succumb most readily to groupthink. But
persons with the most detrimental of these attributes would seldom survive the
career struggles required to reach high executive positions. Nevertheless, my
own observations of the way successful as well as unsuccessful executives
react when they become involved in two-week workshops in group relations
training suggest that none is immune to groupthink. Even individuals who are
generally high in self-esteem and low in dependency and submissiveness are
quite capable of being caught up from time to time in the group madness that
produces the symptoms of groupthink. In certain powerful circumstances that
make for groupthink, probably every member of every policy-making group, no
matter whether strongly or mildly predisposed, is susceptible. I propose to adopt
the general working assumption that all policy-makers are vulnerable whenever
circumstances promote concurrence-seeking.

How widespread is groupthink?

[...]

[...] The archives of other nations might also provide evidence of groupthink
among comparable groups of bureaucrats, as in the case of the decision by
Britain's National Coal Board to ignore warnings about a coal tip slide in
Aberfan, Wales, in order to save the money and time that would have been

required for taking proper precautions. When the predicted slide disaster occurred in October 1966, the local school was completely buried and all the town's school children were killed.

[...]

A lethal decision was made in 1961 by a group of nine directors and scientists of Grünenthal Chemie, the German firm that was making huge profits from marketing Thalidomide as a tranquilizer, to ignore alarming reports from physicians all over the world about dangerous side effects and to advertise that their cherished money-making drug was safe enough to be used by pregnant women, even though the firm had not run a single test to find out its effects on the unborn. Within less than a year after the advertising decision, approximately seven thousand deformed children were born. The German government brought criminal charges against the directors and, as a result of civil suits by parents of 'Thalidomide babies,' the firm had to pay millions of dollars in damages.

[...]

Before looking into such decisions for symptoms of groupthink, we first must check the facts in detail to make sure that each decision in the sample was a group product and not simply based on the judgment of one powerful leader who induced the others to go along with him regardless of whether they thought his decision was good, bad, or indifferent. This consideration has kept me from nominating as candidates a number of fiascoes caused by totalitarian governments – Mussolini's decision to enter the war in 1940 when Italy was completely unprepared, Stalin's failure to anticipate a German invasion while implementing the Nazi–Soviet pact in 1941, Hitler's fatal decision to invade Russia in 1941 – although it is conceivable that in some of these decisions the dictator's advisers participated as genuine policy-makers, not merely as sycophants.

[...]

Hypotheses about when groupthink occurs

When groupthink is most likely to occur pertains to situational circumstances and structural features of the group that make it easy for the symptoms to become dominant. The prime condition repeatedly encountered in the case studies of fiascoes is group cohesiveness. A second major condition suggested by the case studies is insulation of the decision-making group from the judgments of qualified associates who, as outsiders, are not permitted to know about the new policies under discussion until after a final decision has been made. Hence a [...] hypothesis is that the more insulated a cohesive group of executives becomes, the greater are the chances that its policy decisions will be products of groupthink. A third hypothesis suggested by the case studies is that the more actively the leader of a cohesive policy-making group promotes his own preferred solution, the greater are the chances of a consensus based on groupthink, even when the leader does not want the members to be yes-men and the individual members try to resist conforming. To test these hypotheses we would have to compare large samples of high-quality and low-quality decisions made by equivalent executive groups.

The groupthink syndrome: Review of the major symptoms

In order to test generalizations about the conditions that increase the chances of groupthink, we must operationalize the concept of groupthink by describing the symptoms to which it refers. Eight main symptoms run through the case studies of historic fiascoes. Each symptom can be identified by a variety of indicators, derived from historical records, observer's accounts of conversations, and participants' memoirs. The eight symptoms of groupthink are:

1   an illusion of invulnerability, shared by most or all the members, which creates excessive optimism and encourages taking extreme risks;

2   collective efforts to rationalize in order to discount warnings which might lead the members to reconsider their assumptions before they recommit themselves to their past policy decisions;

3   an unquestioned belief in the group's inherent morality, inclining the members to ignore the ethical or moral consequences of their decisions;

4   stereotyped views of enemy leaders as too evil to warrant genuine attempts to negotiate, or as too weak and stupid to counter whatever risky attempts are made to defeat their purposes;

5   direct pressure on any member who expresses strong arguments against any of the group's stereotypes, illusions, or commitments, making clear that this type of dissent is contrary to what is expected of all loyal members;

6   self-censorship of deviations from the apparent group consensus, reflecting each member's inclination to minimize to himself the importance of his doubts and counterarguments;

7   a shared illusion of unanimity concerning judgments conforming to the majority view (partly resulting from self-censorship of deviations, augmented by the false assumption that silence means consent);

8   the emergence of self-appointed mindguards – members who protect the group from adverse information that might shatter their shared complacency about the effectiveness and morality of their decisions.

When a policy-making group displays most or all of these symptoms, the members perform their collective tasks ineffectively and are likely to fail to attain their collective objectives. Although concurrence-seeking may contribute to maintaining morale after a defeat and to muddling through a crisis when prospects for a successful outcome look bleak, these positive effects are generally outweighed by the poor quality of the group's decision-making. My assumption is that the more frequently a group displays the symptoms, the worse will be the quality of its decisions. Even when some symptoms are absent, the others may be so pronounced that we can predict all the unfortunate consequences of groupthink.

[...]

Conclusion

The greater the threats to the self-esteem of the members of a cohesive decision-making body, the greater will be their inclination to resort to concurrence-seeking at the expense of critical thinking. If this explanatory hypothesis is correct, symptoms of groupthink will be found most often when a decision poses a moral dilemma, especially if the most advantageous course of action requires the policy-makers to violate their own standards of humanitarian behavior. Under these conditions, each member is likely to become more dependent than ever on the in-group for maintaining his self-image as a decent human being and accordingly will be more strongly motivated than ever to maintain a sense of group unity by striving for concurrence.

Until the explanation of groupthink in terms of mutual support to cope with threats to self-esteem is verified by systematic research, it is risky to make huge inferential leaps from theory to the practical sphere of prevention. Ultimately, a well-substantiated theory should have valuable practical applications to the formulation of effective prescriptions. As Kurt Lewin pointed out, 'Nothing is so practical as a good theory.' But until we know we have a good theory – one that is well supported by controlled experiments and systematic correlational research, as well as by case studies – we must recognize that any prescriptions we draw up are speculative inferences based on what little we know, or think we know, about when and why groupthink occurs. Still, we should not be inhibited from drawing tentative inferences –so long as we label them as such – in order to call attention to potentially useful means of prevention. Perhaps the worst consequences can be prevented if we take steps to avoid the circumstances in which groupthink is most likely to flourish.

(Janis, 1972, pp. 8–13, 184–206)

Commentary

Janis (1972, p. 9) defined 'groupthink' as 'a mode of thinking that people engage in when they are deeply involved in a cohesive in-group, when the members' strivings for unanimity override their motivation realistically to appraise alternative courses of action'. The word 'groupthink' was meant to be reminiscent of fictional 'Newspeak' in George Orwell's novel *Nineteen Eighty-four.* Janis intended 'groupthink' to take on the same invidious connotations as 'Newspeak' because it refers 'to a deterioration of mental efficiency, reality testing, and moral judgment that results from in-group pressure' (Janis, 1972, p. 9). His use, in Reading 5.1, of the word 'symptoms' takes that metaphor further by suggesting that 'groupthink' is a malady. Janis's ontological assumption seems, therefore, to be somewhat deterministic in implying that people in groups do not have control of what they do and, therefore, that individual decision making is likely to be more rational than group decision making. It is not entirely determinist in that he recognises that the same group of people can make good and bad decisions on different occasions (e.g. the US 1961 Bay of Pigs debacle and the more successful 1962 decisions on the Cuban missile crisis).

According to Janis, 'groupthink' occurs because members of groups are determined to avoid conflict in the process of their decision making and so use a variety of methods to suppress dissensus and maintain high levels of conformity. One of Janis's (1972, p. v) aims was 'to increase awareness of social psychological phenomena in decisions of historic importance, so that *group dynamics* will be taken into account by those who try to understand' the failure of goal-oriented groups. In foregrounding group dynamics, he suggests that group behaviour is a system of reciprocal interactions between groups and individuals and depends on the ways in which members perceive each other and the group. A major contribution of Janis's work is to the understanding of intragroup processes – an area of work that largely disappeared from social psychology in the 1970s (Stasson et al., 1999), but was rejuvenated as research on entitativity burgeoned.

Janis wanted his theory to be tested, including by controlled experiments, and various experiments lend support to his theory. What effect then does entitativity have on groups' decision-making processes? While Janis used the terms 'cohesiveness' and 'concurrence-seeking' rather than Campbell's (1958) term entitativity, recent experimental research is consistent with Janis's analyses in suggesting that groups perceived to be high in entitativity are likely to:

- see entitativity as a positive feature of the group (Yzerbyt et al., 2004b)

- hold stereotypic beliefs about group norms (i.e. prototypes) that accentuate contrasts between their group and others (Hogg et al., 2004)

- assume their group has a psychological essence and so look for features that are common to group members (Yzerbyt et al., 2001)

- be hostile to outgroups (Castano et al., 2002; Hamilton and Sherman, 1996)

- have a group social identity (Spears et al., 2004).

However, the evidence on Janis's theory is mixed (Paulus, 1998). Janis concluded that cohesiveness resulted in poor decision making because it led to less information processing. Recent work on entitativity, however, suggests that more entitative groups may induce more information processing and so can present stronger, more persuasive arguments (Rydell and McConnell, 2005). Janis took a group dynamics approach, based on the interactionist principle that what happens in groups results from the relationship between the group and the individuals within it. In addition, one implication of Janis's work is that groups are likely to make poorer judgements than individuals because they are subject to conformity pressures. This suggests that individuals are likely to be more rational than groups.

While groupthink research is qualitative, its findings are supported by experimental studies of 'group polarisation' that compare individual and group decisions involving risk. Such studies find a tendency for:

> like-minded individuals engaged in discussion with one another to fortify their preexisting views – and indeed to move toward more extreme points of view in the general direction in which they were already tending... For example, a group of people who tend ... to support gun control will, after discussion, do so with greater enthusiasm
>
> (Sunstein, 2001, pp. 5 and 7)

In other words, people make either a 'risky shift' or a 'cautious shift' in groups compared with when they make decisions alone (Stoner, 1968). Research on 'group polarisation' from the social identity and social categorisation theory perspectives, is more nuanced than groupthink in recognising that groups vary in whether they make risky or cautious decisions depending on social context and the social identities that are relevant for the people in the group at that time (Abrams et al., 1990; Wetherell, 1987).

It seems that only directive leadership is consistently crucial for producing the poor decisions Janis studied. Cohesiveness of the group does not necessarily have the impact he expected. This may be because members of cohesive groups can sometimes be sufficiently confident that they will continue to be accepted if they voice dissent (Brown, 2000). Ryan et al. conducted longitudinal research and an experimental study that suggests that:

> uncertainty and desire to be accepted leads new members to focus initially on the similarities among group members and on the development of meaningful group-level impressions of the ingroup and relevant outgroups. This focus results in lower perceived dispersion. [...] As group-level impressions develop, new members gradually shift their focus to developing a more detailed understanding of subgroups and individual group members, especially for the ingroup.
>
> (Ryan et al., 2004, p. 290)

This may explain why the Bay of Pigs decision was ineffective, while the Cuban missile crisis decision a year later was effective despite being 'made by nearly identical cohesive groups of policy-makers headed by the same leader' (Janis, 1972, p. 202). Ryan et al. argue that future research should pay attention to socialisation processes in groups. None the less, there are many publications that build on Janis's suggestions about ways to prevent groupthink (e.g. Hart, 1998).

Janis viewed 'groupthink' as a conflict model of decision making because group members appeared to experience stress when making decisions.

> When we speak of 'decisional conflicts' we are referring to simultaneous opposing tendencies within the individual to accept and reject a given course of action. The most prominent symptoms of such conflicts are hesitation, vacillation, feelings of uncertainty, and signs of acute emotional stress whenever the decision comes within the focus of attention. A major subjective characteristic of decisional conflicts is an unpleasant feeling of distress.
>
> (Janis and Mann, 1977, p. 46)

Janis' work raises the issue of whether people really perceive the group as entitative or instead recognise differences between members but feel pressured to agree – as in classic social psychological studies of conformity (e.g. Asch, 1955).

Reading 5.2, by Jonathan Potter and Stephen Reicher (1987), shows that different people can have contradictory views about what constitutes a particular group (the 'community') and, hence, different understandings of social problems and their solutions. It investigates how insiders and outsiders draw boundaries between groups. Rather than treating cohesiveness (or entitativity) as a fixed background factor as Janis does, Reading 5.2 throws light on how it varies over time, from place to place and according to the groups to which people belong. Potter and Reicher focus on groups of larger size than the membership groups Janis studied because they were interested in how 'community' (in the typology presented at the beginning of this chapter, a 'reference group') is understood. While the groups Janis studied were clearly bounded, definitions of who belongs to 'the community' and the implications of different ways of drawing boundaries around it are central to Potter and Reicher's paper.

A major difference that you should note between the two readings is that Janis's concern was with intragroup processes and so with the effect on insiders of belonging to a group. Potter and Reicher are, however, mostly not concerned with group processes, but with outsider as well as insider constructions of who is considered to belong to a group. Janis and Potter and Reicher, are, therefore, dealing with different objects of study (or units of analysis) – group processes and social constructions of a group respectively. The concept of entitativity enables recognition of linkages between these different objects of study because the research it inspires addresses both group processes and insider and outsider constructions of groups.

Potter and Reicher present an analysis of the discourses of community that circulated after a riot in the St Paul's district of Bristol, UK in 1980. It builds on Reicher's (1987) influential work on crowd behaviour during the riot. Reicher is a social psychologist whose work attempts to theorise both social action and individual–social relationships without treating them as dichotomous or socially determined. He took issue with previous theories of crowd behaviour (e.g. Le Bon, 1896) for desocialising and depoliticising collective action and reifying the individual–society dichotomy. In contrast, he contextualised crowd behaviour in terms of social relationships. According to self-categorisation theory (SCT) (the theoretical framework Reicher uses), when individuals consider that they belong to a group, they tend to foreground group characteristics rather than individual personality. Reicher argued that identity is not lost in a crowd, as Le Bon had suggested, but shifts from an emphasis on the personal to an emphasis on social definitions – i.e. those that are relevant to the values (norms) and history of the group. Incidents of crowd violence such as the St Paul's riot can, therefore, be understood as motivated (not mindless) forms of social action, where behavioural norms and limits result from the crowd's shared social identity and reflect clear and rational political and/or social meanings. However, there are limits to what groups can do because, in any context, history and ideology make certain courses of collective action more possible than others.

ACTIVITY 5.2

As you read the extract below, think about the following points:

1   How is the term 'community' used? Who does it include and who does it exclude?
2   Is the term 'community' constructed as positive or negative?

Note that Potter and Reicher do not mention the concept of entitativity. They conducted this research before the term became widely used.

Reading 5.2 is taken from a 1987 article by Jonathan Potter and Stephen Reicher which appeared in the *British Journal of Social Psychology*. It presents a discursive study of particular ways of constructing community as a group and of including and excluding different people from the category of community.

'Discourses of community and conflict: the organization of social categories in accounts of a "riot"'

This paper has three main goals. First, it is intended to illustrate a novel analytic and theoretical approach based on the systematic analysis of participants' discourse. Second, it will provide a detailed picture of the way the category 'community' is used in a body of discourse which relates to a serious social conflict, the so-called 'St Paul's riot' of 1980. Third, it will extend the boundaries of theorizing about social categorization by focusing on the constitution of categories in everyday discourse. [...]

[...]

The analytic perspective adopted has been termed discourse analysis (Mulkay and Gilbert, 1982; Mulkay et al., 1983; Potter et al., 1984; Potter and Wetherell, [1987]). [...] Discourse analysis is concerned specifically with questions about the organization of discourse and the consequences of this organization. For instance: how are accounts constructed?; what effects do particular accounts have?; and, most generally, how do people construct a coherent social world for the occasion at hand given a particular set of linguistic resources?

There are good reasons for taking discourse analysis as a startpoint to a study of social categories and the 'St Paul's riot'. On the one hand, the principal manner in which conflicts over the nature of events such as St Paul's are carried out is through discourse; both verbal debate and written texts. Insofar as this discourse is all that is available to commentators and those concerned with responding to the events it will, for all intents and purposes, come to *constitute* the events. Or, put another way, the nature of the events will not be *analytically* separable from the nature of the discourse. On the other hand, discourse is readily available to the analyst; it can be transcribed, copied and repeatedly examined, and in this it is in marked contrast to the activities and social processes which are the common currency of social psychological research (see Heritage and Atkinson, 1984).

Our particular concern is with the way conflict is represented. [...] Our analysis deals with the deployment of notions of community in accounts of the street disturbances which occurred in St Paul's, Bristol, on 2 April 1980. Its central argument is that 'community' should be conceptualized as a 'linguistic repertoire' (or perhaps part of a repertoire [...]) which is used for description, evaluation and explanation.

The notion of 'linguistic repertoires' has been developed in a number of studies [...] (e.g. Potter and Mulkay, 1982; Gilbert and Mulkay, 1984; Wetherell, 1986; Yearley, 1985) to account for organized features of the way participants use their language. Linguistic repertoires are constituted through a limited number of lexical items, particular stylistic constructions and use of a range of metaphors and tropes. [...] The suggestion is that selections are made from the available repertoire to best suit the function to which the discourse is put (Litton and Potter, 1985; Potter and Litton, 1985).

[...] We will attempt, first, to document some of the varying facets of the community repertoire and, second, to show how the distinctive features of this repertoire are used in the construction of versions of events. It has been widely noted that contrasting accounts of the 'St Paul's riot' have been offered, particularly with respect to the motives of the various parties involved and the role of the police. Our aim is to describe the details of linguistic usage which go to make up these divergent versions.

Method

Materials

Radio and television programmes which referred to the 'St Paul's riot' were recorded and fully transcribed. A wide range of newspaper reports and editorials were collected. Six subjects who were involved in, or at least present during the disturbance, were interviewed about the events. These interviews were taped and transcribed. The transcription conventions used emphasize readability at some expense of detailed nuances of stress, pronunciation and timing.

Given our theoretical position, no attempt will be made to give a description of the event referred to as the 'St Paul's riot' (but see Joshua et al., 1983; Reicher, 1984). This event dominated the next day's news media and resulted in newspaper headlines such as: '19 POLICE HURT IN BLACK RIOT' (*Telegraph*, 3 April 1980) or 'HUNDREDS OF BLACK YOUTHS BATTLE WITH POLICE IN BRISTOL RIOT' (*The Times*, 3 April 1980). In one of a number of varying descriptions of the consequences of the 'riot' the official police report named 22 officers injured, 21 premises damaged by fire, six vehicles destroyed and 132 arrests. All the incidents appeared to be confined to a small area of Bristol known as St Paul's.

Procedure

The transcribed materials were approached using a systematic analysis of discourse (Potter and Mulkay, 1985; Potter and Wetherell, [1987]). The entire body of transcript and copies of newspaper articles were read and all instances of the terms community, communities, and communal were noted. In further readings, all these instances (totalling 322) were coded as being relevant to one or more of a set of themes. Extracts under each theme were recopied and placed in separate document files for ease of reference.

It is important to stress that we are not claiming that the use of this coding scheme will have identified *all* the relevant instances in these materials. Our claim is that there is a repertoire of terms which are used with stylistic and grammatical regularities, often combined with certain metaphors – by starting with instances which draw upon the term itself we hope to begin to elucidate this repertoire. At the same time, we do not want to suggest that the community repertoire might not be part of some broader linguistic system which might be revealed through further research.

In the analysis that follows we make no sustained attempt at quantification. Instead, our aim is to indicate some of the varying ways in which the category 'community' is constituted and applied, and to suggest some of the functions which these uses serve. We consider this type of analysis to be an essential preliminary to statistical investigation. Where numbers are given, they should only be considered an approximate guide to the prevalence of certain constructions in the transcript. The extracts which are included are meant to indicate the range of uses of 'community' occurring within a particular theme and, in some cases, concentrate on 'important' texts such as Home Office reports and parliamentary debates. In this way we hope to minimize the extent to which the reader has to take our analytic interpretations on trust, for, as far as possible given the available space, they are available for inspection. [...]

Reflexive considerations

[...] In our discussion of 'community' we must emphasize that we are concerned solely with this term's usage in discourse; and are making absolutely no claims about the social organization of people living in St Paul's. Thus the term 'community' and its synonyms should be read as if in quotation marks throughout.

[...] It is worth stressing that we have deliberately avoided the hypothetico–deductive approach common in social psychology, adopting instead a more inductive stance based on repeated and systematic reading of texts. [...]

Analysis

1   The community repertoire

This analytic section has two central goals. In the first place it starts to identify the different facets of what we have termed the community repertoire. To facilitate this it concentrates on accounts which make more or less direct reference to the nature, boundaries or make-up of community. In each case, the way in which the term is deployed is made as explicit as possible. In the second place, this section starts to document the variability in the use of the notion of community. Accounts are examined which present highly inconsistent versions of the existence, scope and make-up of community.

(a) The temporal existence of community. We will examine in turn three accounts which formulate the existence of community over time. The following extract is taken from a newspaper report on the day following the 'riot'. It describes the owners of a nylon shop in St Paul's who claim to be moving out as a response to the previous night's disturbance.

1   (1) The Billingtons began trading in St Paul's about 22 years ago – but last night has driven them away. (2) 'We are packing up – this community is finished. (3) We won't be coming back', said Brian Billington.

In this extract the shop keeper is depicted as moving because the 'community is finished'. This construction implies an important distinction between the physical presence of people in the St Paul's area of Bristol, which will clearly continue, and some aspect of their life-style or social organization – 'community' – which will not. This sort of distinction in uses of 'community' has been noted by Williams (1976). He suggests that 'community' can, first, refer to the physical group of people living in a particular area or district. Second, it can refer to something held in common by a group of people: certain interests, characteristics or identity. The Billingtons clearly express this second usage. They are alluding to some quality of community over and above physical presence, although its exact nature is not made explicit.

In the next extract, the notion of time is also implied, although in a rather different way.

2   (1) I say it doesn't matter how much money you spend within our community if you are not going to let us take an active part in it ourself. (2) And at the end of the day we own what we have, and it is ours, and we can use it for the best ethnic . . . in our culture there. (3) Then we can live alongside in a community.

The extract starts with a reference to spending money 'within our community'. Although this seems to presuppose the existence of a community, in the final sentence its existence is made dependent on the local people being able to determine the way resources are allocated to fit cultural needs best. This quote thus embodies two main uses of 'community' – first, as a local group of people (Extract 2, sentence 1 = 2.1) and later as some (largely unspecified) feature that can arise given certain conditions (2.3).

[...]

[...] we are offered [...] different versions of the temporal existence of community: (i) that it used to exist but does no longer; (ii) that it might exist at some time in the future; (iii) that the community exists at the present time. In addition, each of the extracts expresses the contrast between 'community' as a physical presence and 'community' as a social attribute. What is interesting is that, while each of the passages involves a usage which treats community as an extra quality, not implied by the mere presence of people in an area, this does not necessarily involve outright rejection of a 'physical presence' usage. Indeed, we have seen, in Extract 2, that the two usages can coexist, side by side.

For the analyst, then, there is thus an ambiguity in the referent of 'community' which relates to what it is, when it exists and, as we will show next, what categories it subsumes. This is not, however, to say that participants necessarily find such accounts ambiguous: often the pragmatic context will fix the sense of the term. Yet, as we will show in part 2 of the analysis, the wide range of potential meanings of community allows considerable flexibility in the application of the term which is exploited in the construction of differing versions of events.

(b) Race and community. The discussion of accounts with a temporal dimension starts to flesh out the repertoire of terms which make up the idea of community and some of its uses. By far the largest body of instances (23 out of 32) coded in relation to the general constitution of community were concerned, in one way or another, with its racial basis. This is not surprising because, in the debates conducted in the media and the British parliament after 'the riot', a recurrent theme was whether 'it' should be understood as having racial causes. In the following [...] extracts we indicate some of the alternative forms of discourse through which 'the community' can be racially constituted.

The following extract draws on the notion of time, as in the previous section; yet here what is to be achieved is specifically a 'multiracial community'.

4   (1) Much hard work has gone into promoting good race relations but the lesson has yet to be learned that you cannot engender a multiracial community by spending a lot of money, and appointing a lot of social workers. (2) A community has to grow at its own pace with a balance of interests preserved.

Extract 4 has a lot of similarities with Extract 2. It suggests that a community cannot be achieved by spending money and by input from outside agencies. In this case, however, it is a '*multiracial* community' that is not produced by outside intervention. The alternative offered draws upon the organic metaphor of 'the community' growing 'at its own pace', thus preserving the balance of interests (4.2). [...] Such organic metaphors, which are a common way of characterizing community in the present data, can have important consequences.

[...]

[...] [Extract 4] uses a putative failure to achieve 'a community' to criticize the manner in which the State in general intervenes in order to achieve social solutions. It proposes, as an alternative, 'natural' processes of growth at the community's own rate (4.2). [...]

Other accounts speak of '*the* black community' (31 occurrences) or '*the* West Indian community' (6 occurrences). Given that 'community' is recurrently used to mean something distinct from a mere collective of individual inhabitants in an area, there is, from an analytic perspective, a considerable ambiguity in such accounts. Should they be taken to mean that there is *only* a black community or that there are more communities from which they are selecting the black one for comment? Take the following two extracts.

6   (1) I think we are a very close-knit community. (2) We have good relationship with the white people.

7   (1) We are going to take up some of those underlying grievances with members of the local community. (2) At first I would like to ask you, Councillor Abraham. (3) Do you understand the resentment of so many of the black community, especially young blacks of St Paul's?

Both these extracts imply an identity between the 'black' and 'local community'. In the first, 'black community' is contrasted with 'white people'; in the second, 'black community' is used interchangeably with 'local community'. While these accounts, and others like them, would not directly *contradict* accounts speaking of a 'white community' in St Paul's the recurrent use of 'black community' sharpens the racial focus of discussion of the riot. 'Black community' is formulated as the entity relevant for discussion.

There is one final complexity here. It is that 'black community' need not necessarily refer only to 'black' people (even if one accepts the dubious assumption that there is a neutral definition of who should be included in the category black – Banton, 1977; Reeves, 1983). This term could also refer to people who are 'black defined' either by themselves or others, as in an interviewee's description of St Paul's: 'politically they are all black'.

(c) Positivity and harmony. Thus far, we have been concerned with the make-up and variability of the community repertoire. We have shown differences in descriptions with respect to *what* the relevant community is, *when* it exists, and *what* sorts of people the category covers. Alongside this variability, there is a third dimension over which there is broad agreement: a community should be positively evaluated, it is a good thing.

[...]

[...] The main features of the community repertoire derived from the St Paul's materials are summarized in Table 1.

In the next section we will go on to examine the way this repertoire is used in accounts of conflict, and in particular in attributions of responsibility and suggestions for remedial action.

2   Community relations and the explanation of conflict

[...]

Table 1   The community repertoire

Paradigmatic alternatives
Local residents *or* Local residents with specific social organization
Black community *or* White community *or* Mixed community.
Currently exists *or* Existed in past *or* May exist in future

Sample predicates	Metaphors (where relevant)
Friendly Warm Happy Harmonious	
Close-knit Integrated Tight	Spatial
Mature Grows Evolves	Organic
Acts Knows Feels	Agency

[...]

The notion of 'community relations' is deployed in a number of ways in the corpus and in some form or other makes up for the largest subset of coded accounts – 72 in all. Within this subset there are important variations in reference and in evaluations of the nature and quality of relations.

[...]

Given that 'community relations' is used [...], we can ask what consequences follow. The most basic is that it allows slippage from talking about the police as set over '*against* the community' to depicting them as '*part* of the community'. [...] The significance of this is that, first, if the police are a constituent of 'the community' then, linguistically, any conflict will have been an intragroup phenomenon; it will have taken place between constituent parts of the same social category. Second, drawing the police into the scope of the nominal 'community relations' paves the way for characterizing the police and their actions using the community repertoire. The suggested ways for avoiding further conflict reflect both of these points. [...]

[...]

[...] Take for example the next two extracts.

16   (1) There has never been a lot of friendly relations between the police and the black community.

17   (1) Mr Wilkes said 'There has always been pretty bad relations between the black community and the police'.

In these two examples, attention is focused specifically and explicitly on the relation between police and 'black community'. Furthermore, this relation is described as one that was poor *before* the riot rather than disrupted *by* the riot [...]. These accounts conflict with those stressing good relations [...]. If 'community relations' is read as 'relations between blacks and whites' no contradiction is produced. Such an achievement can be very important in a body of discourse where the clash of versions is endemic. Used in this way 'community relations' can have the effect of softening potential conflicts between versions of events.

[...]

Discussion

[...] The community repertoire [...] can encompass the local residents of an area or the local residents with a specific social organization or set of relationships. It can formulate ethnic categories such as 'black community' or 'mixed community'. It can formulate a condition currently existing in a group of people, a condition which existed in the past or will do so in the future. When community is used to refer to residents with a specific social organization this can be further characterized by notions such as friendliness and warmth; by way of spatial metaphors (close-knit, tight), organic metaphors (growing, mature), and by metaphors of agency (acting, feeling). Crucially, where the term 'community' is used in formulations of an evaluative nature the evaluation is overwhelmingly positive.

[...]

The use of 'community relations' has a number of consequences. On the one hand, attributions of a cause for the conflict are vague and ambiguous [...] and the role of the police will be, in terms of the discourse, less focal (because the reader/hearer is forced to infer it – see Kress and Hodge, 1979). Moreover, the police are depicted as a constituent of 'the community' rather than a group set over against it and, as 'communities' are, linguistically speaking, sources of harmony rather than conflict, are less likely to have initiated any conflict. On the other hand, formulations using 'community relations' go with solutions constructed from the community repertoire. Thus pleas are made to develop trust and personal relationships between police and locals, to see things in human terms and, of course, to introduce 'community policing': the perfect solution to 'community relations problems'!

The other set of accounts we examined eschewed the notion of 'community relations' and instead explicitly formulated conflict between police and 'the community'. The relevant categories are identified and the conflict is specified as an intergroup one. In terms of the attribution of causes, the events are depicted as a consequence of *pre-existing* problems which, in the weaker accounts, are not spelt out, but in the stronger accounts are specified as police repression/ harassment. [...] In terms of solutions, instead of trading on the suggestion that there is a disturbed community that needs healing, the focus is squarely on the police. If their actions are the cause then their power must be curbed or problems dealt with.

Overall, then, two opposing ways of representing and evaluating the role of the police and the nature of the conflict have been described. In each case, the same linguistic repertoire is drawn upon – that of community. But the repertoire is deployed in such a manner that the evaluative implications are markedly different. [...] It is important to emphasize again that the repertoire is a set of *available* resources – we are not suggesting that the entire repertoire will be somehow present in every use of 'community'. At the same time we must stress that no claim is being made about the individual goals of the various participants. Our concern is purely with the consequences of various uses of the community repertoire.

References

Banton, M. (1977) *The Idea of Race*, London, Tavistock.

Gilbert, G.N. and Mulkay, M. (1984) *Opening Pandora's Box: A Sociological Analysis of Scientists' Discourse*, Cambridge, Cambridge University Press.

Heritage, J. and Atkinson, J.M. (1984) 'Introduction' in Atkinson, J.M. and Heritage, J. (eds) *Structures of Social Action: Studies in Conversation Analysis*, Cambridge, Cambridge University Press.

Joshua, H., Wallace, T. and Booth, H. (1983) *To Ride the Storm: The 1980 Bristol 'Riot' and the State*, London, Heinemann.

Kress, G. and Hodge, R. (1979) *Language as Ideology*, London, Routledge and Kegan Paul.

Litton, I. and Potter, J. (1985) 'Social representations in the ordinary explanation of a "riot"', *European Journal of Social Psychology*, vol. 15, pp. 371–88.

Mulkay, M. and Gilbert, G.N. (1982) 'What is the ultimate question? Some remarks in defence of the analysis of scientists' discourse', *Social Studies of Science*, vol. 12, pp. 309–20.

Mulkay, M., Potter, J. and Yearley, S. (1983) 'Why an analysis of scientific discourse is needed' in Knorr-Cetina, K. and Mulkay, M. (eds) *Science Observed: Perspectives on the Social Study of Science*, London, Sage.

Potter, J. and Litton, I. (1985) 'Some problems underlying the theory of social representations', *British Journal of Social Psychology*, vol. 24, pp. 81–90.

Potter, J. and Mulkay, M. (1982) 'Making theory useful: utility accounting in social psychologists' discourse', *Fundamenta Scientiae*, vols 3/4, pp. 259–78.

Potter, J. and Mulkay, M. (1985) 'Scientists' interview talk: interviews as a technique for revealing participants' interpretative practices' in Brenner, M., Brown, J. and Canter, D. (eds) *The Research Interview: Uses and Approaches*, London, Academic Press.

Potter, J., Stringer, P. and Wetherell, M. (1984) *Social Texts and Context: Literature and Social Psychology*, London, Routledge and Kegan Paul.

Potter, J. and Wetherell, M. (1987) *Discourse and Social Psychology*, London, Sage.

Reeves, F. (1983) *British Racial Discourse: A Study of British Political Discourse about Race and Race-related Matters*, Cambridge, Cambridge University Press.

Reicher, S. (1984) 'The St Paul's riot: an explanation of the limits of crowd action in terms of a social identity model', *European Journal of Social Psychology*, vol. 14, pp. 1–21.

Wetherell, M. (1986) 'Linguistic repertoires and literary criticism: new directions for a social psychology of gender' in Wilkinson, S. (ed.) *Feminist Social Psychology*, Milton Keynes, Open University Press.

Williams, R. (1976) *Keywords: A Vocabulary of Culture and Society*, London, Fontana.

Yearley, S. (1985) 'Vocabularies of freedom and resentment: a Strawsonian perspective on the nature of argumentation in science and law', *Social Studies of Science*, vol. 15, pp. 99–126.

(Potter and Reicher, 1987, pp. 25–40)

Conclusion

In this second extract Potter and Reicher focused explicitly on discursive constructions of the entity called 'community' rather than on group processes *per se*. They showed that the same account could construct 'community' in different ways. The variability of the concept made it both ambiguous and flexible. There were multiple *linguistic repertoires* (now more often called 'interpretative repertoires') about the post-riot St Paul's 'community'. Sometimes 'community' referred to all local residents, and at other times to lifestyle, social organisation and relationships. In many accounts, 'community' was treated as synonymous with 'black community' or 'multiracial community'. Both time and space were important; some discourses constructing the community as current and others treating it as finished or as an entity that will exist in the future. Spatial metaphors (e.g. 'close knit', 'tight') were common and the local area was viewed as the site of the community, which was also often treated as an active, feeling agent.

According to SCT (Turner et al., 1987) social categorisation is central to social identity. People in groups (including large crowds) identify with a relevant, overarching social category. Identification makes certain identities, and so certain actions, possible because people in groups tailor their actions to those they consider appropriate for people in that social category. In SCT, self-stereotyping in situations where social identity is salient (e.g. in crowds) can be positive and empowering. Defining oneself as part of a community, therefore, makes certain actions possible and proscribes others (Reicher, 1987). Because discursive constructions of community (which would now be related to the concept of entitativity) affect identification, Potter and Reicher's paper has implications for group processes. Hogg et al. (2004, p. 253) suggest that people think of groups in terms of 'prototypes' – 'fuzzy sets of interrelated attributes that simultaneously capture similarities and structural relationships within groups and differences between the groups, and prescribe group membership-related behavior'. Ingroups differentiate themselves as much as possible from those they view as outgroups (termed the principle of 'metacontrast') in order to accentuate entitativity. As a result, the content of prototypes can vary as groups compare themselves to different outgroups. Quantitative findings on entitativity are supported by newly emerging qualitative research (e.g. Condor, forthcoming).

In the Potter and Reicher paper, the prototypes of community that people produced were all positive (e.g. , friendly, warm, close knit). Some of the local residents differentiated their community (the ingroup) from people in other areas and from other communities as well as the police (outgroups). While the community repertoire was contested, it was entitative in that insiders and outsiders viewed 'the community' as an entity and a source of agency. From a qualitative study of British Muslim identity, Hopkins and Kahani-Hopkins (2004) also found that entitativity is not a pre-given antecedent variable, but is constructed actively in discourse and is contested by activists with different political projects. Just as entitativity in Janis's groups had consequences for group processes and for the decisions taken, so constructions of entitativity had consequences for what different groups of people considered the causes of the St Paul's riot and, hence, for the solutions proposed for preventing further riots. However, the looseness and flexibility of the term 'community' made it difficult to allocate responsibility and blame for the riot. The discourse of 'community relations' was sufficiently flexible to refer either to inter- or intragroup relations. As a result, the potential solutions for preventing further riots varied from suggestions by the police and members of parliament that the community (defined as including the police) needs healing, to some 'community' suggestions that police unfairness was part of a pre-existing problem and the disturbances were not a 'riot', but 'fighting back'. Potter and Reicher thus demonstrate that how groups are defined and who is included and excluded is not a trivial exercise, but has social and political consequences.

There are commonalities and differences between the two readings. Both studies are politically relevant. Both researched naturally occurring (hence ecologically valid) and consequential events in the 'field', using qualitative methods and a range of sources including reports, media accounts and interviews with participants. However, while Potter and Reicher present the details of their then novel methodology, Janis is vaguer about how he carried out his analyses. A major problem with Janis's methods is that he identified events already defined as fiascos and used archival records to investigate them. This meant that he had little evidence about whether or not the same characteristics sometimes led to effective decision-making. Kramer (1998) analysed two of Janis's fiascos using documents declassified since *Victims of Groupthink: A Psychological Study of Foreign-Policy Decisions and Fiascoes* was published, oral histories, and memoirs by key participants. He suggests that Janis overstated the importance of group cohesiveness and small-group dynamics and understated political considerations.

Janis conceptualises group processes as marked by conflict and Potter and Reicher conceptualise constructions of group entities as conflictual. Their different theoretical starting points, however, lead to different emphases. For Janis, 'groupthink' partly results from the stress and anxiety produced when individuals have to make consequential decisions and so face opposing tendencies to accept or to reject a potential course of action, together with pressures to achieve consensus in a group that values cohesiveness. He also identified the fears and anxieties group members reported feeling when they secretly disagreed. This focus on individualised conflict arises because individuals have a major impact on what happens in Janis's small membership groups. By contrast, 'community', a reference group in the typology above, is not necessarily a face-to-face group and is less easy to individualise. However, both sets of theorists would eschew an individual–social dichotomy in favour of an ontology that views them as inextricably linked.

Both Readings 5.1 and 5.2 help increase awareness of the salience of ingroup/ outgroup categorisation and stereotyping and assist understanding of social identities – although neither foregrounded this issue. Janis considered the social identity of the group to have an impact (morally and in terms of perceived invulnerability and stereotyped perceptions of outgroups). Potter and Reicher presented group differences in how the community discourse is deployed, which indicated that intergroup conflict is central to social identities and, hence, to moral and political strategies. Both approaches highlighted effectively the relationship between ingroup identity and perceptions of outgroups. This provides a theoretical means of linking small groups and crowds through common processes of identification and categorisation.

But, how successful are Janis and Potter and Reicher in providing understandings of group dynamics? It is important to remember that they had different objects of study in that they researched different types of groups and that Janis was more concerned with intragroup processes. It is, therefore, not surprising that they had different emphases. Janis emphasised the interaction between *individuals* and *groups* and pinpointed the pivotal role played by a directive leader, by 'mindguards' (group members who protect the leader from contrary opinions) and by individual conflicts. He concluded that it is not 'the policy-makers' personal deficiencies' (Janis, 1972, p. 191) that produce poor decisions, but that their deficiencies are amplified when they participate in groups. Later work has supported Janis's analysis that 'ingroup deviants' are often derogated in order to restore group coherence (Abrams et al., 2004).

Potter and Reicher's analysis remains relevant to political concerns about community cohesion and civil renewal and finds support from experimental studies on entitativity that 'concentrate on possible structural and social factors that may shape a perceiver's propensity to see any given group as a coherent entity or as a looser set of people' (Yzerbyt et al., 2004b, p. 8). However, discourse analysis is not concerned with analysing individuals and Potter and Reicher (1987, p. 37) state that 'we must stress that no claim is being made about the individual goals of the various participants. Our concern is purely with the consequences of various uses of the community repertoire'. They, therefore, produced understandings of the wider social arena, while Janis focused on small-group processes where interpersonal dynamics are of greater significance than are broader social processes.

Although Janis is careful to recognise that there might be exceptions to the behaviour he identifies, his theory is pessimistic in suggesting that if the characteristics he documents are present, groups are highly likely to produce erroneous decisions. He does, however, lay out potential solutions to groupthink. In using discourse analysis, Potter and Reicher take a more distanced view and are neither pessimistic nor optimistic about the implications of different discourses of community. While they indicate the potential solutions that follow from different discourses, they do not themselves advocate solutions. Reicher's (1987) work on the St Paul's riot does, however, suggest ways to minimise violence in crowd situations by, for example, pointing out how certain police actions produce the opposite to their intended results because they exacerbate crowd anger (Drury et al., 2003; Stott and Reicher, 1998). What seems to be missing from Janis's account is the situatedness of group behaviour. His description of the context of decision making does not include the specificity of the decisions to be taken, normative views about the situation or the different social identities that are made salient within the group. This is in contrast to the Potter and Reicher paper, which demonstrates the situatedness of entitativity. Potter and Reicher thus provide a more complex ontology of groups, while Janis provides more insights into group dynamics.

Given these differences, the fact that 'groupthink' was conceptualised more than three decades ago just before the nadir of social psychological research on small-group processes (Stasson et al., 1999), are both theories still of relevance? One test of this is whether they are still influential. This is true for both. Perhaps partly because Janis's neologism is catchy, it is frequently used. For example, the 2004 US Senate Intelligence Committee's *Report of the Select Committee on the US Intelligence Community's Prewar Intelligence Assessments on Iraq* blamed behaviour that has been called 'groupthink' for failures adequately to interpret intelligence about whether or not Iraq had weapons of mass destruction (Wikipedia, 2006). Janis's 'symptoms' and conclusions have been applied to numerous more recent historical examples, including the Challenger spacecraft disaster, some of Margaret Thatcher's cabinet decisions and Bill Clinton's impeachment.

Potter and Reicher's paper is much quoted (e.g. Colombo and Senatore, 2005; Rapley and Pretty, 1999) and the then novel methodology of discourse analysis has proliferated and had a major impact. In addition, Reicher's (1987) research has been influential in shifting the previously widespread view that crowds are mobs that engage in mindless violence and necessarily have negative influences on individuals.

The two papers deal with different processes, groups of different size and composition, are theoretically disparate and take different epistemological, ontological and political approaches (and so have different objects of study). However, both use naturalistic, qualitative methodology to provide insights into groups as entities. Arguably, both helped to pave the way for the resurgence of interest in intragroup processes demonstrated by the burgeoning literature on entitativity, social identity and social categorisation.

References

Abrams, D., Marques, J., Randsley de Moura, G., Hutchison, P. and Brown, N. (2004) 'The maintenance of entitativity: a subjective group dynamics approach' in Yzerbyt, Judd and Corneille (eds) (2004a); also available online at www. psor.ucl.ac.be/personal/yzerbyt [Vincent Yzerbyt's homepage] (Accessed 28 January 2006).

Abrams, D., Wetherell, M., Cochrane, S., Hogg, M.A. and Turner, J.C. (1990) 'Knowing what to think by knowing who you are: self-categorization and the nature of norm formation, conformity and group polarization', *British Journal of Psychology*, vol. 29, pp. 97–119.

Allport, F. (1962) 'A structuronomic conception of behaviour: individual and collective', *Journal of Abnormal and Social Psychology*, vol. 64, pp. 3–30.

Asch, S. (1952) *Social Psychology*, Englewood Cliffs, NJ, Prentice Hall.

Asch, S. (1955) 'Opinions and social pressure', *Scientific American*, pp. 31–5.

Brown, R. (2000) *Group Processes* (2nd edn), Oxford, Blackwell.

Buys, C. (1978) 'Humans would do better without groups', *Personality and Social Psychology Bulletin*, vol. 4, pp. 123–5.

Campbell, D. (1958) 'Common fate, similarity, and other indices of the status of aggregates of person as social entities', *Behavioural Science*, vol. 3, pp. 14–25.

Castano, E., Yzerbyt, V., Paladino, M.P. and Sacchi, S. (2002) 'I belong therefore I exist: ingroup identification, ingroup entitativity, and ingroup bias', *Personality and Social Psychology Bulletin*, vol. 28, no. 2, pp. 135–43.

Colombo, M. and Senatore, A. (2005) 'The discursive construction of community identity', *Journal of Community and Applied Social Psychology*, vol. 15, pp. 48–62.

Condor, S. (forthcoming) 'Temporality and collectivity: diversity, history and the rhetorical construction of national entitativity', *British Journal of Social Psychology*.

Drury, J., Stott, C.J. and Farsides, T. (2003) 'The role of police perceptions and practices in the development of "public disorder"', *Journal of Applied Social Psychology*, vol. 33, pp. 1480–500.

Erikson, E. (1968) *Identity: Youth and Crisis*, New York, Norton.

Hamilton, D.L. and Sherman, S.J. (1996) 'Perceiving persons and groups', *Psychological Review*, vol. 103, pp. 336–55.

Hart, P.T. (1998) 'Preventing groupthink revisited: evaluating and reforming groups in government', *Organizational Behavior and Human Decision Processes*, vol. 73, pp. 306–26.

Hogg, M., Abrams, D., Otten, S. and Hinkle, S. (2004) 'The social identity perspective: intergroup relations, self-conception, and small groups', *Small Group Research*, vol. 35, no. 3, pp. 246–76.

Hopkins, N. and Kahani-Hopkins, V. (2004) 'The antecedents of identification: a rhetorical analysis of British Muslim activists' constructions of community and identity', *British Journal of Social Psychology*, vol. 43, pp. 41–57.

Janis, I. (1972) *Victims of Groupthink: A Psychological Study of Foreign-Policy Decisions and Fiascoes* (2nd edn), Boston, MA, Houghton Mifflin.

Janis, I. and Mann, L. (1977) *Decision Making: A Psychological Analysis of Conflict, Choice and Commitment*, New York, The Free Press.

Kelly, C. and Breinlinger, S. (1996) *The Social Psychology of Collective Action: Identity, Injustice and Gender,* London, Taylor and Francis.

Kramer, R.M. (1998) 'Revisiting the Bay of Pigs and Vietnam decisions 25 years later: how well has the groupthink hypothesis stood the test of time?', *Organizational Behavior and Human Decision Processes,* vol. 73, nos 2–3, pp. 236–71.

Le Bon, G. (1896) *The Crowd: A Study of the Popular Mind,* Macmillan, New York; also available online at http://etext.lib.virginia.edu/toc/modeng/public/ BonCrow.html (Accessed 29 December 2005).

Lewin, K. (1948) 'Resolving social conflicts; selected papers on group dynamics' in Lewin, G.W. (ed.) *Resolving Social Conflicts,* New York, Harper and Row.

McDougall, W. (1920) *The Group Mind,* Cambridge, Cambridge University Press.

Mead, G.H. (1934) *Mind, Self, and Society,* Chicago, IL, University of Chicago Press.

Paulus, P. (1998) 'Developing consensus about groupthink after all these years', *Organizational Behavior and Human Decision Processes,* vol. 73, pp. 362–74.

Potter, J. and Reicher, S. (1987) 'Discourses of community and conflict: the organization of social categories in accounts of a "riot"', *British Journal of Social Psychology,* vol. 26, pp. 25–40.

Rapley, M. and Pretty, G. (1999) 'Playing Procrustes: the interactional production of a "psychological sense of community", *Journal of Community Psychology,* vol. 27, no. 6, pp. 695–715.

Reicher, S.D. (1987) 'Crowd behaviour as social action' in Turner, Hogg, Oakes, Reicher, and Wetherell (eds) (1987).

Ryan, C., Robinson, D. and Hausmann, L. (2004) 'Group socialization, uncertainty reduction, and the development of new members' perceptions of group variability' in Yzerbyt, Judd and Corneille (eds) (2004a).

Rydell, R. and McConnell, A. (2005) 'Perceptions of entitativity and attitude change', *Personality and Social Psychology Bulletin,* vol. 31, no. 1, pp. 99–110.

Senate Intelligence Committee (2004) *Report of the Select Committee on the US Intelligence Community's Prewar Intelligence Assessments on Iraq,* US Government Printing Office; also available online at: www.gpoaccess.gov/ serialset/creports/iraq.html (Accessed 22 August 2006).

Sherif, M. (1966) *In Common Predicament: Social Psychology of Intergroup Conflict and Cooperation,* Boston, MA, Houghton-Mifflin.

Smith, M.B. (1992) 'Obituary: Irving L. Janis', *American Psychologist,* vol. 47, no. 6, pp. 812–13.

Spears, R. Scheepers, D., Jetten, J., Doosje, B., Ellemers, N. and Postmes, T. (2004) 'Entitativity, group distinctiveness and social identity: getting and using social structure' in Yzerbyt, Judd and Corneille (eds) (2004a).

Stainton-Rogers, W. (2003) *Social Psychology: Experimental and Critical Approaches*, Maidenhead, Open University Press.

Stangor, C. (2004) *Social Groups in Action and Interaction*, New York, Psychology Press.

Stasson, M.F., Markus, M.J. and Hart, J.W. (1999) 'Theory and research on small groups', *Group Dynamics: Theory, Research, and Practice*, vol. 3, no. 4, pp. 313–16.

Stoner, J. (1968) 'Risky and cautious shifts in group decisions: the influence of widely held values', *Journal of Experimental Social Psychology*, vol. 4, pp. 442–59.

Stott, C. and Reicher, S. (1998) 'How conflict escalates', *Sociology*, vol. 32, no. 2, pp. 353–77.

Sunstein, C. (2001) *Echo Chambers: Bush v. Gore, Impeachment, and Beyond*, New Jersey, Princeton University Press; also available online at www.pupress. princeton.edu/sunstein/echo.pdf (Accessed 26 February 2006).

Tajfel, H. (1982) *Social Identity and Intergroup Relations*, Cambridge, Cambridge University Press.

Turner, J.C., Hogg, M.A., Oakes, P.J., Reicher, S.D. and Wetherell, M.S. (eds) (1987) *Rediscovering the Social Group: A Self-categorization Theory*, Oxford, Basil Blackwell.

Wetherell, M. (1987) 'Social identity and group polarization' in Turner et al. (eds) (1987) pp. 171–202.

Wikipedia (2006) 'Groupthink', http://en.wikipedia.org/wiki/Groupthink (Accessed 1 January 2006).

Yzerbyt, V., Corneille, O. and Estrada, C. (2001) 'The interplay of subjective essentialism and entitativity in the formation of stereotypes', *Personality and Social Psychology Review*, vol. 5, no. 2, pp. 141–55.

Yzerbyt, V., Judd, C. and Corneille, O. (eds) (2004a) *The Psychology of Group Perception: Perceived Variability, Entitativity, and Essentialism*, London, Psychology Press.

Yzerbyt, V., Judd, C. and Corneille, O. (2004b) 'Perceived variability, entitativity, and essentialism: introduction and overview' in Yzerbyt et al. (eds) (2004a).

Further reading

Janis, I. and Mann, L. (1977) *Decision Making: A Psychological Analysis of Conflict, Choice and Commitment*, New York, The Free Press.
Develops further the groupthink analysis.

Reicher, S.D. (1987) 'Crowd behaviour as social action' in Turner, J.C., Hogg, M.A., Oakes, P.J., Reicher, S.D. and Wetherell M.S. (eds) *Rediscovering the Social Group: A Self-categorization Theory*, Oxford, Basil Blackwell, pp. 171–202.
Describes in more detail the study on which the Potter and Reicher discourse analysis is based.

Yzerbyt, V., Judd, C., and Corneille, O. (2004) 'Perceived variability, entitativity, and essentialism: introduction and overview' in Yzerbyt, V., Judd, C., and Corneille, O. (eds) *The Psychology of Group Perception: Perceived Variability, Entitativity, and Essentialism*, London, Psychology Press.
Provides a clear explanation of entitativity and brings recent quantitative research in this area together with work on stereotyping (the variability part of the title) and on categorisation processes and the ways in which people treat categories as if they are naturally occurring and fixed – i.e. in essentialist ways. The title of the book signals that the ways in which these three issues are perceived are of (social) psychological importance.

Chapter 6

Intergroup processes: social identity theory

by Steven D. Brown, Loughborough University

Introduction

Attempts to theorise the constitutive role played by the membership of social groups have a mixed history in social psychology. It may seem an entirely banal observation to argue that the way a person behaves and comes to think of themselves is related to the social groups in which they live and dwell. None the less, this individual–group relation has proven frustratingly difficult to theorise. There is first of all an inherent problem of scale.

To live in any society is to find oneself by default a member of many different kinds of groups – from family groups and local communities, through to more diffuse social groups defined in terms of gender, ethnicity, religion, sexuality and nationality. By and large, early social psychological work eschewed these larger forms of collectivity in favour of defining groups narrowly in terms of small-scale sets of people who routinely meet face to face. For instance, Triplett's (1898) classic study of social facilitation defined groups in this way – his study of children working in pairs to perform a mechanical task promoted the idea that a 'group setting' involves merely the presence of another person. It is this narrow approach to social groups which has formed the dominant tradition in social psychology. This tradition is often referred to as the study of intragroup relations. It is usually concerned with the immediate effects of other group members on a given individual. For example, Floyd Allport's (1924) then influential review of the field asserted that groups act merely to intensify the habits and responses of individuals, meaning that group processes are really nothing more than the aggregation of the personal behaviour of group members. Similarly, Solomon Asch's (1956) studies of the normative social influence that group situations place upon individuals, which results in conformity of a minority to the apparent views or behaviour of the majority of the group, treat social groups as contexts which affect individual behaviour rather than as meaningful objects in their own right.

McGarty's and Haslam's (1997) work on the immediate effect of other group members on the individual usefully summarises this as the effect of social influence (i.e. the presence of others) on social interaction (i.e. behaviour in social contexts) and social perception (i.e. the efforts to make sense of those contexts and behaviour). When groups are defined in this way, however, the relation between the person and the collective tends to be seen in highly *individualistic* terms. Nevertheless, it is worth noting that the group dynamics tradition (which draws on the psychoanalysis of groups) does stress the conscious and unconscious flows between individuals working together and therefore succeeds in retaining a perspective on the group that does not reduce it to the sum of its individual members.

However, in general, in social psychology the group is seen as an influence which distorts the otherwise rational thinking of the individual, often resulting in the production of conflict. As a result, 'the social' is seen simply in terms of how it affects given people. It is a backdrop against which the 'real action' of individual behaviour is studied. This tendency is reinforced by social psychological experiments which adopt single individuals, placed in improbable and often outlandishly staged situations, as the unit of analysis.

The work of Henri Tajfel belongs to a slightly different tradition, the study of intergroup relations. This approach, which has its roots in the study of crowd behaviour initiated by Le Bon (1896), subsequently developed in the wave of research on prejudice that accompanied the racial and national conflicts of the mid-twentieth century (e.g. Adorno et al., 1950; Allport, 1954; Clark and Clark, 1947; Pettigrew, 1958; Sherif and Sherif, 1956). The intergroup approach is concerned with how people identify with the larger social groups to which they belong and how this identification has an impact upon the social judgements people make. As a result, research in this tradition has grappled with broader questions of the links between *individual identity* and *societal dimensions,* such as ethnicity and class. Groups are often considered as the point where the individual and the social come together – the question then for social psychologists is to conceptualise and clarify the relevant processes through which this occurs.

Tajfel was a major figure in the creation of distinctively European social psychology. As a French national, born a Polish Jew who had survived as a prisoner of war during 1940–5 (and was obliged to disguise his origins to do so), who settled in Britain, Tajfel had a lifelong concern with the impact of the attribution of membership of social groups on social interaction. In his autobiographical introduction to a collection of selected papers, Tajfel captures this concern in the following way:

> social psychology can and must include in its theoretical and research
> preoccupations a direct concern with the relationship between human
> psychological functioning and the large-scale processes and events which shape
> this functioning and are shaped by it

(Tajfel, 1981, p. 7)

The kind of social psychology which is up to this task is one which is not afraid of theoretical exploration. In a series of articles, including the classic 'Experiments in a vacuum' (1981), Tajfel rejected what he saw as a dominant North American trend in social psychology towards experimentation with little concern for matters of social context and validity, along with any reference to broader social and cultural issues. Tajfel argued for the importance of theories which could throw a bridge between macro-social work in sociology and politics and the micro-social work in psychology (so-called 'mid-range theorising'). Such theories would display the interdependence of the social and the cultural with the psychological.

What is perhaps surprising about Tajfel's work is the way he set about pursuing these goals. Tajfel's research in the late 1950s and early 1960s dealt with social perception. Tajfel described a phenomenon around the judgement of the size of coins, whereby people tend to overestimate the physical difference between high- and low-value coins, and as a result underestimate the size difference between coins of similar value. Tajfel's (1957, 1959) explanation for this was that it was the result of combining a continuous dimension of judgement (monetary value) with a second dimension made up of apparently clear-cut categories (the different sizes of the coins). Combining the two dimensions triggers a 'cognitive bias', which results in a distorted judgement about actual differences within and between different categories of objects (for example, the coins).

In later work, Tajfel reasoned that cognitive biases of this kind might also be at work in how we perceive other people. Here we also have to combine judgements about continuous variables (e.g. intelligence, laziness, attractiveness, friendliness) with categorisation of people into clear-cut *social* groups (e.g. nationality, ethnicity, socio-economic status). Tajfel (1969) argued the same phenomenon then occurs – we tend to see people who belong together in the same group as alike in most ways, and simultaneously exaggerate the differences between groups. This phenomenon of categorising whole groups of people as 'all the same' coupled with making sharp distinctions between groups is, Tajfel observed, at the root of prejudice in all its forms.

Tajfel set about developing an approach to relations between groups based on an analysis of cognitive biases of this type. For Tajfel, a 'cognitive' approach could help clarify the individual variables contributing to intergroup processes, but this would need to be supplemented by a 'social' approach which described the societal, cultural and economic variables that shaped the relations between social groups. Tajfel's approach came to be known as social identity theory (SIT). SIT is now the major approach to intergroup processes, at least in European social psychology, and is rivalled only by the dominant social cognition approach, against which it is often contrasted (Abrams and Hogg, 1999).

At its core, SIT proposes that the way in which people identify with social categories (i.e. groups of various degrees of scale) shapes how they perceive the immediate social context and how they are prepared to act within that perceived context. It also holds that contrasts between social categories serve an important function. By differentiating our own group clearly from other groups ('us versus them'), we tend to reinforce our identification with our group, and contrast its positive attributes with the relative failings of other groups. This is fertile ground indeed for intergroup conflict, which SIT sees as practically inevitable under many circumstances.

Reading 6.1 is drawn from the key 1979 piece by Tajfel and John C. Turner which first drew together Tajfel's ideas on categorisation into a coherent account of intergroup conflicts systematically. What you should note in this selection is the way Tajfel and Turner try to blend cognitive and social approaches, and attempt to offer a range of ideas about what conditions might lead towards conflict.

ACTIVITY 6.1

As you read the following extract, consider these points:

1   What are the difficulties that we encounter in understanding conflict between groups in terms of a struggle for limited material resources?

2   To what extent does the SIT approach to intergroup relations allow us to understand changes to social values over time and social change more generally?

Reading 6.1, by Tajfel and Turner, presents social identity theory. This theory was initiated by Tajfel and is the basis of a major tradition of social psychology theory and research on groups.

READING 6.1

'An integrative theory of intergroup conflict'

Introduction

[...]

Much of the work on the social psychology of intergroup relations has focused on patterns of individual prejudice and discrimination and on the motivational sequences of interpersonal interaction. Outstanding examples of these approaches can be found, respectively, in the theory of authoritarian personality (Adorno et al., 1950) and in the various versions and modifications of the theory of frustration, aggression, and displacement (such as Berkowitz, 1962, 1969, 1974). The common denominator of most of this work has been the stress on the intraindividual or interpersonal psychological processes leading to prejudiced attitudes or discriminatory behavior. [...]

The alternative to these approaches is represented in the work of Muzafer Sherif and his associates [...], and has been referred to [...] as the 'realistic group conflict theory' (RCT). Its point of departure for the explanation of intergroup behavior is in what Sherif (1966) has called the functional relations between social groups. Its central hypothesis – 'real conflict of group interests causes intergroup conflict' (Campbell, 1965, p. 287) – is deceptively simple, intuitively convincing, and has received strong empirical support [...].

RCT was pioneered in social psychology by the Sherifs, who provided both an etiology of intergroup hostility and a theory of competition as realistic and instrumental in character, motivated by rewards which, in principle, are extrinsic to the intergroup situation [...]. Opposed group interests in obtaining scarce resources promote competition, and positively interdependent (superordinate) goals facilitate cooperation. Conflicting interests develop through competition into overt social conflict. It appears, too, that intergroup competition enhances intragroup morale, cohesiveness, and cooperation [...]. Thus, the real conflicts of group interests not only create antagonistic intergroup relations but also heighten identification with, and positive attachment to, the in-group.

This identification with the in-group, however, has been given relatively little prominence in the RCT as a theoretical problem in its own right. The development of in-group identifications is seen in the RCT almost as an epiphenomenon of intergroup conflict. As treated by the RCT, these identifications are *associated* with certain patterns of intergroup relations, but the theory does not focus either upon the processes underlying the development and maintenance of group identity nor upon the possibly autonomous effects upon the in-group and intergroup behavior of these 'subjective' aspects of group membership. [...] In this sense, the theoretical orientation to be outlined here is intended not to replace the RCT, but to supplement it in some respects that seem to us essential for an adequate social psychology of intergroup conflict – particularly as the understanding of the psychological aspects of social change cannot be achieved without an appropriate analysis of the social psychology of social conflict.

The social context of intergroup behavior

Our point of departure for the discussion to follow will be an *a priori* distinction between two extremes of social behavior, corresponding to what we shall call *interpersonal* versus *intergroup* behavior. At one extreme (which most probably cannot be found in its 'pure' form in 'real life') is the interaction between two or more individuals that is *fully* determined by their interpersonal relationships and individual characteristics, and not at all affected by various social groups or categories to which they respectively belong. The other extreme consists of interactions between two or more individuals (or groups of individuals) which are *fully* determined by their respective memberships in various social groups or categories, and not at all affected by the interindividual personal relationships between the people involved. Here again, it is unlikely that 'pure' forms of this extreme can be found in 'real' social situations. Examples nearing the interpersonal extreme would be the relations between wife and husband or between old friends. Examples near the intergroup extreme are provided by the behavior of soldiers from opposing armies during a battle, or by the behavior at a negotiating table of members representing two parties in an intense intergroup conflict.

The main empirical questions concern the conditions that determine the adoption of forms of social behavior nearing one or the other extreme. The first – and obvious – answer concerns intergroup conflict. It can be assumed, in accordance with our common experience, that the more intense is an intergroup conflict, the more likely it is that the individuals who are members of the opposing groups will behave toward each other as a function of their respective group memberships, rather than in terms of their individual characteristics or interindividual relationships. [...]

[...]

Social categorization and intergroup discrimination

The initial stimulus for the theorizing presented here was provided by certain experimental investigations of intergroup behavior. The laboratory analogue of real-world ethnocentrism is in-group bias – that is, the tendency to favor the in-group over the out-group in evaluations and behavior. Not only are incompatible group interests not always sufficient to generate conflict [...], but there is a good deal of experimental evidence that these conditions are not always *necessary* for the development of competition and discrimination between groups [...].

All this evidence implies that in-group bias is a remarkably omnipresent feature of intergroup relations. The phenomenon in its extreme form has been investigated by Tajfel and his associates. There have been a number of studies [...], all showing that the mere perception of belonging to two distinct groups – that is, social categorization per se – is sufficient to trigger intergroup discrimination favoring the in-group. In other words, the mere awareness of the presence of an out-group is sufficient to provoke intergroup competitive or discriminatory responses on the part of the in-group.

In the initial experimental paradigm (Tajfel, 1970; Tajfel et al., 1971), the subjects (both children and adults have acted as subjects in the various studies) are randomly classified as members of two nonoverlapping groups – ostensibly on the basis of some trivial performance criterion. They then make 'decisions', awarding amounts of money to pairs of *other* subjects (excluding self) in specially designed booklets. The recipients are anonymous, except for their individual code numbers and their group membership (for example, member number 51 of the X group and member number 33 of the Y group). The subjects, who know their own group membership, award the amounts individually and anonymously. The response format of the booklets does not force the subjects to act in terms of group membership.

In this situation, there is neither a conflict of interests nor previously existing hostility between the 'groups'. No social interaction takes place between the subjects, nor is there any rational link between economic self-interest and the strategy of in-group favoritism. Thus, these groups are purely cognitive, and can be referred to as *minimal*.

The basic and highly reliable finding is that the trivial, ad hoc intergroup categorization leads to in-group favoritism and discrimination against the out-group. Fairness is also an influential strategy. There is also a good deal of evidence that, within the pattern of responding in terms of in-group favoritism, maximum difference (MD) is more important to the subjects than maximum in-group profit (MIP). Thus, they seem to be competing with the out-group, rather than following a strategy of simple economic gain for members of the in-group. [...]

The question that arises is whether in-group bias in these 'minimal' situations is produced by some form of the experimenter effect or of the demand characteristics of the experimental situation – in other words, whether explicit references to group membership communicate to the subjects that they are expected to, or ought to, discriminate. The first point to be made about this interpretation of the results is that explicit references to group membership are logically necessary for operationalizing in these minimal situations the major independent variable – that is, social categorization per se. This requires not merely that the subjects perceive themselves as similar to or different from others as *individuals*, but that they are members of discrete and discontinuous categories – that is, 'groups'. Second, a detailed analysis of the subjects' postsession reports (Billig, 1972; Turner, 1975) shows that they do not share any common conception of the 'appropriate' or 'obvious' way to behave, that only a tiny minority have some idea of the hypothesis, and that this minority does not always conform to it.

[...]

Social identity and social comparison

[...]

We can conceptualize a group [...] as a collection of individuals who perceive themselves to be members of the same social category, share some emotional involvement in this common definition of themselves, and achieve some degree of social consensus about the evaluation of their group and of their membership of it. Following from this, our definition of intergroup behavior is basically identical to that of Sherif (1966, p. 62): any behavior displayed by one or more actors toward one or more others that is based on the actors' identification of themselves and the others as belonging to different social categories.

Social categorizations are conceived here as cognitive tools that segment, classify, and order the social environment, and thus enable the individual to undertake many forms of social action. But they do not merely systematize the social world; they also provide a system of orientation for *self*-reference: they create and define the individual's place in society. Social groups, understood in this sense, provide their members with an identification of themselves in social terms. These identifications are to a very large extent relational and comparative: they define the individual as similar to or different from, as 'better' or 'worse' than, members of other groups. [...] It is in a strictly limited sense, arising from these considerations, that we use the term *social identity*. It consists, for the purposes of the present discussion, of those aspects of an individual's self-image that derive from the social categories to which he perceives himself as belonging. With this limited concept of social identity in mind, our argument is based on the following general assumptions:

1   Individuals strive to maintain or enhance their self-esteem: they strive for a positive self-concept.

2   Social groups or categories and the membership of them are associated with positive or negative value connotations. Hence, social identity may be positive or negative according to the evaluations (which tend to be socially consensual, either within or across groups) of those groups that contribute to an individual's social identity.

3   The evaluation of one's own group is determined with reference to specific other groups through social comparisons in terms of value-laden attributes and characteristics. Positively discrepant comparisons between in-group and out-group produce high prestige; negatively discrepant comparisons between in-group and out-group result in low prestige.

From these assumptions, some related theoretical principles can be derived:

1   Individuals strive to achieve or to maintain positive social identity.

2   Positive social identity is based to a large extent on favorable comparisons that can be made between the in-group and some relevant out-groups: the in-group must be perceived as positively differentiated or distinct from the relevant out-groups.

3   When social identity is unsatisfactory, individuals will strive either to leave their existing group and join some more positively distinct group and/or to make their existing group more positively distinct.

The basic hypothesis, then, is that pressures to evaluate one's own group positively through in-group/out-group comparisons lead social groups to attempt to differentiate themselves from each other [...]. There are at least three classes of variables that should influence intergroup differentiation in concrete social situations. First, individuals must have internalized their group membership as an aspect of their self-concept; they must be subjectively identified with the relevant in-group. It is not enough that the others define them as a group, although consensual definitions by others can become, in the long run, one of the powerful causal factors for a group's self-definition. Second, the social situation must be such as to allow for intergroup comparisons that enable the selection and evaluation of the relevant relational attributes. Not all between-group differences have evaluative significance [...], and those that do vary from group to group. [...] Third, in-groups do not compare themselves with every cognitively available out-group; the out-group must be perceived as a relevant comparison group. Similarity, proximity, and situational salience are among the variables that determine out-group comparability, and pressures toward in-group distinctiveness should increase as a function of this comparability. [...]

[...]

Retrospectively, at least, the social-identity/social-comparison theory is consistent with many of the studies mentioned in the preceding section of this chapter. In particular, in the paradigm of the 'minimal group' experiments (such as Tajfel et al., 1971), the intergroup discrimination can be conceived as being due not to conflict over monetary gains, but to differentiations based on comparisons made in terms of monetary rewards. Money functioned as a dimension of comparison (the only one available within the experimental design), and the data suggest that larger absolute gains that did not establish a difference in favor of the in-group were sacrificed for smaller comparative gains, when the two kinds of gains were made to conflict.

[...]

Status hierarchies and social change

[...] Status is not considered here as a scarce resource or commodity, such as power or wealth; it is the *outcome* of intergroup comparison. It reflects a group's relative position on some evaluative dimensions of comparison. Low subjective status does not promote intergroup competition directly; its effects on intergroup behavior are mediated by social identity processes. The lower is a group's subjective status position in relation to relevant comparison groups, the less is the contribution it can make to positive social identity. [...]

1 *Individual Mobility.* The more an individual approaches the structure of beliefs [...] described [...] as that of 'social mobility', the more it is likely that he will try to leave, or dissociate himself from, his erstwhile group. This usually implies attempts, on an individual basis, to achieve upward social mobility, to pass from a lower- to a higher-status group. [...] Tendencies to dissociate oneself psychologically from fellow members of low-prestige categories are known to many of us from everyday experience; they have been noted more systematically by Jahoda (1961) and Klineberg and Zavalloni (1969), among others, and indirectly by the whole literature on racial identification and preference. The most important feature of individual mobility is that the low status of one's own group is not thereby changed: it is an individualist approach designed, at least in the short run, to achieve a personal, not a group, solution. Thus, individual mobility implies a disidentification with the erstwhile in-group.

2 *Social Creativity.* The group members may seek positive distinctiveness for the in-group by redefining or altering the elements of the comparative situation. This need not involve any change in the group's actual social position or access to objective resources in relation to the out-group. It is a group rather than an individualistic strategy that may focus upon:

(a) *Comparing the in-group to the out-group on some new dimension.* Lemaine (1966) found, for example, that children's groups which could not compare themselves favorably with others in terms of constructing a hut – because they had been assigned poorer building materials than the out-group – tended to seek out other dimensions of comparison involving new constructions in the hut's surroundings. The problems that obviously arise here are those of legitimizing the value assigned to the new social products – first in the in-group and then in the other groups involved. To the extent that this legitimization may threaten the out-group's superior distinctiveness, an increase in intergroup tension can be predicted.

(b) *Changing the values assigned to the attributes of the group, so that comparisons which were previously negative are now perceived as positive.* The classic example is 'Black is beautiful'. The salient dimension – skin color – remains the same, but the prevailing value system concerning it is rejected and reversed. The same process may underlie Peabody's (1968) finding that even when various groups agree about their respective characteristics, the trait is evaluated more positively by the group that possesses it.

(c) *Changing the out-group (or selecting the out-group) with which the in-group is compared – in particular, ceasing or avoiding to use the high-status out-group as a comparative frame of reference.* Where comparisons are not made with the high-status out-group, the relevant inferiority should decrease in salience, and self-esteem should recover. Hyman's (1942) classic paper on the psychology of status suggested that discontent among low-status-group members is lessened to the degree that intraclass rather than intergroup comparisons are made. [...] It follows that self-esteem can be enhanced by comparing with other lower-status groups rather than with those of higher status. This is consistent with the fact that competition between subordinate groups is sometimes more intense than between subordinate and dominant groups – hence, for example, lower-class or 'poor white' racism.

3. *Social Competition.* The group members may seek positive distinctiveness through direct competition with the out-group. They may try to reverse the relative positions of the in-group and the out-group on salient dimensions. To the degree that this may involve comparisons related to the social structure, it implies changes in the groups' objective social locations. We can hypothesize, therefore, following the RCT, that this strategy will generate conflict and antagonism between subordinate and dominant groups insofar as it focuses on the distribution of scarce resources. [...]

Let us assume as an ideal case some stratification of social groups in which the social hierarchy is reasonably correlated with an unequal division of objective resources and a corresponding status system (based on the outcomes of comparisons in terms of those resources). Under what conditions will this *not* lead to intergroup conflict – or, more precisely, to the development of competitive ethnocentrism on the part of the subordinate group?

First, to the extent that the objective and the subjective prohibitions to 'passing' are weak [...], low status may tend, in conditions of unsatisfactory social identity, to promote the widespread adoption of individual mobility strategies, or at least initial attempts to make use of these strategies. Insofar as individual mobility implies disidentification, it will tend to loosen the cohesiveness of the subordinate group. This weakening of subjective attachment to the in-group among its members will tend: (a) to blur the perception of distinct group interests corresponding to the distinct group identity; and (b) to create obstacles to mobilizing group members for collective action over their common interests.

Thus, the low morale that follows from negative social identity can set in motion disintegrative processes that, in the long run, may hinder a change in the group status.

Second, assuming that the barriers (objective, moral, and ideological prohibitions) to leaving one's group are strong, unsatisfactory social identity may stimulate social creativity that tends to reduce the salience of the subordinate/dominant group conflict of interest. Strategy 2(c) mentioned above is likely to be crucial here since, in general, access to resources such as housing, jobs, income, or education is sufficiently central to the fate of any group that the relevant comparisons are not easily changed or devalued. Few underprivileged groups would accept poverty as a virtue, but it may appear more tolerable to the degree that comparisons are made with even poorer groups rather than with those that are better off (see Runciman, 1966).

[...]

For the moment, we can note that both individual mobility and some forms of social creativity can work to reduce intergroup conflict over scarce resources – though with different implications. The former is destructive of subordinate-group solidarity and provides no antidote to negative social identity at group level. The latter may restore or create a positive self-image but, it can be surmised, at the price either of a collective repression of objective deprivation or, perhaps, of spurious rivalry with some other deprived group. [...]

By reversing the conditions under which social stratification does not produce intergroup conflict, we can hypothesize that negative social identity promotes subordinate-group competitiveness toward the dominant group to the degree that: (a) subjective identification with the subordinate group is maintained; and (b) the dominant group continues or begins to be perceived as a relevant comparison group. [...] Let us consider a comparison between two football teams that have come first and second in their league, respectively. There is no argument about which has the higher status, but alternative comparative outcomes were and, in the future, still will be possible. When the new season begins, the teams will be as comparable and competitive as they had been before. In this instance, the status difference does not reduce the meaningfulness of comparisons because *it can be changed*.

This example illustrates Tajfel's (1974) distinction between *secure* and *insecure* intergroup comparisons. The crucial factor in this distinction is whether *cognitive alternatives* to the actual outcome are available – whether other outcomes are conceivable. Status differences between social groups in social systems showing various degrees of stratification can be distinguished in the same way. Where status relations are perceived as immutable, a part of the fixed order of things, then social identity is secure. It becomes insecure when the existing state of affairs begins to be questioned. An important corollary to this argument is that the dominant or high-status groups, too, can experience insecure social identity. Any threat to the distinctively superior position of a group implies a potential loss of positive comparisons and possible negative comparisons, which must be guarded against. Such a threat may derive from the activity of the low-status group or from a conflict within the high-status group's own value system (for example, the sociopolitical morality) and the actual foundations of its superiority. Like low-status groups, the high-status groups will react to insecure social identity by searching for enhanced group distinctiveness.

In brief, then, it is true that clear-cut status differences may lead to a quiescent social system in which neither the 'inferior' nor the 'superior' groups will show much ethnocentrism. But this 'ideal type' situation must be considered in relation to the perceived stability and legitimacy of the system. Perceived illegitimacy and/or instability provide new dimensions of comparability that are directly relevant to the attitudes and behavior of the social groups involved, whatever their position in the system. This is the social-psychological counterpart to what is widely known today as 'the revolution of rising expectations'. Providing that individual mobility is unavailable or undesirable, consensual inferiority will be rejected most rapidly when the situation is perceived as both unstable and illegitimate. [...]

[...]

Many of the points and hypotheses we have advanced in this chapter are not, in themselves, new (see, for instance, Sherif, 1966; Runciman, 1966; Milner, 1975; Billig, 1976). What is new, we think, is the integration of the three processes of social categorization, self-evaluation through social identity, and intergroup social comparison, into a coherent and testable framework for contributing to the explanation of various forms of intergroup behavior, social conflict, and social change. This framework contains possibilities of further development, and, to this extent, we hope that it may stimulate theoretically directed research in areas that have not been considered here.

[...]

'Objective' and 'subjective' conflicts

None of the arguments outlined in this chapter must be understood as implying that the social-psychological or 'subjective' type of conflict is being considered here as having priority or a more important causal function in social reality than the 'objective' determinants of social conflict of which the basic analysis must be sought in the social, economic, political, and historical structures of a society. The major aim of the present discussion has been to determine what are the points of insertion of social-psychological variables into the causal spiral; and its argument has been that, just as the effects of these variables are powerfully determined by the previous social, economic, and political processes, so they may also acquire, in turn, an *autonomous* function that enables them to deflect in one direction or another the subsequent functioning of these processes.

It is nearly impossible in most natural social situations to distinguish between discriminatory intergroup behavior based on real or perceived conflict of 'objective' interests between the groups and discrimination based on attempts to establish a positively valued distinctiveness for one's own group. However, as we have argued, the two can be distinguished theoretically, since the goals of actions aimed at the achievement of positively valued in-group distinctiveness often retain no value outside of the context of intergroup comparisons. An example would be a group that does not necessarily wish to increase the level of its own salaries but acts to prevent other groups from getting nearer to this level so that differentials are not eroded. But the difficulty with this example – as with many other similar examples – is that, in this case, the preservation of salary differentials is probably associated with all kinds of 'objective' advantages that cannot be defined in terms of money alone. In turn, *some* of these advantages will again make sense only in the comparative framework of intergroup competition. Despite this confusing network of mutual feedbacks and interactions, the distinctions made here are important because they help us to understand some aspects of intergroup behavior which have often been neglected in the past.

References

Adorno, T.W., Frenkel-Brunswik, E., Levinson, D.J. and Sanford, R.N. (1950) *The Authoritarian Personality*, New York, Harper & Row.

Berkowitz, L. (1962) *Aggression: A Social Psychological Analysis*, New York, McGraw-Hill.

Berkowitz, L. (1969) 'The frustration-aggression hypothesis revisited' in Berkowitz, L. (ed.) *Roots of Aggression. A Re-examination of Frustration-aggression Hypothesis*, New York, Atherton Press.

Berkowitz, L. (1974) 'Some determinants of impulsive aggression: role of mediated associations with reinforcements for aggression', *Psychological Review*, vol. 81, pp. 165–76.

Billig, M. (1972) 'Social categorisation in intergroup relations', unpublished doctoral dissertation, University of Bristol.

Billig, M. (1976) *Social Psychology and Intergroup Relations*, London Academic Press, European Monographs in Social Psychology.

Campbell, D.T. (1965) 'Ethnocentric and other altruistic motives' in Levine, D. (ed.) *Nebraska Symposium on Motivation*, vol. 13, Lincoln, NE, University of Nebraska Press.

Hyman, H.H. (1942) 'The psychology of status', *Archives of Psychology*, p. 269.

Jahoda, G. (1961) *White Man*, London, Oxford University Press for Institute of Race Relations.

Klineberg, O. and Zavalloni, M. (1969) *Nationalism and Tribalism Among African Students*, The Hague and Paris, Mouton.

Lemaine, G. (1966) 'Inegalité, comparison et incomparabilité: esquisse d'une théorie de l' originalité sociale, *Bulletin de Psychologie*, vol. 252, no. 20, pp. 1–2, 1–9.

Milner, D. (1975) *Children and Race*, Harmondsworth, Penguin.

Peabody, D. (1968) 'Group judgments in the Philippines: evaluative and descriptive aspects', *Journal of Personality and Social Psychology*, vol. 10, pp. 290–300.

Runciman, W.G. (1966) *Relative Deprivation and Social Justice*, London, Routledge and Kegan Paul.

Sherif, M. (1966) [sic] *Group Conflict and Cooperation: Their Social Psychology*, London, Routledge and Kegan Paul.

Sherif, M. (1966) [sic] *In Common Predicament: Social Psychology of Intergroup Conflict and Cooperation*, Boston, MA, Houghton Mifflin.

Tajfel, H. (1970) 'Experiments in intergroup discrimination', *Scientific American*, vol. 223, no. 5, pp. 96–102.

Tajfel, H. (1974*)* 'Intergroup behaviour, social comparison and social change', unpublished Katz-Newcomb lectures, University of Michigan, MI, Ann Arbor.

Tajfel, H., Billig, M.G., Bundy, R.P. and Flament, C. (1971) 'Social categorization and intergroup behaviour', *European Journal of Social Psychology*, vol. 1, pp. 149–78.

Turner, J.C. (1975) 'Social comparison and social identity: some prospects for intergroup behaviour', *European Journal of Social Psychology*, vol. 5, pp. 5–34.

(Tajfel and Turner, 1979, pp. 33–47)

Commentary

The article from which Reading 6.1 is taken begins with a discussion of a tradition of research on groups ('realistic group conflict theory' (RCT)) which states that conflict between groups is the result of a genuine competition over scarce resources. Members of a group work together and against members of rival groups because doing so earns some reward for the group as a whole. Tajfel and Turner (1979) point out that while that is all well and good as an explanation when there are explicit and objective conditions which define groups (e.g. rival teams in a game; competing groups in a workplace), a great deal of the groups to which we all belong are simply not formed along these lines. How does RCT explain hostility between members of different religious groups, for instance, where there is rarely any 'objective' basis for competition or 'material' pay-off as reward?

Tajfel and Turner propose that conflict between groups depends upon how individuals identify with the social groups to which they belong. They propose that social interaction between individuals may be classified along an 'interpersonal'–'intergroup' continuum. At the one end, personal characteristics are all important – we relate to one another purely in terms of individual impressions. At the other end, we treat one another purely in terms of group membership (e.g. as 'one of them' or 'not one of us'). While Turner and Tajfel admit that most interactions fall somewhere in between these two poles, they argue that it is conflict near the intergroup pole – where there is no material basis for conflict – that realistic group conflict theory finds particularly difficult to explain.

The relevant question then is what moves social interaction towards the intergroup pole, or more simply 'why would a given individual treat another as "one of them" rather than as a unique person?' According to Tajfel and Turner this is explained by a second 'belief continuum' that ranges between a strong belief in social mobility (i.e. it is possible to change group membership if desired) to a strong belief in social change (i.e. groups are 'set for life' and it is not possible to change membership). Strong beliefs in social change tend to be associated with intergroup social interactions. In other words, the more someone believes in the permanent, unchanging nature of group membership (that society is 'highly stratified' as sociologists would put it), the more likely they are to focus on social identity – what group someone belongs to – rather than personal identity – what someone is typically like as a person.

This distinction between personal and social identity is at the core of SIT. In work following this paper, the transition from behaviour at the 'interpersonal' pole to behaviour at the 'intergroup' pole became referred to as 'depersonalisation' (Brown, 2000). The phrase usually implies some kind of loss of self (the related term 'deindividualisation', from Zimbardo's classic 1971 Stanford Prison Experiment, is used in this way), but Tajfel and his followers were keen to stress that depersonalisation means acting with the interests and values of one's group uppermost in mind, rather than acting in terms of one's own personal motivations and beliefs. The minimal group paradigm (MGP) is a type of experiment which randomly separates participants into two groups on an entirely arbitrary basis – for example, liking the work of one modern painter more than another (Billig and Tajfel, 1973). Participants are then asked to write down how they wish to distribute monetary rewards to pairs of other participants. The only relevant information they are given is to which group each participant belongs. The well-replicated finding is that participants tend to reward people who belong to the same group as themselves ('ingroup favouritism') at the expense of those who belong to the rival group ('outgroup discrimination'). During the 1970s, Tajfel and his co-workers at Bristol conducted a series of MGP experiments (see Billig and Tajfel, 1973), the results of which are discussed in Reading 6.1. As Tajfel and Turner (1979) note, what was remarkable about these studies is that this effect – which they see as a direct analogue of 'real-world' intergroup conflict – is brought about by the mere fact of dividing people into groups. These groups only really exist inside the heads of participants who have been told which group they belong to. The groups have no real objective basis, since there is no reason or point to their existence; they are entirely 'minimal'. This suggests that, at a subjective level, categorising oneself as a member of a group functions in much the same way as categorising different coins. Focusing on differences between different classes of things (groups as well as coins) leads people to become biased in their judgements.

Tajfel and Turner then go on to argue that group membership, from a social psychological point of view, is primarily a cognitive matter. So long as a person feels themself to belong to a group and is prepared to define themself in terms of this membership, it need not matter how often the group actually meets etc. A social identity can then be properly defined as 'those aspects of an individual's self-image that derive from the social categories to which he perceives himself [sic] as belonging' (Tajfel and Turner, 1979). To this they add some key assumptions:

1   Individuals try to maintain positive self-esteem.

2   This self-esteem is related to the positive or negative values associated with group membership.

3   These values arise through comparing one's own group with relevant outgroups.

Taken together, these ideas demonstrate the unique way in which SIT combines the cognitive with the social. The way in which we classify and categorise the world, as humans who are driven by a need to maintain our self-esteem, inevitably leads to biases in judgement. But since the actual categories we work with (the 'content' of our judgements) are social in origin, this means that the structure of the society the individual inhabits exerts a fundamental influence on how these cognitive processes operate. For example, the selection of a relevant outgroup against which to compare one's own group depends on social and cultural factors, such as the relative importance accorded to skin colour or language.

It is possible, Tajfel and Turner argue, to see conflicts between groups as the need to favourably compare one's own group against another group. Clearly, however, some groups will be disadvantaged in such comparisons – notably those which have a generally low social status. Under these conditions, Tajfel and Turner hypothesise three general strategies that will be followed:

1   Individual mobility: this is where group members try to dissociate or 'dis-identify' themselves from their own group. Clearly, this depends on the individual possessing beliefs towards the 'social mobility' end of the continuum, and also being literally able to separate or 'cut and run' from their ingroup.

2   Social creativity: this is what Tajfel and Turner (1979) define as the 'redefining or altering the elements of the comparative situation' to the favour of the ingroup. This can include, for instance, finding a new, more favourable, basis on which to compare groups, or re-evaluating a negative attribute in a positive light, or simply changing the target outgroup for one which is of a lower status. The examples which Tajfel and Turner use to illustrate this strategy are particularly well chosen.

3   Social competition, or a direct struggle to secure resources or otherwise change the existing social structure: it is notable that Tajfel and Turner provide only a limited discussion of this, the most overtly political of the three hypothesised strategies. Indeed social competition remains the least well researched aspect of SIT (see Reicher, 1984, 1987).

Tajfel and Turner conclude with the statement that, in general, intergroup conflict becomes more likely when group members can perceive not only the inequity of the current social structure but also possibilities for change. Hence, conflict is an inevitable part of how societies develop.

It is this last point – the inevitability of conflict – that is the point of departure for Reading 6.2, taken from a 2002 paper by Michael Billig. This reading is unusual in that it seeks to critically evaluate SIT by returning to what Billig regards as the origins of the approach in a short piece published by Tajfel in 1969 called 'Cognitive aspects of prejudice'. As we shall see, Billig reads this paper as a well-intentioned attempt to break with simplistic accounts of conflict and prejudice as biologically determined. However, Billig suggests that the cognitive approach Tajfel advocates actually creates as many problems as it solves.

ACTIVITY 6.2

As you read the following extract, consider these points:

1   How does Tajfel's cognitive approach enable us to reject a 'blood and guts' model of human conflict?

2   What are the limitations of Tajfel's approach, particularly in relation to emotion?

Reading 6.2 is by Michael Billig, who originally worked with Tajfel. Billig is one of a number of key figures (including Margaret Wetherell (see Chapter 3) and Steve Reicher (see Chapter 5) involved in the development of both SIT and self-categorisation theory (SCT), who have turned towards other approaches such as discursive psychology, to pursue their interests in intergroup conflict.

'Henri Tajfel's "Cognitive aspects of prejudice" and the psychology of bigotry'

Michael Billig, Department of Social Sciences, Loughborough University

It will soon be 20 years since the death of Henri Tajfel. His influence throughout social psychology persists, especially in work on social identity (Robinson, 1996). As Brown and Capozza (2000) have shown, interest in Social Identity Theory (SIT) continues to grow, with an increasing number of studies being published yearly. As with any major figure in the social sciences, Tajfel's writings repay careful study and reinterpretation. This article examines the rhetoric and argument of Henri Tajfel's classic article 'Cognitive aspects of prejudice', which was first published in the *Journal of Biosocial Sciences* in 1969 and which has been reprinted a number of times since. [...]

[...]

Over and above paying tribute to Tajfel's enduring intellectual legacy, there is another reason for returning to 'Cognitive aspects of prejudice'. This is to understand the nature of prejudice. It is not suggested that 'Cognitive aspects' holds all the keys, nor even that we should follow rigidly the message that Tajfel was advocating there. Far from it, the strategy is to examine critically the omissions in the article. [...]

The omissions in 'Cognitive aspects', it will be suggested, enable us to understand the context of Tajfel's theorizing, especially in relation to his background. They are also theoretically revealing, inasmuch as they point towards the limitations of the cognitive approach for understanding extreme prejudice. In this respect, the present tribute to 'Cognitive aspects' is also an argument. To argue, however, is not necessarily to reject, but to develop. As Tajfel (1981) emphasized, no social psychology is value-free, for all social psychology reflects the cultural climate in which it is produced. That was why he argued that it was vital to have multiple perspectives in social psychology (Tajfel, 1981, p. 6). The political climate of today is different from that of the late 1960s and early 1970s, when Tajfel was developing his ideas. So must social psychology reflect these changed times. Today's social psychology cannot be a mere repetition of that which was formulated a generation ago. Tajfel may have argued that motivational themes should be put to one side, but, by considering one of the finest pieces of writing, it will be suggested that such themes cannot, and should not, be excluded entirely if one wishes to understand extreme prejudice.

Image of humanity

[...]

Typically, an academic argument is directed towards a rival position. Therefore, to understand the meaning of an academic position, not only must one determine the specific case that is being advocated, but one must also know what positions are being argued against (Billig, 1987). Tajfel's assertion of a common rational humanity was an argument against a counter-position. As he noted, when observers try to explain human social activity, especially warfare, they discard the rational image of humanity, adopting instead 'a blood-and-guts model for social phenomena' (Tajfel, 1981, p. 128). [...] Tajfel had in mind populist versions of Freudian and ethological theories that postulated an instinct for aggression. Foremost amongst the blood-and-guts writers was the [...] ethologist, Konrad Lorenz, who was to publish his ideas in a number of best-selling books (e.g. Lorenz, 1974, 1976). [...] Lorenz proposed that human conflict should be explained in terms of this innate aggressive instinct, and, thus, he was proposing a biological source of irrationality at the core of human nature. [...]

Against the blood-and-guts model

Tajfel recognized that there were compelling intellectual and political reasons for combating the blood-and-guts model. [...] First, there was the waxing-and-waning argument, which powerfully yet simply undermined the theoretical adequacy of an instinctivist explanation of human warfare. [...] In short, the positing of an invariant and unchangeable instinct cannot explain the waxing and waning of social conflict (nor of individual aggressiveness). To explain why wars occur at one time and not another, one must go beyond the hypothesis of an aggressive instinct and look at social and historical conditions. This involves examining the beliefs and ideologies that groups hold about each other. Thus, the study of conflict must embrace the study of group attitudes, and, in consequence, there should be a social psychological dimension.

Tajfel also had a moral/political argument against the blood-and-guts perspective. To offer an account of social conflict in terms of an unchanging instinct is, at best, to suggest that nothing can be done to alleviate prejudice. At worst, it is to justify prejudice and chauvinism as an innate part of the human condition. [...]

[...]

Cognition and prejudice

The next step in Tajfel's argument was a bold one: to show that the seeming irrationalities in human social conduct owed their origin to this essential rationality. [...]

In prejudiced thinking, judgments are made about the members of other groups regardless of their individual characteristics: members of the out-group are judged negatively, or unfavourably stereotyped, simply because they belong to the out-group. Tajfel related this type of stereotyping to ordinary sense-making. In order to understand the world – both the physical and the social world – humans need to make cognitive short cuts. There is too much sensory information available at any one point to deal with every detail. Unless this information is cognitively organized – unless it is categorized – there can be no meaning. Therefore, humans need to organize the social world into categories. However, when we do this, we are liable to distort the world, even as we make it meaningful. As Tajfel had shown in his line-estimation studies, imposing a categorization on a continuum of stimuli creates a tendency towards two sorts of exaggeration: there is the tendency to overestimate the extent to which instances of the same category resemble each other and a tendency to overestimate the differences between instances of different categories (Tajfel and Wilkes, 1963). Tajfel argued that the effects of categorization on the judgment of physical stimuli resembled the exaggerations of social stereotypes. Thus, the tendency to prejudge members of out-groups was, at root, similar to the more general tendency to exaggerate the differences between categories and to minimize differences within categories.

The notion of 'categorization' was one of three key concepts that Tajfel used in 'Cognitive aspects' to outline the cognitive dynamics of prejudice. The other two concepts were 'assimilation' and 'coherence'. In line with Tajfel's attempt to construct a genuinely social approach to prejudice, he stressed the importance of 'assimilation'. Individuals do not create their own categories but assimilate the categories that are culturally available, thereby accepting culturally determined patterns of prejudgment and stereotyping.

Individuals use these social categories to make sense of, and thereby bring coherence to, their understanding of the world. The search for coherence provides a clue about how individuals cope with understanding the constantly changing social world. Individuals will attempt to use categories in ways that preserve their self-image or integrity. According to Tajfel, 'this need to preserve the integrity or the self-image is the only motivational assumption that we need to make in order to understand the direction that the search for coherence will take' (1981, p. 137). A similar motivational assumption was to appear in Social Identity Theory, which assumed a need for a positive social identity (i.e. Tajfel and Turner, 1979).

'Cognitive aspects' provides a brilliant rebuttal of an instinctual theory of prejudice. Tajfel takes an aspect of human behaviour that appears to be inherently irrational but argues that this irrationality should be understood in terms of a psychological perspective that is based on the assumption of human rationality. There is, in consequence, no need to posit an underlying motivational force. Yet, as can be seen, motivational premises are not entirely excluded. The cognitive approach includes the motivation to understand, as well as the motive for preserving the self-image. As such, the cognitive approach is not entirely cognitive.

There are a number of criticisms that can be made of the cognitive approach to prejudice. Recently, critics have suggested that cognitive social psychology is mistaken in taking a perceptual, rather than discursive, view of categorization (Billig, 1985, 1987; Potter and Wetherell, 1987; Wetherell, 1996). According to this argument, the categories of prejudice are essentially language categories. Speakers can use language flexibly and, thus, are not restricted merely to minimizing within-category differences or between-category similarities (Edwards, 1991). Indeed, with language, we can both categorize in our judgments as well as particularize, not to mention talk critically about our categories (Billig, 1987). All this makes the use of categories in language very different from the use of perceptual categorization. Moreover, this duality of particularization and categorization can be found in the language of those who are prejudiced and, more generally, in the talk of those who hold strong views (Billig, 1985, 1991).

The present purpose is not to pursue this discursive critique of the cognitive approach. [...] The intention is to probe the absences, in order to clarify which aspects of prejudice the cognitive approach best addresses and which aspects it tends to ignore.

Holocaust and explanation

There is a paradox in the limitation of Tajfel's approach to prejudice. He did not apply either his cognitive approach, or his Social Identity Theory, to explain the one historical event that brought him to social psychology – the Holocaust. [...] Unlike the majority of the people whom he had grown up with, Tajfel survived the massacre of European Jews. For the rest of his life, he was to reflect on what happened. [...]

Yet, apart from occasional comments, Tajfel rarely in his written work applied his powerful theories of prejudice to the one event that preoccupied him (for a more detailed discussion of this omission, see Billig, 1996). In part, this reflects a more general phenomenon. There was little written or spoken about the Holocaust for a generation after the Second World War. Survivors at that time would rarely risk telling their stories to a world that seemingly had more important things to do than listen. In addition there are specific reasons against offering academic explanations, especially psychological explanations, of the Holocaust.

If we claim to have explained an event, we are claiming to have understood it. Moreover, the explanation by providing understanding – by giving a set of adequate causes – seems to 'wrap up' that event. Further detailed thought becomes unnecessary; after all, we know and understand what happened. Any explanation of the Holocaust would be claiming too much. More than any other event in history, the Holocaust should not be explained away; it demands further thought. A psychological explanation runs a further risk: *tout comprendre c'est tout pardonner*. If an account explains the motives and thought processes of the perpetrators in psychological terms, such an account may present the perpetrators in an understandable light that wittingly or unwittingly invites empathy (see Billig, 1996; Mandel, 1998). Primo Levi expressed this better than anyone in *If This Is a Man* (Levi, 1987). He argues that one should not understand what happened in the Holocaust because to understand is almost to justify. Understanding would mean putting oneself in the place of, and thus identifying with, the perpetrators. Better not to understand, argued Levi, than risk such identification.

In addition to such general considerations, there are specific features of Tajfel's cognitive approach that would make it unsuitable, at least on its own, as an explanation of the Holocaust. In 'Cognitive aspects', Tajfel was describing universal processes. 'Categorization', 'assimilation' and 'coherence' were not assumed to be culturally specific, as if they only occur in certain socio-historic contexts and not others. They were intended to represent features of all human thinking. [...]

It would be neither appropriate, nor informative, to say that the Germans systematically murdered the Jews in the Second World War, because they were seeking to understand the world and to protect their self-integrity. Of course, such processes may have played their part, but constitute only a small part in a wider picture (Mandel, 1998, 2001). We can say – indeed we must say – that the German murder of the Jews should be understood in terms of what the Nazis thought about Jews. But this is very different from offering an 'explanation' in terms of cognitive processes such as the search for understanding and the protection of self-integrity. There is nothing intrinsic about these processes, nor about the universal processes of categorization, assimilation and coherence, that would account for the historical specificity of Nazi ideology.

[...]

Prejudice and bigotry

[...] Just as the blood-and-guts position could not account for the waxing and waning of warfare, so we can say that there can be a waxing and waning of prejudice. Sometimes there is socially shared bigotry; sometimes there is not; sometimes an ideology of tolerance might be widespread. A cognitive approach that links prejudice to categorization (and also to assimilation and coherence) cannot of itself account for this waxing and waning: some additional element is called for.

This, of course, does not necessarily imply a return to the blood-and-guts model that Tajfel criticized so powerfully. Just to say that the cognitive model needs an added element is not to say that the additional factor must be an assumed innate instinct for aggression. It might be suggested that the additional elements are not psychological factors but are historical and cultural elements, which, according to Tajfel's account, would need to be assimilated by the individual. If this were the case, the distinguishing features between different intensities of prejudice would not be psychological. It would be implausible, however, to assert that the difference between prejudice, as a cognitive interpretation of the social world, and bigotry, as an intense group hatred, must only be cultural and historical. There surely could be some socio-psychological distinctions between the two types of phenomena.

The difference between prejudice and bigotry, or hatred, can be considered further. Whereas the notion of prejudice seems to invite a cognitive interpretation, since its literal sense refers to prejudgment, bigotry seems to include the very psychological components that the cognitive approach sought to exclude, or at least to put to one side. These are emotional or motivational factors, adding an intensity and wilfulness to mere categorical exaggerations. [...]

[...]

This can be seen in 'Cognitive aspects of prejudice'. At one point, Tajfel writes 'if a man is prejudiced, he has an emotional investment in preserving differentiations between his own group and "others"' (p. 134). Here Tajfel is using the description 'prejudiced' in a different way than he used 'prejudice' when describing the cognitive implications of categorization. To be 'prejudiced' in this statement is to do more than use a social category in a way that overestimates the differences between in-group and out-group members. The sentence significantly suggests that prejudice can be a condition of a person's being ('to *be* prejudiced', he writes), not something that is a by-product of inevitable cognitive processing. In this case, the condition of being includes an extra dimension, namely an 'emotional investment'.

Tajfel has little to say about what this 'emotional investment' might be and how it might operate. There was a good theoretical reason why Tajfel would have avoided drawing out this theme. To talk of emotional motivations might seem to be leading back to individual dynamics. Significantly, in the statement just quoted, Tajfel refers to an individual being prejudiced, and not a group. Reducing social events to individual motives was something he consistently sought to avoid. The problem of bigotry was not to be resolved by the psychological analysis – or psychoanalysis – of individual bigots.

However, the reductionism, that Tajfel opposed, is not a necessary consequence of considering motivational factors. Recently, within social constructionist psychology, there is an awareness that emotions must be considered as socially constituted (Edwards, 1997; Harré and Gillett, 1994). This position stresses that emotions do not exist as wordless impulses, lying beneath social life, but are constituted within social, discursive interaction. This is even true of unconscious emotions (Billig, 1999). Thus, hatred need not be seen as an individual condition, located within the body of the individual. There can be ideologies of hatred that produce 'hate-talk' (e.g. Whillock and Slayden, 1995). The hatred is not separate from the discourse. To hate is not merely, or principally, to feel something at a bodily or visceral level – but to believe and to utter particular sorts of things about others (Billig, 2001). Without that, there can be no hatred. To put it crudely, we do not need to know the hidden, inner psychological mechanisms of the Nazis, in order to know that they hated Jews. Their actions and their words were not a *sign* of their hatred, as if the hatred really was elsewhere; those actions and words were, in the most literal sense, pure hatred.

[...]

Depersonalization and dehumanization

In Social Identity Theory, there is a further absence, paralleling the cognitive approach's failure to distinguish between prejudice and bigotry. In his writings about social identity, Tajfel introduced the notion of 'depersonalization' – a concept that was to feature significantly in Turner's Self-Categorization Theory (see, for instance, Turner et al., 1987). [...]

Tajfel suggested that the use of categories was necessary for human thinking, but that this entailed prejudgment and, thus, prejudice. However, an extra emotional investment was required to turn such inevitable cognitive prejudice into the state of 'being prejudiced'. Depersonalization was similar to categorization in being a common aspect of intergroup phenomena. [...]

Significantly, Tajfel, in his comments about depersonalization, also used a stronger term, namely 'dehumanization'. Depersonalization might be the 'common denominator' in the minimal intergroup experiments and in actual warfare, but there is a crucial difference between the two situations. In actual warfare, out-group members are often not merely depersonalized but commonly dehumanized. Thus, Tajfel wrote that depersonalization of out-group members may be just a beginning, and 'the next stage is often their dehumanization' (1981, p. 241). Depersonalization, thus, is a milder form of the way that in-group members can treat out-groups: 'Our social history is full of familiar and horrifying examples of dehumanization of outgroups and even more so of milder forms of their depersonalization' ([Tajfel,] 1981, pp. 52–3). As such, there is a 'continuum' stretching between depersonalization and dehumanization (Tajfel, 1981, p. 241). One might suggest a ratio: depersonalization is to dehumanization as cognitive prejudice is to bigotry.

[...]

Towards a study of bigotry

There is not space here to do anything more than make suggestions about recasting the social psychological study of bigotry. [...] Several factors would need to be taken into account to develop the continuum between prejudice and bigotry or between depersonalization and dehumanization. Some preliminary points can be made about such a development.

(i) ***Bigotry as ideological***. In line with Tajfel's argument in 'Cognitive aspects', it can be reaffirmed that the study of bigotry should not be reduced to the personal dynamics of individual bigots. Bigotry typically is more than an individual emotional investment. It is a feature of group relations. In this regard, the ideological basis of bigotry needs to be recognized, as indeed Tajfel acknowledged with his concept of assimilation.

(ii) ***Discursive basis of ideology***. The discursive position in social psychology stresses the key role of language in the social world (i.e. Billig, 1987; Edwards, 1997; Potter and Wetherell, 1987). Ideologies are above all discursive, instantiated within discursive actions (Billig, 1991). Thus, the categories of ideology, together with shared stereotyping and commonplace social explanations, are framed in language. If this is accepted, it is no longer necessary to understand categorization in terms of models that are derived from perceptual processes, as is commonly found in most cognitive social psychology, including Tajfel's 'Cognitive aspects'. Instead, categorization and stereotyping can be investigated within discursive interaction.

(iii) *Emotional aspects of ideology*. The ideology of bigotry cannot be seen merely as a cognitive appraisal of social reality. [...] What is required is not merely the addition of 'emotional variables' to the prevailing cognitive perspective but a theoretical reassessment of the apparent distinction between cognition and emotion. If ideologies are said to encompass emotions, this does not mean that emotions should be seen as free-floating psychological impulses, lying behind ideologies or social categories. They exist within socially shared explanations, blamings, accountings and so on. The emotion within an ideology of hatred is not something extra that is added to a cognitive interpretation; it is part of that interpretation. When Tajfel was writing, it was customary for psychologists to assume a rigid split between cognition and emotion, or between rational and irrational aspects of human functioning. The social constructionist position, which has been developed subsequently, attempts to bridge this gap. Thus, social constructionists have stressed the social and discursive constitution of emotions (Billig, 1999; Edwards, 1997; Harré and Gillett, 1994). In consequence, to say that bigotry involves emotions does not imply that there must be an emotional force behind the bigotry. The emotions will be contained within the hate-talk that comprises the bigotry.

(iv) *Reconceptualizing depersonalization and dehumanization in discursive terms*. Following Tajfel, one can assert that the notions of depersonalization and dehumanization are vital to an understanding of bigotry. Depersonalization should not be restricted to the depersonalization of the self, nor should it be seen as a cognitive process that somehow lies behind language. Instead, the focus should be on the ways that particular ways of speaking might depersonalize the 'other'. To probe this further, one would want to examine the language of stereotyping as used in actual social interaction. Dehumanization will be an extreme form of depersonalization, as the 'other' is depicted as somehow less than human. Dehumanization may, for instance, occur in ethnic jokes, and it will certainly be found in the extremes of hate-talk (Billig, 2001). The ideology of bigotry, in which the discourse of dehumanization will occur, might be presumed to be an emotion-laden discourse.

(v) *Repressed and unrepressed emotions*. Tajfel, in common with most cognitive social psychologists, was resolutely anti-Freudian. He did not wish the study of ideology to be reduced to individual or interpersonal dynamics. However, a discursive approach offers the possibility of reconstituting Freudian theory around the notion of repression in a way that avoids individual reductionism (Billig, 1997, 1999). This perspective assumes that language is both expressive and repressive: in order to speak appropriately, speakers must learn to repress routinely the desire to speak inappropriately. In any social context, there will be norms and routines that permit certain discursive actions and that forbid others. What is socially forbidden can become an object of desire and pleasure. If there are taboos on the expression of bigotry in contemporary society, outward prejudice may take the form of a forbidden pleasure. Bigotry, then, becomes a temptation.

(vi) *Pleasure in bigotry*. This would lead to the disturbing possibility that there is pleasure in bigotry. As Sartre recognized in his *Portrait of the Anti-Semite* (1948), the bigot might enjoy the act of hatred, especially if this includes the pleasure of doing something that is forbidden. Dehumanizing the other can be enjoyable as the bigot is freed from the constraints of respect, tolerance and reasonableness. Thus one should not expect extreme racist propaganda to be devoid of humour and mockery (Billig, 2001). The complex relations between language and pleasure in extreme racist humour involve, as Sartre realized, mocking the restraints of logic and reason. [...]

These notions are sketched out in order to stress a simple point. A turn towards the study of bigotry and the emotions contained with hate-discourse does not mean a return to the sort of blood-and-guts psychology that Tajfel explicitly rejected. When Tajfel was writing, the choice seemed to be between concentrating on either cognitive or instinctual dynamics, as if the two belonged to entirely separated psychological realms. Faced with that choice, Tajfel understandably, and with good reason, chose the cognitive aspects. Today, such a stark choice is unnecessary. The academic, cultural and political climate has changed. In many spheres, there has been a blurring of boundaries that were previously thought to be impermeable. [...] Within social psychology, social constructionism is a product of this changed mood. More generally there might be a theoretical gain if the previously accepted divisions between emotion and cognition, or between rationality and irrationality, no longer have to be accepted at least in the old manner. The challenge is to explore the interconnections, especially in relation to the continuing problems of prejudice and bigotry.

The political context of today should not be forgotten. The current age is not one of confident political ideological truth. Nevertheless, bigotry remains a major social issue in Europe with fascist parties appealing to anti-foreigner sentiments, and the re-emergence of extreme, often violent, nationalist politics. Fascism in Western Europe refuses to wane to the point of disappearance, and there is a marked waxing in the East. These forces are not the products of individual motivations, nor do they represent mere systems of social categorization. They represent powerful and dangerous mixtures. So long as this ideological mixture continues to threaten, the need to attend to the social psychological dynamics of bigotry persists.

References

Billig, M. (1985) 'Prejudice, categorization and particularization: from a perceptual to a rhetorical approach', *European Journal of Social Psychology*, vol. 15, pp. 79–103.

Billig, M. (1987) *Arguing and Thinking*, Cambridge, Cambridge University Press.

Billig, M. (1991) *Ideology and Opinions*, London, Sage.

Billig, M. (1996) 'Remembering the background of social identity theory' in Robinson, (ed.) (1996).

Billig, M. (1997) 'The dialogic unconscious: psychoanalysis, discursive psychology and the nature of repression', *British Journal of Social Psychology*, vol. 36, pp. 139–59.

Billig, M. (1999) *Freudian Repression*, Cambridge, Cambridge University Press.

Billig, M. (2001) 'Humour and hatred: the racist jokes of the Ku Klux Klan', *Discourse and Society*, vol. 12, pp. 291–313.

Brown, R. and Capozza, D. (2000) 'Social identity theory in retrospect and prospect' in Capozza, D. and Brown, R. (eds) *Social Identity Processes: Trends in Theory and Research*, London, Sage.

Edwards, D. (1991) 'Categories are for talking', *Theory and Psychology*, vol. 1, pp. 515–42.

Edwards, D. (1997) *Discourse and Cognition*, London, Sage.

Harré, R. and Gillett, G. (1994) *The Discursive Mind*, London, Sage.

Levi, P. (1987) *If This Is a Man*, London, Abacus.

Lorenz, K. (1974) *Civilized Man's Eight Deadly Sins*, London, Methuen.

Lorenz, K. (1976) *Behind the Mirror*, London, Methuen.

Mandel, D.R. (1998) 'The obedience alibi: Milgram's account of the Holocaust reconsidered', *Analyse und Kritik*, vol 20, pp. 74–94.

Mandel, D.R. (2001) 'Instigators of genocide: examining Hitler from a social psychological perspective' in Newman, L.S. and Erber, R. (eds) *What Social Psychology Can Tell Us About The Holocaust*, Oxford, Oxford University Press.

Potter, J. and Wetherell, M. (1987) *Discourse and Social Psychology*, London, Sage.

Robinson, W.P. (ed.) (1996) *Social Groups and Identities: Developing the Legacy of Henri Tajfel*, London, Butterworth-Heinemann.

Sartre, J.P. (1948) *Portrait of the Anti-Semite*, London, Secker and Warburg.

Tajfel, H. (1969) 'Cognitive aspects of prejudice', *Journal of Biosocial Sciences*, Supplement no. 1, pp. 173–91.

Tajfel, H. (1981) *Human Groups and Social Categories*, Cambridge, Cambridge University Press.

Tajfel, H. and Turner, J.C. (1979) 'An integrative theory of intergroup conflict' in Austin, W. G. and Worchel, S. (eds) *The Social Psychology of Intergroup Relations*, Monterey, CA, Brooks/Cole, pp. 33–47.

Tajfel, H. and Wilkes, A.L. (1963) 'Classification and quantitative judgement', *British Journal of Psychology*, vol. 54, pp. 101–14.

Turner, J.C., Hogg, M.A., Oakes, P.J., Reicher, S.D. and Wetherell, M.S. (1987) *Rediscovering the Social Group: A Self-Categorisation Theory*, Oxford, Blackwell.

Wetherell, M. (1996) 'Constructing social identities: the individual/social binary in Henri Tajfel's social psychology' in Robinson (ed.) (1996).

Whillock, R.K. and Slayden, D. (1995) *Hate Speech,* Thousand Oaks, CA, Sage.

(Billig, 2002, pp. 171–88)

Conclusion

Billig is a social psychologist whose work has dealt with nationalism, prejudice, racism, fascism and ideology. Billig was also a student and researcher with Tajfel at Bristol in the late 1960s/early 1970s and was involved in the design of the MGP and subsequent research (see Billig and Tajfel, 1973; Tajfel and Billig, 1974). The article from which Reading 6.2 is taken is, then, unique in presenting a critical commentary on Tajfel's work, and on the SIT tradition, from the perspective of someone who was closely involved in the original research. Throughout the article, Billig is keen to stress both the historical context in which the research evolved, and the personal choices made by Tajfel in formulating the key tenets of SIT. Billig then describes SIT not as an abstract theory but as the outcome of a situated set of intellectual choices made by researchers who had definite beliefs and political commitments. Billig's own intellectual choices have led him away from the SIT tradition and towards the study of discourse and rhetoric (see Billig, 1991, 1996, 2005). He is a key contributor to discursive psychology (for more on this topic see Chapters 3 and 5). From a discursive perspective, the social categories which are central to the expression of prejudice are discursively formed and re-formed in ongoing interaction between group members.

Reading 6.2 opens with a commentary on Tajfel's 'Cognitive aspects of prejudice', which Billig considers to be among Tajfel's key work. The style of the article the reading is taken from is seen as critical to the nature of the piece; unlike traditional 'scientific reviews', Tajfel ranges across disciplines, dwelling at length on anthropology. In the full article (Billig, 2002), Billig proposes that this style is intended to set out what follows as a 'political and moral position', as an argument about how human nature ought to be viewed, rather than engage in the pretence that social psychology could ever be entirely 'experimental' or purely 'value-free' (in this respect it is instructive to compare both Readings 6.1 and 6.2 with a great deal of publications on SIT). Tajfel's political and moral position is taken up against the 'blood and guts' model of human nature, where conflict is seen as the inevitable outcome of our savage, biologically-based instincts. Billig notes that although Tajfel was writing before the fascist leanings of Konrad Lorenz's early work were known, the 'deeply reactionary implications' (Billig, 2002) (i.e. that nothing can be done to stem prejudice and irrationality, that it is part of 'human nature') were clear. Against this model, Tajfel proposes instead to focus on the inherent rationality of persons – to stress human behaviour as intentional, thoughtful and, ultimately, grounded in rational principles.

Billig describes how Tajfel's key ideas in the paper – categorisation, assimilation, search for coherence – build up a model of people as possessing a 'universal rationality' (Billig, 2002). In this sense, Tajfel's cognitive approach supports his moral and political opposition to the biological-based 'blood and guts' model. Billig, however, takes issue with the extent to which the cognitive approach can by itself provide a compelling account of social phenomena. He points to places in Tajfel's article where an appeal is made to factors that are not cognitive, such as the motive to preserve a good self-image. Billig argues that these shortcomings are not in themselves grounds for rejecting Tajfel's work, since all theories inevitably have weak points or 'absences' (Billig, 2002). None the less, it does suggest that a cognitive approach could never by itself fully account for social phenomenon since it relies upon other sorts of explanations.

Billig goes on to describe how a discursive approach, which treats categorisation as a linguistic rather than purely cognitive activity, is better able to account for the flexible and complex ways that we use categories on a daily basis. The discursive critique of SIT is that categorisation is not a constraint on our thinking, which forces us to see the world in terms of clear-cut distinctions between groups or any classes of objects. Categorisation is instead something we actively do through language; it is a form of social action in its own right (Wetherell, 1996). We use our language to both generalise and to particularise in talking about group members, according to the demands of the circumstances and conversations we are involved with. Most importantly, the categories we use, including social categories to describe ourselves, are always there to be potentially challenged by others and consequently revised. It is this subtle and dynamic quality of categorisation as an interactional process that SIT misses (see Billig, 1985, 1996; Edwards, 1997; Wetherell and Potter, 1992).

Reading 6.2 goes on to examine why Tajfel, a survivor of the Holocaust, never applied SIT to explain the historical event which was central to his moral and political position. Billig suggests that to apply SIT in this way would amount to trying to 'explain' the Holocaust in such a way that it would no longer be necessary to continue reflection. To explain is to 'come to terms' with some event, to have understood it in such a way that there is no longer any need to spare it further thought, and even, perhaps, to have excused or justified it. Yet there are some things it is simply not possible to come to terms with, and certainly not to ever justify. We remember the Holocaust better precisely by not claiming to have fully explained how or why it was possible. But although Tajfel's refusal to theorise the Holocaust was a principled position, if we were to seek to apply SIT to events of such magnitude, the shortcomings of the theory would become clear. As Billig observes, the cognitive processes of categorisation and intergroup comparison do not tell us how it is possible for prejudice, as a routine cognitive operation, to mutate into the kind of bigotry and extreme ideology that accompanies genocide. In order to think about this social phenomenon, we need to explore the non-cognitive or motivational basis which leads people to invest in or commit themselves to extremism. Billig notes that Tajfel does point to the role played by 'emotional investment' (Billig, 2002), but it was never developed adequately in his own work or in the SIT research that followed.

For Billig, SIT since Tajfel has for the most part turned away from what he feels were Tajfel's central concerns in 'Cognitive aspects of prejudice'. For example, the notion of 'depersonalisation', which appears in SCT, is treated as a positive aspect of categorisation – we become broader, richer individuals as we learn to categorise ourselves in terms of social identities (see Turner et al., 1987). But for Tajfel, depersonalisation could be the first step towards treating others not as people but as 'non-humans'. Later SIT work entirely denies this link between depersonalisation and dehumanisation (see Brown, 2000). Similarly, for Tajfel, even though prejudice is produced by rational cognitive processes, it continues to be a problem, a negative social phenomenon. Later work has tended to see prejudice and stereotyping not as social problems in their own right, but merely as features of the broader model of intergroup relations that SIT provides (see, for instance, Ellemers et al., 1999).

How should we then evaluate SIT as a whole? In which ways does it preserve the legacy of Tajfel's work? For Billig, contemporary SIT and SCT squanders that legacy. He characterises SIT, as Tajfel envisaged it, as a 'theory of liberation' (Billig, 2002), which tries to understand the conditions under which social change operates at the level of groups. It ought also to be a morally and politically engaged project which treats prejudice and bigotry as social problems. Billig suggests that in order for SIT to develop in this way it must begin to explore the relationship between bigotry and ideology. Although Tajfel made reference to ideology, as with so much else in SIT he thought it best approached as a cognitive matter where individual 'beliefs' interact with group dynamics and general cultural constraints. For Billig, this does not go far enough. Ideology, especially extreme ideology and bigotry, is collectively produced and re-produced through interaction. It is not a static constraint on thinking, but the outcome of concerted collective efforts to promote categories and interpretations of social relations. Moreover, Billig points out the significant emotional dimension to ideology. Bigots do not simply make biased cognitive judgements; they also invest emotionally in the categories to which they orient – they express hatred and loathing, they speak words and insults which express 'forbidden' thoughts, and in doing so, they may even experience a kind of enjoyment in their denigration of the other.

So while Tajfel did a profound service to social psychology, in promoting the idea that prejudice has its roots in ordinary, normative rational thought, he ultimately failed to see that this thought, and prejudice itself, might take on fluid, complex and even wilfully perverse and irrational forms that could not, in themselves, be explained by a purely cognitive approach. Although Billig does not make this point, we might see the discursive psychology that he, along with another former student of Tajfel's, Margaret Wetherell, has helped to develop, as a continuation and radical redevelopment of the intergroup approach that Tajfel represented. Billig's article powerfully demonstrates both what this approach contributes, and the significant number of outstanding problems with which the approach has only just begun to grapple.

References

Abrams, D. and Hogg, M.A. (eds) (1999) *Social Identity and Social Cognition*, Oxford, Blackwell.

Adorno, T.W., Frenkel-Brunswik, E., Levinson, D.J. and Sanford, R.N. (1950) *The Authoritarian Personality*, New York, Harper & Row.

Allport, F. (1924) *Social Psychology*, Boston, MA, Houghton Mifflin.

Allport, G.W. (1954) *The Nature of Prejudice*, Reading, MA, Addison-Wesley.

Asch, S.E. (1956) 'Studies of independence and conformity: a minority of one against a unanimous majority', *Psychological Monographs*, vol. 70 (Whole no. 416).

Billig, M. (1985) 'Prejudice, categorisation and particularisation: from a perceptual to a rhetorical approach', *European Journal of Social Psychology*, vol. 15, pp. 79–103.

Billig, M. (1991) *Ideology and Opinions*, London, Sage.

Billig, M. (1996) *Arguing and Thinking*, 2nd edn, Cambridge, Cambridge University Press.

Billig, M. (2002) 'Henri Tajfel's "Cognitive aspects of prejudice" and the psychology of bigotry', *British Journal of Social Psychology*, vol. 41, pp. 171–88.

Billig, M. (2005) *Laughter and Ridicule: Towards a Social Critique of Humour*, London, Sage.

Billig, M. and Tajfel, H. (1973) 'Social categorisation and similarity in intergroup behaviour', *European Journal of Social Psychology*, vol. 3, pp. 37–52.

Brown, R. (2000) 'Social identity theory: past achievements, current problems and future challenges', *European Journal of Social Psychology*, vol. 30, no. 5, pp. 745–78.

Clark, K. and Clark, M. (1947) 'Racial identification and preference in Negro children' in Newcomb, T.M. and Hartley, E.L. (eds) *Readings in Social Psychology*, New York, Holt.

Edwards, D. (1997) *Discourse and Cognition*, London, Sage.

Ellemers, N., Spears, R. and Doosje, B. (eds) (1999) *Social identity: Context, Commitment, Content*, Oxford, Blackwell.

Le Bon, G. (1896) *The Crowd: A Study of the Popular Mind*, Kitchener, Ontario, CA, Batoche Books.

McGarty, C. and Haslam, S.A. (eds) (1997) *The Message of Social Psychology*, Oxford, Blackwell.

Pettigrew, T.W. (1958) 'Personality and sociocultural factors in intergroup attitudes: a cross-national comparison', *Journal of Conflict Resolution*, vol. 2, pp. 29–42.

Reicher, S. (1984) 'Social influence in the crowd: an explanation of the limits of crowd action in terms of a social identity model', *European Journal of Social Psychology*, vol. 14, pp. 1–21.

Reicher, S. (1987) 'Crowd behaviour as social action' in Turner et al. (eds) (1987).

Sherif, M. and Sherif, C.W.V. (1956) *An Outline of Social Psychology* (revised edn), New York, Harper & Row.

Tajfel, H. (1957) 'Value and the perceptual judgement of magnitude', *Psychological Review*, vol. 64, pp. 192–204.

Tajfel, H. (1959) 'Quantitative judgement in social perception', *British Journal of Psychology*, vol. 50, pp. 16–29.

Tajfel, H. (1969) 'Cognitive aspects of prejudice', *Journal of Social Issues*, vol. 25, pp. 79–97.

Tajfel, H. (1981) *Human Groups and Social Categories*, Cambridge, Cambridge University Press.

Tajfel, H. and Billig, M. (1974) Familiarity and categorisation in intergroup behavior', *Journal of Experimental Social Psychology*, vol. 10, pp. 159–70.

Tajfel, H. and Turner, J. (1979) 'An integrative theory of intergroup conflict' in Austin, W.G. and Worchel, S. (eds) *The Social Psychology of Intergroup Relations*, Monterey, CA, Brooks/Cole.

Triplett, N.D. (1898) 'The dynamogenic factor in pacemaking and competition', *American Journal of Psychology*, vol. 9, pp. 507–33.

Turner, J.C., Hogg, M.A., Oakes, P.J., Reicher, S.D. and Wetherell, M.S. (1987) *Rediscovering the Social Group: A Self-categorisation Theory*, Oxford, Blackwell.

Wetherell, M. (1996) 'Constructing social identities: the individual/social binary in Henri Tajfel's social psychology' in Robinson, W.P. (ed.) *Social Groups and Identities: Developing the Legacy of Henri Tajfel*, Oxford, Butterworth-Heinemann, pp. 269–84.

Wetherell, M. and Potter, J. (1992) *Mapping the Dynamics of Racism: Discourse and the Legitimation of Exploitation*, Hemel Hempstead, Harvester Wheatsheaf.

Further reading

Brown, S.D. and Lunt, P. (2002) 'A genealogy of the social identity tradition: Deleuze and Guattari and social psychology', *British Journal of Social Psychology*, vol. 41, no. 1, pp. 1–23.
A critical genealogy of SIT which suggests that recent continental philosophy might assist in a radical re-working of the approach.

Capozza, D. and Brown, R. (eds) (2000) *Social Identity Processes: Trends in Theory and Research*, London, Sage.
A collection of recent essays on SIT, of interest as an example of 'the state of the art' in SIT research to both supporters and critics.

Robinson, W.P. (ed.) (1996) *Social Groups and Identities: Developing the Legacy of Henri Tajfel*, Oxford, Butterworth-Heinemann.
This is a collection of essays written in memory of Tajfel by former colleagues and students. It has numerous excellent pieces broadly supporting SIT (Abrams, Brown, Hogg) and critically evaluating and extending the tradition (Billig, Condor, Wetherell).

Tajfel, H. (1981) *Human Groups and Social Categories*, Cambridge, Cambridge University Press.
A collection of work taken throughout Tajfel's career, organised chronologically, which provides an excellent overview, including a very useful biographical introduction.

Turner, J.C., Hogg, M.A., Oakes, P.J., Reicher, S.D. and Wetherell, M.S. (1987) *Rediscovering the Social Group: A Self-categorisation Theory*, Oxford: Blackwell.
A presentation of self-categorisation theory (a modification of SIT) which argues for a 'cognitive conception of the group', and, somewhat implausibly, for more experimental answers to fundamental conceptual questions.

Wetherell, M. and Potter, J. (1992) *Mapping the Dynamics of Racism: Discourse and the Legitimation of Exploitation*, Hemel Hempstead, Harvester Wheatsheaf.

An extended argument for discursive psychology which takes care to show how a discursive approach can extend SIT concerns with social categories.

Chapter 7

Bystander intervention

by Viv Burr, University of Huddersfield

Introduction

The key event which led to research into bystander intervention was the murder of a young woman, Kitty Genovese, in New York in 1964. Public and academic attention was drawn to the killing by an account of the incident in the *New York Times* in March 1964. Kitty Genovese was murdered on the street by a man she did not know, Winston Mosely. He followed her as she walked home in the early hours of the morning, and stabbed her numerous times. He then raped her as she lay dying. What seemed incredible to those who read of the attack is that, although thirty-eight people heard her cries or witnessed some part of the events, no-one came to her aid or even called the police. They were all bystanders to the emergency, but none intervened. Many people were understandably appalled at this, and research into 'bystander intervention' aimed to investigate, among other things, why bystanders sometimes fail to act.

All kinds of people subsequently wrote letters to the newspaper, giving their own opinions for this seeming lack of concern. However, John Darley and Bibb Latané (1968) were not persuaded by the popular view that it was the apathy and indifference of the average New Yorker that was the cause. They point out that, when faced with an apparent emergency, people may be pulled in opposite directions by their desire to help, on the one hand, and their fears about what might happen to them if they do, on the other. Their main suggestion, however, is that, where several people witness an attack, each individual feels less responsible for taking action than they would if they were the only person available to help. In Darley and Latané's terms, the responsibility to help is 'diffused' or spread across all the bystanders, so that no individual feels that it is up to them to do something. Furthermore, they argue that as well as this diffusion of responsibility, there is also a diffusion of blame. They cite research evidence in support of the view that, where several people are involved in a blameworthy act (such as failing to come to the aid of Kitty Genovese), each person is likely to feel that they personally are not to blame for this neglect. Moreover, in any case, they conclude, if we cannot actually see the responses of other bystanders, we might legitimately conclude that they have already offered their help or called for assistance. In the light of these considerations, Darley and Latané predict that as the number of bystanders to an emergency increases, the less likely it is that any one of them will actually intervene, or they may be slower to take action. This prediction is supported by their research findings.

The study chosen as Reading 7.1 is one of a series of experiments conducted by Darley and Latané and their co-workers in which some crisis would typically be enacted: an epileptic fit, smoke suggesting a fire in an adjacent room or the sound of someone falling and calling out nearby. Darley and Latané's (1968) journal article 'Bystander intervention in emergencies' was chosen as it is a good example of the extensive series of experiments conducted into bystander intervention by these researchers, whose work is recognised as foundational to this field. It is also typical of experimental research, the predominant paradigm in social psychology in the 1960s, and probably still so today. By manipulating a limited number of situational variables (in this case, group size and sex of subjects), the experimenters aimed to identify the effect these had upon the likelihood and speed of someone helping in an emergency.

One of the aims of laboratory experiments is to study a phenomenon in a situation where it is not 'contaminated' by incidental variables that could affect the results, and so experimenters are careful to exclude or control many features that may be present in real emergencies, and this of course includes the events and social context that would have led up to the emergency. Some of this context may be very wide-ranging, for example the personal histories and demographic details (such as sex, 'race', age and social class) of the people involved, and the prevailing attitudes and values of the society and communities they inhabit. Many of these things are virtually impossible to control in experimental settings and experimenters often do not attempt to do so.

But there is also an unwritten assumption, underlying experimental social psychology, that explanations for social phenomena can be found by examining the behaviour of individuals and groups irrespective of their social context, and it is this assumption that forms one of the strands of critique of bystander intervention research put forward by Frances Cherry (1995a). Cherry devotes a chapter to bystander intervention in her book *The Stubborn Particulars of Social Psychology*, and this chapter has been chosen as Reading 7.2. Cherry was writing at a time when (in today's parlance) 'mainstream' social psychology had for some time been thought of as 'in crisis' (see, for example, Armistead, 1974; Brown, 1973; Harré and Secord, 1972), and part of that crisis had to do with what was seen as its over-reliance upon experimental method (Hollway, 2006). The social and historical context and personal meaning of people's behaviour was thought by an increasing number of 'critical' social psychologists to be crucial to understanding social phenomena, and qualitative methods were becoming more acceptable as research tools (Sloan, 2000; Smith et al., 1995a, 1995b).

Second-wave feminism had also begun to have an impact on psychology, and a number of writers (for example, Harding, 1991; Stanley and Wise, 1983) had expressed concern about the way that women's experience was often distorted by research and theory. Furthermore, these critical writers were keen to point out that psychology, while dressing itself as apolitical and value free, often subtly reinforced and legitimated oppressive attitudes and practices.

Cherry's chapter brings these issues into focus in her analysis of bystander intervention research and in particular of the usefulness of this research in helping us to understand the murder of Kitty Genovese.

So, by comparing the approach to bystander intervention research taken by Darley and Latané with that of Cherry, a number of important issues can be explored which have implications, beyond the field of bystander intervention, for our research and theory more generally.

ACTIVITY 7.1

As you read the following extract, think about these points:

■ Does the experiment help us to understand why some people may fail to act in an emergency?

■ To what extent does the experiment reproduce enough of the important features of Kitty Genovese's murder to be a useful parallel?

Reading 7.1 is from a 1968 journal article by John Darley and Bibb Latané, which presents their work on bystander intervention.

READING 7.1

'Bystander intervention in emergencies: Diffusion of responsibility'

Several years ago, a young woman was stabbed to death in the middle of a street in a residential section of New York City. Although such murders are not entirely routine, the incident received little public attention until several weeks later when the New York Times disclosed another side to the case: at least 38 witnesses had observed the attack – and none had even attempted to intervene. Although the attacker took more than half an hour to kill Kitty Genovese, not one of the 38 people who watched from the safety of their own apartments came out to assist her. Not one even lifted the telephone to call the police (Rosenthal, 1964).

Preachers, professors, and news commentators sought the reasons for such apparently conscienceless and inhumane lack of intervention. Their conclusions ranged from 'moral decay,' to 'dehumanization produced by the urban environment,' to 'alienation,' 'anomie,' and 'existential despair.' An analysis of the situation, however, suggests that factors other than apathy and indifference were involved.

A person witnessing an emergency situation, particularly such a frightening and dangerous one as a stabbing, is in conflict. There are obvious humanitarian norms about helping the victim, but there are also rational and irrational fears about what might happen to a person who does intervene (Milgram and Hollander, 1964). 'I didn't want to get involved,' is a familiar comment, and behind it lies fears of physical harm, public embarrassment, involvement with police procedures, lost work days and jobs, and other unknown dangers.

In certain circumstances, the norms favoring intervention may be weakened, leading bystanders to resolve the conflict in the direction of nonintervention. One of these circumstances may be the presence of other onlookers. For example, in the case above, each observer, by seeing lights and figures in other apartment house windows, knew that others were also watching. However, there was no way to tell how the other observers were reacting. These two facts provide several reasons why any individual may have delayed or failed to help. The responsibility for helping was diffused among the observers; there was also diffusion of any potential blame for not taking action; and finally, it was possible that somebody, unperceived, had already initiated helping action.

When only one bystander is present in an emergency, if help is to come, it must come from him. Although he may choose to ignore it (out of concern for his personal safety, or desires 'not to get involved'), any pressure to intervene focuses uniquely on him. When there are several observers present, however, the pressures to intervene do not focus on any one of the observers; instead the responsibility for intervention is shared among all the onlookers and is not unique to any one. As a result, no one helps.

A second possibility is that potential blame may be diffused. However much we may wish to think that an individual's moral behavior is divorced from considerations of personal punishment or reward, there is both theory and evidence to the contrary (Aronfreed, 1964; Miller and Dollard, 1941; Whiting and Child, 1953). It is perfectly reasonable to assume that, under circumstances of group responsibility for a punishable act, the punishment or blame that accrues to any one individual is often slight or nonexistent.

Finally, if others are known to be present, but their behavior cannot be closely observed, any one bystander can assume that one of the other observers is already taking action to end the emergency. Therefore, his own intervention would be only redundant – perhaps harmfully or confusingly so. Thus, given the presence of other onlookers whose behavior cannot be observed, any given bystander can rationalize his own inaction by convincing himself that 'somebody else must be doing something.'

These considerations lead to the hypothesis that the more bystanders to an emergency, the less likely, or the more slowly, any one bystander will intervene to provide aid. To test this proposition it would be necessary to create a situation in which a realistic 'emergency' could plausibly occur. Each subject should also be blocked from communicating with others to prevent his getting information about their behavior during the emergency. Finally, the experimental situation should allow for the assessment of the speed and frequency of the subjects' reaction to the emergency. The experiment reported below attempted to fulfill these conditions.

Procedure

Overview. A college student arrived in the laboratory and was ushered into an individual room from which a communication system would enable him to talk to the other participants. It was explained to him that he was to take part in a discussion about personal problems associated with college life and that the discussion would be held over the intercom system, rather than face-to-face, in order to avoid embarrassment by preserving the anonymity of the subjects. During the course of the discussion, one of the other subjects underwent what appeared to be a very serious nervous seizure similar to epilepsy. During the fit it was impossible for the subject to talk to the other discussants or to find out what, if anything, they were doing about the emergency. The dependent variable was the speed with which the subjects reported the emergency to the experimenter. The major independent variable was the number of people the subject thought to be in the discussion group.

Subjects. Fifty-nine female and thirteen male students in introductory psychology courses at New York University were contacted to take part in an unspecified experiment as part of a class requirement.

Method. Upon arriving for the experiment, the subject found himself in a long corridor with doors opening off it to several small rooms. An experimental assistant met him, took him to one of the rooms, and seated him at a table. After filling out a background information form, the subject was given a pair of headphones with an attached microphone and was told to listen for instructions.

Over the intercom, the experimenter explained that he was interested in learning about the kinds of personal problems faced by normal college students in a high pressure, urban environment. He said that to avoid possible embarrassment about discussing personal problems with strangers several precautions had been taken. First, subjects would remain anonymous, which was why they had been placed in individual rooms rather than face-to-face. (The actual reason for this was to allow tape recorder simulation of the other subjects and the emergency.) Second, since the discussion might be inhibited by the presence of outside listeners, the experimenter would not listen to the initial discussion, but would get the subject's reactions later, by questionnaire. (The real purpose of this was to remove the obviously responsible experimenter from the scene of the emergency.)

The subjects were told that since the experimenter was not present, it was necessary to impose some organization. Each person would talk in turn, presenting his problems to the group. Next, each person in turn would comment on what the others had said, and finally, there would be a free discussion. A mechanical switching device would regulate this discussion sequence and each subject's microphone would be on for about 2 minutes. While any microphone was on, all other microphones would be off. Only one subject, therefore, could be heard over the network at any given time. The subjects were thus led to realize when they later heard the seizure that only the victim's microphone was on and that there was no way of determining what any of the other witnesses were doing, nor of discussing the event and its possible solution with the others. When these instructions had been given, the discussion began.

In the discussion, the future victim spoke first, saying that he found it difficult to get adjusted to New York City and to his studies. Very hesitantly, and with obvious embarrassment, he mentioned that he was prone to seizures, particularly when studying hard or taking exams. The other people, including the real subject, took their turns and discussed similar problems (minus, of course, the proneness to seizures). The naive subject talked last in the series, after the last prerecorded voice was played.

When it was again the victim's turn to talk, he made a few relatively calm comments, and then, growing increasingly louder and incoherent, he continued:

> I-er-um-I think I-I need-er-if-if could-er-er-some-body er-er-er-er-er-er-er give me a little-er-give me a little help here because-er-I-er-I'm-er-er-h-h-having a-a-a real problem-er-right now and I-er-if somebody could help me out it would-it would-er-er s-s-sure be-sure be good ... because-er-there-er-er-a cause I-er-I-uh-I've got a-a one of the-er-se- - - - -er-er-things coming on and-and-and I could really-er-use some help so if somebody would-er-give me a little h-help-uh-er-er-er-er-er c-could somebody-er-er-help-ef-uh-uh-uh (choking sounds) ... . I'm gonna die-er-er-I'm ... gonna die-er-help-er-er-seizure-er-[chokes, then quiet].

The experimenter began timing the speed of the real subject's response at the beginning of the victim's speech. Informed judges listening to the tape have estimated that the victim's increasingly louder and more disconnected ramblings clearly represented a breakdown about 70 seconds after the signal for the victim's second speech. The victim's speech was abruptly cut off 125 seconds after this signal, which could be interpreted by the subject as indicating that the time allotted for that speaker had elapsed and the switching circuits had switched away from him. Times reported in the results are measured from the start of the fit.

Group size variable. The major independent variable of the study was the number of other people that the subject believed also heard the fit. By the assistant's comments before the experiment, and also by the number of voices heard to speak in the first round of the group discussion, the subject was led to believe that the discussion group was one of three sizes: either a two-person group (consisting of a person who would later have a fit and the real subject), a three-person group (consisting of the victim, the real subject, and one confederate voice), or a six-person group (consisting of the victim, the real subject, and four confederate voices). All the confederates' voices were tape-recorded.

Variations in group composition. Varying the kind as well as the number of bystanders present at an emergency should also vary the amount of responsibility felt by any single bystander. To test this, several variations of the three-person group were run. In one three-person condition, the taped bystander voice was that of a female, in another a male, and in the third a male who said that he was a premedical student who occasionally worked in the emergency wards at Bellevue hospital.

In the above conditions, the subjects were female college students. In a final condition males drawn from the same introductory psychology subject pool were tested in a three-person female-bystander condition.

Time to help. The major dependent variable was the time elapsed from the start of the victim's fit until the subject left her experimental cubicle. When the subject left her room, she saw the experimental assistant seated at the end of the hall, and invariably went to the assistant. If 6 minutes elapsed without the subject having emerged from her room, the experiment was terminated.

As soon as the subject reported the emergency, or after 6 minutes had elapsed, the experimental assistant disclosed the true nature of the experiment, and dealt with any emotions aroused in the subject. Finally the subject filled out a questionnaire concerning her thoughts and feelings during the emergency and completed scales of Machiavellianism, anomie, and authoritarianism (Christie, 1964), a social desirability scale (Crowne and Marlowe, 1964), a social responsibility scale (Daniels and Berkowitz, 1964), and reported vital statistics and socioeconomic data.

Results

Plausibility of manipulation

Judging by the subjects' nervousness when they reported the fit to the experimenter, by their surprise when they discovered that the fit was simulated, and by comments they made during the fit (when they thought their microphones were off), one can conclude that almost all of the subjects perceived the fit as real. There were two exceptions in different experimental conditions, and the data for these subjects were dropped from the analysis.

Effect of group size on helping

The number of bystanders that the subject perceived to be present had a major effect on the likelihood with which she would report the emergency (Table 1). Eighty-five percent of the subjects who thought they alone knew of the victim's plight reported the seizure before the victim was cut off, only 31% of those who thought four other bystanders were present did so.

TABLE 1
Effects of groups size on likelihood and speed of response

Group size	N	% responding by end of fit	Time in sec.	Speed score
2 (S & victim)	13	85	52	.87
3 (S, victim, & 1 other)	26	62	93	.72
6 (S, victim, & 4 others)	13	31	166	.51

Note.—> p value of differences: $x^2 = 7.91$, $p < .02$; $F = 8.09$, $p < .01$, for speed scores.

Every one of the subjects in the two-person groups, but only 62% of the subjects in the six-person groups, ever reported the emergency. The cumulative distributions of response times for groups of different perceived size (Figure 1) indicates that, by any point in time, more subjects from the two-person groups had responded than from the three-person groups, and more from the three-person groups than from the six-person groups.

Ninety-five percent of all the subjects who ever responded did so within the first half of the time available to them. No subject who had not reported within 3 minutes after the fit ever did so. The shape of these distributions suggest that had the experiment been allowed to run for a considerably longer time, few additional subjects would have responded.

Speed of response

To achieve a more detailed analysis of the results, each subject's time score was transformed into a 'speed' score by taking the reciprocal of the response time in seconds and multiplying by 100. The effect of this transformation was to deemphasize differences between longer time scores, thus reducing the contribution to the results of the arbitrary 6-minute limit on scores. A high speed score indicates a fast response.

An analysis of variance indicates that the effect of group size is highly significant ($p < .01$). Duncan multiple-range tests indicate that all but the two- and three-person groups differ significantly from one another ($p < .05$).

[...]

Effect of group composition on helping the victim

Several variations of the three-person group were run. In one pair of variations, the female subject thought the other bystander was either male or female; in another, she thought the other bystander was a premedical student who worked in an emergency ward at Bellevue hospital. As Table 2 shows, the variations in sex and medical competence of the other bystander had no important or detectable effect on speed of response. Subjects responded equally frequently

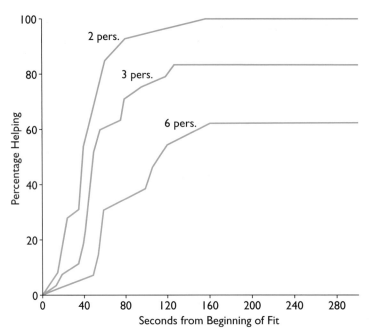

Figure 1   Cumulative distributions of helping responses

and fast whether the other bystander was female, male, or medically experienced.

TABLE 2
Effects of group composition on likelihood and speed of response*

Group composition	N	% responding by end of fit	Time in sec.	Speed score
Female S, male other	13	62	94	74
Female S, female other	13	62	92	71
Female S, male medic other	5	100	60	77
Male S, female other	13	69	110	68

*Three-person group, male victim.

Sex of the subject and speed of response

Coping with emergencies is often thought to be the duty of males, especially when females are present, but there was no evidence that this was the case in this study. Male subjects responded to the emergency with almost exactly the same speed as did females (Table 2).

Reasons for intervention or nonintervention

After the debriefing at the end of the experiment each subject was given a 15-item checklist and asked to check those thoughts which had 'crossed your mind when you heard Subject 1 calling for help.' Whatever the condition, each subject checked very few thoughts, and there were no significant differences in number or kind of thoughts in the different experimental groups. The only thoughts checked by more than a few subjects were 'I didn't know what to do' (18 out of 65 subjects), 'I thought it must be some sort of fake' (20 out of 65), and 'I didn't know exactly what was happening' (26 out of 65).

It is possible that subjects were ashamed to report socially undesirable rationalizations, or, since the subjects checked the list *after* the true nature of the experiment had been explained to them, their memories might have been blurred. It is our impression, however, that most subjects checked few reasons because they had few coherent thoughts during the fit.

We asked all subjects whether the presence or absence of other bystanders had entered their minds during the time that they were hearing the fit. Subjects in the three- and six-person groups reported that they were aware that other people were present, but they felt that this made no difference to their own behavior.

[...]

Discussion

Subjects, whether or not they intervened, believed the fit to be genuine and serious. 'My God, he's having a fit,' many subjects said to themselves (and were overheard via their microphones) at the onset of the fit. Others gasped or simply said 'Oh.' Several of the male subjects swore. One subject said to herself, 'It's just my kind of luck, something has to happen to me!' Several subjects spoke aloud of their confusion about what course of action to take, 'Oh God, what should I do?'

When those subjects who intervened stepped out of their rooms, they found the experimental assistant down the hall. With some uncertainty, but without panic, they reported the situation. 'Hey, I think Number 1 is very sick. He's having a fit or something.' After ostensibly checking on the situation, the experimenter returned to report that 'everything is under control.' The subjects accepted these assurances with obvious relief.

Subjects who failed to report the emergency showed few signs of the apathy and indifference thought to characterize 'unresponsive bystanders.' When the experimenter entered her room to terminate the situation, the subject often asked if the victim was 'all right.' 'Is he being taken care of?' 'He's all right isn't he?' Many of these subjects showed physical signs of nervousness; they often had trembling hands and sweating palms. If anything, they seemed more emotionally aroused than did the subjects who reported the emergency.

Why, then, didn't they respond? It is our impression that nonintervening subjects had not decided *not* to respond. Rather they were still in a state of indecision and conflict concerning whether to respond or not. The emotional behavior of these nonresponding subjects was a sign of their continuing conflict, a conflict that other subjects resolved by responding.

The fit created a conflict situation of the avoidance-avoidance type. On the one hand, subjects worried about the guilt and shame they would feel if they did not help the person in distress. On the other hand, they were concerned not to make fools of themselves by overreacting, not to ruin the ongoing experiment by leaving their intercom, and not to destroy the anonymous nature of the situation which the experimenter had earlier stressed as important. For subjects in the two-person condition, the obvious distress of the victim and his need for help were so important that their conflict was easily resolved. For the subjects who knew there were other bystanders present, the cost of not helping was reduced and the conflict they were in more acute. Caught between the two negative alternatives of letting the victim continue to suffer or the costs of rushing in to help, the nonresponding bystanders vacillated between them rather than choosing not to respond. This distinction may be academic for the victim, since he got no help in either case, but it is an extremely important one for arriving at an understanding of the causes of bystanders' failures to help.

Although the subjects experienced stress and conflict during the experiment, their general reactions to it were highly positive. On a questionnaire administered after the experimenter had discussed the nature and purpose of the experiment, every single subject found the experiment either 'interesting' or 'very interesting' and was willing to participate in similar experiments in the future. All subjects felt they understood what the experiment was about and indicated that they thought the deceptions were necessary and justified. All but one felt they were better informed about the nature of psychological research in general.

Male subjects reported the emergency no faster than did females. These results (or lack of them) seem to conflict with the Berkowitz, Klanderman, and Harris (1964) finding that males tend to assume more responsibility and take more initiative than females in giving help to dependent others. Also, females reacted equally fast when the other bystander was another female, a male, or even a person practiced in dealing with medical emergencies. The ineffectiveness of these manipulations of group composition cannot be explained by general insensitivity of the speed measure, since the group-size variable had a marked effect on report speed.

It might be helpful in understanding this lack of difference to distinguish two general classes of intervention in emergency situations: direct and reportorial. Direct intervention (breaking up a fight, extinguishing a fire, swimming out to save a drowner) often requires skill, knowledge, or physical power. It may involve danger. American cultural norms and Berkowitz's results seem to suggest that males are more responsible than females for this kind of direct intervention.

A second way of dealing with an emergency is to report it to someone qualified to handle it, such as the police. For this kind of intervention, there seem to be no norms requiring male action. In the present study, subjects clearly intended to report the emergency rather than take direct action. For such indirect intervention, sex or medical competence does not appear to affect one's qualifications or responsibilities. Anybody, male or female, medically trained or not, can find the experimenter.

In this study, no subject was able to tell how the other subjects reacted to the fit. (Indeed, there were no other subjects actually present.) The effects of group size on speed of helping, therefore, are due simply to the perceived presence of others rather than to the influence of their actions. This means that the experimental situation is unlike emergencies, such as a fire, in which bystanders interact with each other. It is, however, similar to emergencies, such as the Genovese murder, in which spectators knew others were also watching but were prevented by walls between them from communication that might have counteracted the diffusion of responsibility.

The present results create serious difficulties for one class of commonly given explanations for the failure of bystanders to intervene in actual emergencies, those involving apathy or indifference. These explanations generally assert that people who fail to intervene are somehow different in kind from the rest of us, that they are 'alienated by industrialization,' 'dehumanized by urbanization,' 'depersonalized by living in the cold society,' or 'psychopaths.' These explanations serve a dual function for people who adopt them. First, they explain (if only in a nominal way) the puzzling and frightening problem of why people watch others die. Second, they give individuals reason to deny that they too might fail to help in a similar situation.

The results of this experiment seem to indicate that such personality variables may not be as important as these explanations suggest. Alienation, Machiavellianism, acceptance of social responsibility, need for approval, and authoritarianism are often cited in these explanations. Yet they did not predict the speed or likelihood of help. In sharp contrast, the perceived number of bystanders did. The explanation of bystander 'apathy' may lie more in the bystander's response to other observers than in presumed personality deficiencies of 'apathetic' individuals. Although this realization may force us to face the guilt-provoking possibility that we too might fail to intervene, it also suggests that individuals are not, of necessity, 'non-interveners' because of their personalities. If people understand the situational forces that can make them hesitate to intervene, they may better overcome them.

References

Aronfreed, J. (1964) 'The origin of self-criticism', *Psychological Review*, vol. 71, pp. 193–219.

Berkowitz, L., Klanderman, S., and Harris, R. (1964) 'Effects of experimenter awareness and sex of subject on reactions to dependency relationships', *Sociometry*, no. 27, pp. 327–9.

Christie, R. (1964) 'The prevalence of Machiavellian orientations', Paper presented at the meeting of the American Psychological Association, Los Angeles.

Crowne, D. and Marlowe, D. (1964) *The Approval Motive*, New York, Wiley.

Daniels, L. and Berkowitz, L. (1964) 'Liking and response to dependency relationships', *Human Relations*, vol. 16, pp. 141–8.

Milgram, S. and Hollander, P. (1964) 'Murder they heard', *Nation*, vol. 198, pp. 602–4.

Miller, N. and Dollard, J. (1941) *Social Learning and Imitation*, New Haven, Yale University Press.

Rosenthal, A.M. (1964) *Thirty-eight witnesses*, New York, McGraw-Hill.

Whiting, J.W.M. and Child, I. (1953) *Child Training and Personality*, New Haven, Yale University Press.

(Darley and Latané, 1968, pp. 377–83)

Commentary

There are a number of very positive features of Darley and Latané's paper. First, they explain the background of social events, that is, the murder of Kitty Genovese and the subsequent letters to the press, which led to their research. This immediately gives the experiment social relevance, and also helps the reader to understand the motives behind the research. Although the practice of psychology as a scientific endeavour is usually represented as objective, free from human passions and concerns, many critical psychologists and critical social psychologists (for example, Fox and Prilleltensky, 1997; Gough and McFadden, 2001; Tuffin, 2005) believe that such objectivity is an unattainable fiction and that all research projects inevitably arise, at least to some degree, from the beliefs, desires and interests of the researchers. Therefore, if we are given some background information about the research, it helps us to be aware of such influences and to consider their impact. It is likely that, in the case of the present piece of research, the experimenters were also shocked by the Kitty Genovese murder and were keen to shed some light on the event in the hope that this would help to avoid such instances in the future. However, sometimes the values and beliefs underpinning research are more diffuse and may lie outside the conscious awareness of the researchers themselves. I will explore this point in more depth later in this section.

Second, Darley and Latané are not prepared to take popular common sense at face value. The people who sent their opinions to the *New York Times* suggested that city life had become alienating and inhuman, that relatively well-off New Yorkers no longer cared about what happened to others, or that the bystanders were gratifying their own sadistic impulses. But of course none of these people felt that they themselves were alienated, indifferent or sadistic. Darley and Latané felt that at least some of these views were self-serving rationalisations: if shocking acts can be explained by the negative personality characteristics of a sick minority, then the people offering this explanation need not worry about their own behaviour. They could be sure that, in the same situation, they would certainly have come to Kitty's aid. However, Darley and Latané thought it likely that most people, if put in the same situation as those witnesses, would have found themselves behaving in exactly the same way. They challenged an intra-psychic explanation (personality) by presenting evidence for a social one (situational factors). None of the personality measures they took predicted helping, and, whether they intervened or not, their participants were not indifferent: they were clearly distressed by the event and confused about what they should do.

The results of this experiment suggest that the number of people present at an emergency is a key factor affecting whether and how quickly someone is likely to help. At the end of their discussion, Darley and Latané claim that understanding the 'situational forces' present in such circumstances will help us to overcome these. Understood in its own terms, this experiment seems well designed and has provided some results that have valuable applications. But if we step outside of the assumptions most fundamental to the research we can ask further, perhaps more searching, questions.

As noted in the introduction, this research is typical of the experimental tradition in psychology, which has dominated the discipline since the rise of behaviourism early in the twentieth century (Jones and Elcock, 2001). In an experiment we manipulate a small number of variables and observe the consequences. But what if the important factors in a phenomenon cannot be operationalised in this way? One of the differences between people and the inanimate objects that are studied by the natural sciences (on which the experimental paradigm in psychology is modelled) is that people's behaviour is often complex; it is not just a straightforward reaction to a stimulus or some measurable aspect of the immediate surroundings (for instance, the number of people present). Rather, it is framed and given meaning by people's personal histories and by the beliefs, values and moral principles of the society and communities to which they belong. These things cannot be conceptualised adequately as experimental variables, and such concerns have led to an increase in the use of qualitative methods. When critical psychologists talk about experiments 'decontextualising' behaviour (for example, Hepburn, 2003), they are often referring to this more 'distant' personal and societal context as well as to features of the more immediate situational context that can inform our understanding of a person's conduct.

So, if we want to understand more about why people failed to come to the aid of Kitty Genovese, we may need a fuller awareness of context than is demanded by the experimental paradigm. Furthermore, as noted in the introduction, the principles of value freedom and objectivity are key assumptions in the experimental tradition, and the use of scientific language (for example, talking about 'variables' and writing in the third person) helps persuade us that they are real. But this language serves to disguise the world of assumptions, values and vested interests that the researchers themselves inhabit and that inevitably influences the research questions they pose (Howitt, 1991 offers a good discussion of values and vested interests in psychology).

In the second reading, Cherry (1995b) explores these issues, adopting a broadly feminist approach. This involves two major critiques. First, she questions whether women are adequately represented in psychological research; much experimental work has been conducted by male researchers, on male undergraduates as subjects, and has taken male experience and behaviour as the norm. Second, she challenges the assumptions underlying the experimental paradigm. In particular, she questions whether research can be objective and value free – the 'God's eye view' (Haraway, 1988) – and indeed even whether it *ought* to be so. Instead, feminist researchers argue that research should attend to the social and cultural factors surrounding the phenomena being investigated. This also involves examining how a researcher's own biography and location in society might affect her interpretation of the issues, referred to as 'reflexivity'. It is this second critical strand to feminist theory that Cherry adopts.

ACTIVITY 7.2

As you read the following extract, think about these points:

■   How does Cherry understand her own changing theoretical position?

■   What kind of methodological approach(es) might be appropriate for researching
    bystander intervention as Cherry conceptualises it?

Reading 7.2, taken from a 1995 book by Frances Cherry, was written as a
direct critique of the experimental work by Darley and Latané presented in
Reading 7.1.

READING 7.2

'Kitty Genovese and culturally embedded theorizing'

When I reflect on how I generate hunches or come up with explanations for
contemporary events I am often aware of the boundedness imposed by my
experiences thus far. Often I can see the assumptive framework in the family
that shaped me, the larger society that shaped my family, the educational
system in which I learned, the books I've read, the communities and countries
I've lived in and the people with whom I've shared my life. Construed this way, I
am unable to think of the social scientist as an isolated individual with sound and
rational private abstractions about cultural experience. Rather, the social
scientist appears to me as a passionate and public person. As one such person,
the social psychologist constructs an understanding of the social world that she
or he inhabits. An imagined line is broken between the past and the present,
between 'historical research' and 'social science research'. Social psychology
becomes a powerful post-dictive science of meaning more than a predictive
science of control based on the model of the physical sciences. Generating
hypotheses about social situations involves constructing meaning from one's
own cultural experience, sharing that meaning publicly, and finding tension and
conflict with other points of view through public discussion and enquiry. It
necessitates more than one understanding of the same event and exposes the
difficulty of resolving conflicting viewpoints.

The link between an historical event and the social and political practice of
theorizing about it that engages me as a social psychologist can be illustrated by
my discipline's account of bystander intervention. Through introductory social
psychology textbooks most North American students of social psychology have
become familiar with the murder in 1964 of Catherine (Kitty) Genovese in
Queens, New York. We have learned to think of this event as an instance of the
failure of bystanders to intervene in emergency situations. Our contact with the
event has for three decades been shaped by the social psychological research
of Bibb Latané and John Darley, who both graduated with PhDs in
1964 and 1965 respectively. They were responding to the event in 1964 and to
numerous headlines, many of which reported the incident as an instance of
'apathy': 'Apathy at stabbing of Queens woman shocks inspector' (*New York
Times* [NYT], 27 March 1964). 'Apathy is puzzle in Queens killing' (NYT, 28
March 1964), In a later interview with Rand Evans (1980), Darley described their
thinking. 'Latané and I, shocked as anybody else, met over dinner a few days
after this terrible incident had occurred and began to analyze this process in
social psychological terms ...' (Evans, 1980, p. 216). These researchers were

not satisfied to think of the event in terms of the 'personality' characteristics of the onlookers, such as apathy, or to set the event in the context of social norms. Instead, they explained the passivity of the onlookers to this murder by using theoretical concepts that focused on immediate situational factors that might inhibit helping in emergencies. Concepts of group-inhibition and diffusion of responsibility in large groups were invoked and became the focus of later empirical work.

[...]

In the *Letter to the Times* section of the *New York Times* that followed from 31 March to 24 May, numerous attempts to find a meaningful way to interpret this event were submitted. These constructions represented diverse views: there was a failure of morality at its worst in large cities; people were immersed in themselves; they were apathetic, much as the Germans were to the plight of the Jews; there was a fear of police reprisal; a failure of the American male to do the manly and courageous thing; what could one expect with so much violence in the mass media? What better argument for keeping weapons in one's house! On 3 May 1964 A.M. Rosenthal, then Metropolitan editor for the *New York Times*, wrote a lengthier analysis for the *New York Times Magazine* (*NYTM*) focusing on the apathy of the bystanders, but noting also that

> Each individual obviously approaches the story of Catherine Genovese, reacts to it and veers away from it against the background of his own life experience, and his own fears and shortcomings and rationalizations.
>
> (Rosenthal, in *NYTM*, 1964, p. 69)

A professional identification with experimental social psychology carries with it a strong tendency towards behavioural and situational explanations. Not surprisingly, the analysis offered by Latané and Darley in the 1960s was a theoretical construction based on the immediate situational determinants of behaviours such as noticing, judging and taking personal responsibility through action. An inverse relationship between group size and helping behaviour figured prominently in their empirical work, and reflected a longstanding preoccupation with social psychology defined as the influence of people in one another's lives (Latané and Darley, 1970). However, by moving in as closely as possible to the behavioural phenomenon and casting the event in terms of independent variables such as size of group that affect dependent variables such as intervening behaviour, these researchers chose to 'veer away' from a sociocultural analysis of the event.

Here's how I think theorizing happens. During an initial period of reflection, the social psychologist, like other members of society, asks him/herself and others, 'Did you see the headlines?' 'Did you read about Kitty Genovese?' 'So what was that about?' 'Why did that happen?' In addition, the academic theorizer is subtly guided by his or her socialization into a discipline's normative beliefs about appropriate intellectual frameworks and scientifically respectable methodologies for bringing together hunch and evidence. It is in this effort to *construct* the meaning of an event where we also *constrict* our vision, where we fail to ask the question, 'Of what else is this event an instance?' Here is where 'normal science' begins, where Kitty Genovese's murder becomes an instance of a seemingly larger category of social behaviour designated as 'bystander intervention'.

Consider for a moment that Kitty Genovese and her assailant, Winston Moseley, were living in a society at a time when its members did little to intervene in violence directed towards women. Such details were not the central part of the abstraction/construction process by which 'general processes' of social behaviour were hypothesized and later empirically tested. In the mid-1960s, what was abstracted as the general phenomenon of interest was something like this: there was an emergency and no one intervened to help.

As a graduate student in the early 1970s, in the heyday of bystander intervention research and at the pre-dawning of my own feminist consciousness, I can't claim to have seen anything other than Latané and Darley's point of view. Only later, while reviewing literature relevant to the social psychology of rape (Cherry, 1983), did I come across information that shifted the context for the event and altered my framework for thinking about the meaning of Kitty Genovese's death.

The murder of Kitty Genovese in 1964 was described in detail by Susan Brownmiller in her book on rape, *Against Our Will* (1975). Brownmiller was writing about known rapists who continued unchecked by police, and to her the 'event' symbolized something quite different from the inaction of bystanders:

> It comes as a surprise to most people that the murder of Kitty Genovese, stalked and stabbed to death shortly after 3 a.m. on a bleak commercial-residential street in Queens on March 13, 1964 – a much discussed case in the nineteen sixties because thirty-eight people heard the victim's cries or witnessed some part of her ordeal without calling the police – ended in her rape as she lay dying. Winston Moseley, Genovese's 29-year-old killer, later made an extraordinary confession. 'I just set out to find any girl that was unattended and I was going to kill her,' he calmly announced in court.
>
> (Brownmiller, 1975, p. 199)

Brownmiller, writing in the mid-1970s for a North American audience becoming increasingly vocal about violence towards women, called attention to the 'stubborn particulars' of gender implicated in this incident. By the 1980s, my thinking about this incident might be better expressed this way: violence was directed at yet another woman by a man and no one intervened to help her. What has changed over the years is the way I name the incident as well as the cultural framework in which the incident is reinterpreted.

In early accounts, only one onlooker was reported to have expressed a reluctance to intervene in what might have been a 'lovers' quarrel' (Rosenthal, 1964), thereby specifying something gendered about the meaning of the situation. In fact, what followed this incident at the time were the numerous experimental simulations of generalized bystander behaviour in emergency situations: hearing someone having an epileptic seizure and reporting it; reporting a room filling with smoke; coming to the aid of a woman in distress as she is heard to fall and apparently hurt herself. None of these simulations involved situations of attack.

However, all were excellent examples of how research can strip meaning from events at the creative phase of theorizing about the world. Sex/gender violence was excluded at the phase of abstracting hypotheses about social reality. The link to the Kitty Genovese incident was stripped of its original gendered particulars, that is, an *attack* on a woman was no longer an essential component in the laboratory exploration of what the event meant.

This is not surprising given that in 1964 we lived in a world that did not recognize by name the widespread abuse of women. Feminist movement throughout the 1970s 'enlarged our definition of violence to take in abuse of children, and the discussion of rape, spousal abuse, incest and pornography, clitorectomy'

(Apfelbaum and Lubek, 1983). The increasing momentum of the women's movement to confront violence in the 1970s allowed for a different framework for my understanding of the murder of Kitty Genovese. This shift in framework was part of a larger ongoing shift to view social psychology as an interpretive rather than predictive science. In my own training as an experimental social psychologist, I was urged to conceptualize my understanding of events in terms of 'variables' rather than 'persons'. I would more easily ask the question – 'Is sex of subject a significant variable in my multivariate analysis of helping behaviour?' than 'What is this about for people particularized with respect to their sex, race and class, namely those aspects of persons which form the material and psychological experience of the world?' I remember being trained to think that it is more elegant to strip questions of their social embeddedness, such that 'bystander behaviour' is considered scientifically purer than what you can learn from trying to make sense of the specifics of the murder/rape of a woman. However, my own experiences with the women's movement and my own feminist politicization prevented me from seeing this event exclusively within the framework of unresponsive bystander intervening behaviour. Rather, I found myself returning to view Genovese's murder first within the framework of sex/gender relationships and then within an even larger framework of multiple structures of powerlessness (sex, race, age and class) that play themselves out in our daily lives.

As my perspective shifted, I began to take more seriously the view of social psychology as a science that thrives within historical and cultural contexts and with that my views on experimentation were also altered. I found it difficult to believe that there were critical experiments rather than just historically important ones that foster a greater understanding of the world we live in. Social experiments are not crucial tests of the truth of competing hypotheses but reflect the experimenter's cultural knowledge by locating an appropriate social context for displaying that knowledge (Gergen, 1978). Given this approach, understanding and insight will be augmented by research that does not decontextualize social phenomena, but rather attempts to address the social context in which phenomena are located.

There were two such experimental studies in social psychology that I kept for a long time in a file folder marked 'these mean something'. The two studies were conceptual anomalies in the unresponsive bystander literature which later allowed me to see how social context informs hypothesis generation. The studies did not decontextualize the Genovese incident but rather viewed her plight as an aspect of generalized sex-role reactions to women under attack. In the first study Borofsky et al. (1971) conducted a role-playing experiment with male and female dyads where an attack was simulated. They found that none of six male observers tried to stop a man assaulting a woman while in other dyads, male helping was at a higher rate. Women were unlikely to intervene in any of the four role-played dyads, a finding that received no explanation. The researchers explained the male behaviour by the possible 'vicarious sexual and/or hostile gratification from seeing a man injure a woman' (Borofsky et al, 1971, p. 317). It was too early for this study to become an overnight classic spawning further research on the general question of unimpeded violence towards women.

A second study, by Shotland and Straw, appeared in 1976, at a time when feminist activism was becoming increasingly focused on collective intervention in the form of rape crisis centres and homes for battered wives run by women. The authors conducted a rather elaborate set of experiments to examine more carefully the Genovese attack as it occurred in its original context. In their study of staged assaults and reactions to these assaults they found that 'intervention occurred much more frequently when subjects perceived the attacker and victim as strangers (65%) rather than married (19%)' (Shotland and Straw, 1976, p. 992), and subjects were more likely to infer an intimate connection between the man and woman when they were unsure about the relationship. In the 1960s, bystander behaviour was the general phenomenon of which sex-paired dyads were a subcase. In the 1980s, gender-role expectations became the general phenomenon and bystander behaviour became a subcase.

Shotland and Straw ended their research by making a plea for knowing one's neighbours as a way of reducing faulty inferences and as a means of facilitating 'social control' in the community. They were operating on the assumption that violence (rape included) is largely a phenomenon between strangers, which we now know is not the case. They concluded: 'If we could obtain this control in terms of a man beating up a woman, we might be able to restrict the victimization of women to their husbands or close associates' (Shotland and Straw, 1976, p. 999), acknowledging in a footnote that 'If bystanders and, one would guess, society do not regard wife beating seriously, this act cannot be controlled' (Shotland and Straw, 1976, p. 999). It should be remembered that these authors were writing at a time when the extent of wife battering was not well documented, when a wife could not legally claim to have been raped and when violence against women was interpreted from the perspective of psychopathology of either the offender or the victim. Despite such limitations, the two studies managed to produce an experimental analogue for another interpretation of the original Kitty Genovese incident.

These two anomalous studies were not focused on bystander apathy or diffusion of responsibility as the major theoretical explanation but on the nature and perception of male–female relatedness. Despite all the training to see the world in gender-neutral terms, these two studies were early evidence that some researchers could not ignore what was going on around them, namely, an increasing awareness of the prevalence of violence towards women. A footnote in the Shotland and Straw study bears this out. Describing the social milieu on the campus on which the study was conducted in 1974, Shotland and Straw stated that 'approximately six to nine months prior to the experiment there were a number of assaults, on campus and in town, on women, of both a sexual and non-sexual nature. The attacks had caused much concern and a great deal of publicity' (Shotland and Straw, 1976, p. 991). These two studies form a bridge between understanding Genovese's murder in terms of the unresponsive bystander paradigm and understanding it in the context of changing sex/gender relations.

If theorizing is an historically situated activity, it becomes dangerous to canonize events and the research that follows as having one meaning for all time. Over the course of a decade, the 'Genovese incident' changed for me from being about the behavioural problem of bystanders failing to intervene in emergencies to being about the social problem of violence towards women. [...]

[...]

At some point, I began to reconsider that Genovese's murder, while an instance of violence towards women, had still broader implications. It signalled a growing expression of a community's sense of powerlessness to prevent violence. Increased reporting of attacks on women also seemed to indicate that some communities were more vulnerable than others, because of race and social class. I became curious to discover whether race or class were ever presented as part of the understanding of Genovese's murder. I turned back to the press coverage in the *New York Times* that covered the initial murder-rape and has continued to discuss it. I systematically traced each reference to Genovese and/ or Moseley in the *New York Times* from 1964 to 1988, including Letters to the Editor, editorial opinions and special comments in the *Times Supplement*. The original report of the murder of Catherine Genovese appeared on 14 March 1964, with the headline 'Queens woman is stabbed to death in front of home'. In the course of this analysis, the contexts of gender, race and class emerged at different points to provide an understanding of the event as part of a more complex picture of violence in American communities than could be revealed in laboratory studies of bystander intervention.

The story of the murder did not end with a brief one-column report but accelerated when an in-depth investigation revealed that thirty-eight onlookers (safe in the privacy of their own apartments) failed to intervene even by contacting the police. Rosenthal subsequently interviewed witnesses and other professionals, and he quite candidly described the race and class dimensions of victimization that affected the very way in which the story was constructed. He wrote in his book, *Thirty-Eight Witnesses*:

> The truth also is that if Miss Genovese had been killed on Park Avenue or Madison Avenue an assistant would have called the story to my attention, I would have assigned a top man and quite possibly we would have had a front-page story the next morning. If she had been a white woman killed in Harlem, the tension of the integration story would have provided her with a larger obituary. If she had been a Negro killed in Harlem she would have received a paragraph or two.
>
> (Rosenthal, 1964, p. 16)

We know about Catherine Genovese partly because she was a white woman killed in a predominantly middle-class neighbourhood, and no one intervened to help her. As for the assailant, Rosenthal wrote further that 'during the life of the story we received a few nasty letters demanding to know why we had "concealed" the fact that Moseley was Negro. The answer is really quite simple. Where the fact that a man is a Negro is directly relevant to the story we print the fact. Where it is not, we do not' (Rosenthal, 1964, pp. 18–19). In his testimony, Moseley indicated that he went out looking for 'any girl' and the *New York Times* coverage made little of his actions as racially motivated. More was made of how such a thing could have happened in a middle-class neighbourhood.

In all the social psychological experimentation that followed the focus shifted to the bystanders, away from the victim and the assailant. [...]

[...]

Indeed, this particular historical event will continue to raise questions about how we are to prevent violence towards women. However, if we stay too focused on violence towards women, we lose sight of other systemic factors that structure violence – poverty, race and class. While not absolving Moseley of his crime, we still need to understand the world that formed him in his 'early years in Detroit and Pittsburgh' in the 1930s and 1940s. Furthermore, the 'commitment to anti-sexist and anti-racist work' (Hooks, 1990, p. 64) requires that we are always looking at the political context of the crime despite our outrage at the victimizers. The daily experience of violence in people's lives is a story too easily decontextualized by social psychological theories that operate at the individual behavioural level. If we theorize at the level of community, then we begin to consider that some groups or communities are more vulnerable to violence than others and have been so historically. By understanding the overlap of racism, sexism and poverty, we can understand both the personal suffering and the political significance of any particular attack. Theorizing about the Genovese incident involves us in theorizing about the relative power or powerlessness of groups and communities to protect themselves from violence. This theme slowly emerged through the 1980s and was reflected in some of the later commentary on the Genovese murder.

Maureen Dowd, in a piece entitled '20 years after the murder of Kitty Genovese – the question remains: Why?', wrote that this murder 'crystallized what people were only beginning to feel about urban life in America: the anonymity, the lack of human contact, the feeling of not being able to control one's environment' (*NYT*, 12 March 1984). Indeed, the incident occurred before American national crime rates soared. Dowd reported on views put forward at a Catherine Genovese Memorial Conference at Fordham University marking the twentieth anniversary of Genovese's murder. In the opinion of a university administrator:

> Kitty Genovese died because we didn't have a sense of community. We're finally coming out of it now because people are tired of being afraid to walk on the streets or go in the subways.
>
> (Sexter, in Dowd *NYT*, 12 March 1984)

And of subsequent incidents, the conference was told by the then Surgeon General of the United States that they would decline:

> [W]hen people learn to care, when they accept the fact that there may be risks to caring, and when they agree to take those risks in order to preserve their place in the community.
>
> (Koop, in Dowd *NYT*, 12 March 1984)

The speaker claimed that risks are required to preserve 'community' but one wants to ask whose community will be preserved? Since 1964 several stories have been reported in the *New York Times* that were reminiscent of the Genovese incident. By the mid-1980s, a magazine editor, L.J. Davis, living nearby the scene of another woman's murder lamented that 'fights – violent, destructive fights, often accompanied by the display if not the use of murderous hardware – are roughly as common as trips to the post office. The wonder, therefore, is not that many people failed to summon the police; the wonder is that anybody bothered' (*NYT*, 19 December 1984); and that poorer communities were more vulnerable: 'everyone knows what happens when you lock a sane man up in a madhouse. ... Until we address the reality of the poor, they will remain locked in the same hermetic and unbroken cycle of rage, and sometimes they will kill each other' (*NYT*, 19 December 1984).

Rosenthal, whose accounts of the Genovese murder and the police's response to crime were cited earlier, wrote an article entitled 'The 39th witness' (*NYT*, 12 February 1987). He described his reaction to New York City's homeless, perhaps the most powerless community of all:

> I hoped that I would never be a silent witness. ... Almost every day of my life I see a body sprawled on the sidewalk. ... They do not scream, as did Catherine Genovese, but if they did I would probably walk even faster, because they are dirty, sometimes foul persons, a most unattractive and unsympathetic kind of victim. ... Sometimes I get very angry. ... Then, sometimes and more often recently, I think of Catherine Genovese and the way she died and the 38 witnesses. I check out a little book I wrote about the case then and find that I didn't really attack the 38 and wrote that any one of us might have done the

same. I am glad I was not too high and mighty about them because now I am the 39th. And whether you live in New York or any other city where living bodies lie in the streets or roam them in pain, and walk by, so are you.

(Rosenthal in NYT, 12 February 1987)

When we theorize about violence in communities, it is important to look at how understanding and experience are structured by the material conditions of poverty and systemic exclusion from power. Intervening or turning away are behaviours best understood in historical and cultural context. The circumstances of Genovese's murder that I originally understood in individual behavioural terms became, during the 1970s, an instance of the general failure to intervene in the prevention of violence towards women. Now I use that incident as a springboard to understand how whole communities can be seen as vulnerable to unchecked violence. I think it is the task of social psychology to theorize a socio-politics of intervention starting with increased knowledge of the long and complex history of non-intervention in instances of violence against powerless groups – women, the aged, children, racial minorities and the poor, among others.

References

Apfelbaum, E. and Lubek, I. (1983) 'Setting human violence into its historical and socio-psychological contexts', Paper given at Understanding Human Violence: An Interdisciplinary Conference on Violence in the Individual, The Portman Clinic, London, September.

Borofsky, G., Stollak, G. and Messe, L. (1971) 'Bystander reactions to physical assault: Sex differences in reactions to physical assault', *Journal of Experimental Social Psychology*, vol. 7, pp. 313–18.

Brownmiller, S. (1975) *Against Our Will: Men, Women and Rape*, New York, Simon and Schuster.

Cherry, F. (1983) 'Gender roles and sexual violence' in Allgeier, E.R. and McCormick, N. B. (eds) *Changing Boundaries: Gender Roles and Sexual Behavior*, Palo Alto, Ca., Mayfield Publishing.

Evans, R. (1980) *The Making of Social Psychology*, New York, Gardner Press.

Gergen, K. (1978) 'Toward generative theory', *Journal of Personality and Social Psychology*, vol. 36, pp. 1344–60.

Hooks, B. (1990) *Yearning: Race, Gender and Cultural Politics*, Toronto, Between the Lines.

Latané, B. and Darley, J.M. (1970) *The Unresponsive Bystander: Why Doesn't He Help?*, New York, Meredith.

Rosenthal, A.M. (1964) *Thirty-Eight Witnesses*, New York, McGraw-Hill.

Shotland, R.L. and Straw, M.K. (1976) 'Bystander response to an assault: when a man attacks a woman', *Journal of Personality and Social Psychology*, vol. 34, pp. 990–9.

(Cherry, 1995b, pp. 16–29)

Conclusion

The title of the chapter from which Reading 7.2 is taken, 'Kitty Genovese and culturally embedded theorizing', tells us that Cherry will be attending to the social context surrounding both Kitty's murder and its interpretation within psychological theory. She argues that bystander intervention research stripped Kitty Genovese's murder of vital aspects of the social and cultural context which can help us to understand both the crime and bystanders' responses to it. In Reading 7.2, Cherry points out that 'Kitty Genovese and her assailant, Winston Mosely, were living in a society at a time when its members did little to intervene in violence directed towards women'; one of the onlookers did not want to get involved in what they thought might have been a 'lover's quarrel'. Furthermore, she argues that 'in 1964 we lived in a world that did not recognize [...] the widespread abuse of women'. Challenging the myth that violence towards women is perpetrated by men who are strangers to them, she points out that such violence includes domestic abuse, incest and the rape of women by men who are familiar to them. At the time of Kitty's murder, it is likely that the police would have been reluctant to respond to calls for assistance in cases of domestic conflict.

Darley and Latané's experimental design incorporated some of the features of Kitty Genovese's murder: they staged an 'emergency' where there were several bystanders, and none of them were able to tell whether the others were taking action. But Cherry draws our attention to the fact that key features were not incorporated into most bystander intervention research. She points out that Kitty was not only murdered but also raped, a fact often omitted from accounts reproduced in many psychology text books, and so gender and power relations are surely important issues in understanding this event. But in Darley and Latané's experiment the 'victim' was always presented as male and the range of simulated emergencies they used throughout their series of experiments did not include a man attacking a woman, an essential feature of the original crime. Instead, this crime became seen as just one example of the broader psychological phenomenon of bystander apathy. The result is that one of the most important means of understanding this crime, in terms of gender and sexual relations, together with their prevailing societal norms, has been removed from our view, and replaced by a series of situational variables such as size of group. The meaning of both the emergency itself and bystanders' responses is thoroughly suffused with societal assumptions, norms and values. The meaning of, and explanation for, a person's behaviour is often only apparent when we see it in the context of shared cultural assumptions and social inequalities.

However, this is not to say that experiments are unable to recognise and take into consideration some of these sociocultural issues. Cherry cites later experimental evidence supporting the view that gender relations is the vital factor here rather than situational variables. Borofsky et al. (1971), using simulated attacks, found that men were less likely to intervene in an attack by a man on a woman than in any other gender combination of attacker/victim, and Shotland and Straw (1976) found that intervention was less likely when the attacker and victim were perceived as married rather than strangers.

Nevertheless, if our aim is to study those societal and cultural factors which form the context for social behaviour, then laboratory experiments are probably not the research tools of choice. This is why critical and feminist psychologists have argued for the use of qualitative methods such as ethnographic studies, depth interviews and narrative analysis, as these are more able to give researchers access to the meanings that events hold for us as individuals, communities and societies.

Why did the early bystander intervention research (including the paper by Darley and Latané that you have read) ignore what now seem to be important sociocultural issues surrounding Kitty Genovese's murder? Cherry's account suggests that the reason may have less to do with the experimental design (although, as she points out, this exerts a strong 'pull' towards framing questions in terms of situational variables) and more to do with the societal assumptions about gender, 'race' and other unquestioned inequalities that were embedded in US culture in the 1960s, assumptions that would be invisible especially to white, middle-class, male researchers. Cherry also points out that the murder of Kitty Genovese would probably have gone relatively unnoticed if the victim had not been a white woman living in a respectable, middle-class area, thus placing the event within an even broader context that goes beyond gender to include class, racial inequalities and poverty. She also makes salient the fact that the murderer was a black man – a fact that received no comment in most news reports. It is worth remembering that the mid-1960s was a period when anti-black racism was taken for granted in the USA and 'race riots' occurred in many southern states. It may well have been that the 'race' of the murderer was so unsurprising to the white, middle-class reporters that it needed no comment and even seemed irrelevant to their stories. Had he been white, they may have considered that this required comment. Bystander intervention is therefore an example of research where it seems vital to place the phenomenon in its social context of gender, class and race in order to understand it adequately.

But Cherry does not simply argue that one form of analysis (feminist) should be preferred over another (experimental). She suggests that a feminist reading of Kitty Genovese's murder, and therefore a feminism-informed research response, would not have been readily 'available' in the 1960s. In a reflexive account of the development of her own thinking, she admits that she herself found the 'diffusion of responsibility' theory persuasive as a student and that it was only when she later developed her feminist awareness that an alternative interpretation became possible for her. In this way, she challenges the objectivity of theory by illustrating how theory is always to some degree the product of its time and place; theories can therefore never be 'for all time'.

Cherry's account of bystander intervention therefore raises a number of important epistemological issues that have implications beyond this single area of research. The feminist critique of objectivity and experimentalism and the arguments for reflexivity are highlighted here, and it is worth taking the opportunity to examine the implications of these arguments in a little more depth. The concern with objectivity is characteristic of psychological research that is located within the predominant positivist epistemology. This concern is seen as reflecting a principally masculine preoccupation with a dispassionate detachment from the research material and from individual participants; instead of producing 'objectivity' it is argued that scientific language and experimental procedures serve only to mask the values and assumptive world of the researcher. Some feminist writers have argued instead for a 'standpoint epistemology' (for example, Henwood et al., 1998). This recommends that we are open and explicit about, literally, 'where we are coming from' in approaching the research since it is not humanly possible to have no perspective at all; the research questions that we see fit to ask are inevitably a product of our cultural and personal heritage. Harding (1991) additionally calls for what she terms 'strong objectivity'. This is the requirement that we systematically examine the background beliefs and assumptions that inevitably inform our research questions and findings, and is part of what feminist researchers today mean by 'reflexivity'.

However, if we pursue this line of thinking, we can see that there are as many potential ways of understanding or interpreting a phenomenon as there are 'standpoints' or people. Even the philosophical framework we choose for our research is just this – a choice. The purpose of reflexivity, then, becomes not only to ensure that the researcher takes account of and discusses the implications of their own social identities for the research process and findings, what Willig (2001) calls 'personal reflexivity' (Ussher, 2000 offers an example of a reflexive account, in this instance of her own position within critical psychology); it also enables them to reflect upon how the choice of theory and method has 'produced' a particular way of understanding the phenomenon ('epistemological reflexivity'). Willig (2001) helpfully provides an example of how to include reflexivity in a research report.

If we take seriously the idea of multiple standpoints and interpretations, we can no longer defend the idea that there can be only one true description of the world and the people in it, to be 'discovered' by objective observation (positivism). Our knowledge as social scientists becomes seen as a product of the questions we have chosen to ask and of the unique interaction between our own biography, that of our participants and the broader social and cultural context in which the research takes place. This argument for seeing knowledge as socially contingent and fluid rather than discoverable and fixed is a 'social constructionist' epistemology (see Burr, 2003) that contrasts with the realist epistemology of the experimental method.

The investigation of 'bystander intervention' has in recent times been abandoned in favour of a focus on 'helping' behaviours in general and altruism (for example, Batson, 1998) bringing with it a new range of theories. However, the methodological framework for investigating these has not changed significantly, and you are unlikely to find Cherry's critique cited in research reports. Nonetheless, critical and feminist psychologists have had some impact upon the discipline; they have helped to raise the profile of qualitative methods and of an epistemological focus on 'situated knowledges' and they have encouraged the investigation of a wide range of human experiences, including those of women and marginalized groups, that earlier might not have been regarded as worthy of study.

References

Armistead, N. (1974) *Reconstructing Social Psychology*, Harmondsworth, Penguin.

Batson, C.D. (1998) 'Altruism and prosocial behaviour' in Gilbert, D.T., Fiske, S.T. and Lindzey G. (eds) *The Handbook of Social Psychology* (4th edn), vol. 2, New York, McGraw-Hill.

Borofsky, G.L., Stollak, G.E. and Messe, L.A. (1971) 'Sex differences in bystander reactions to physical assault', *Journal of Experimental Social Psychology*, vol. 7, pp. 313–18.

Brown, P. (1973) *Radical Psychology*, London, Tavistock.

Burr, V. (2003) *Social Constructionism* (2nd edn), London, Routledge.

Cherry, F. (1995a) *The Stubborn Particulars of Social Psychology: Essays on the Research Process*, London, Routledge.

Cherry, F. (1995b) 'Kitty Genovese and culturally embedded theorizing' in Cherry (1995a).

Darley, J.M. and Latané, B. (1968) 'Bystander intervention in emergencies: Diffusion of responsibility', *Journal of Personality and Social Psychology*, vol. 3, no. 4, p. 377–83.

Fox, D. and Prilleltensky, I. (eds) (1997) *Critical Psychology: An Introduction*, London, Sage.

Gough, B. and McFadden. M. (2001) *Critical Social Psychology: An Introduction*, Basingstoke, Palgrave.

Haraway, D.J. (1998) 'Situated knowledges: The science question in feminism and the privilege of partial perspective', *Feminist Studies*, vol. 14, no. 3, pp. 575–97.

Harding, S. (1991) *Whose Science? Whose Knowledge? Thinking from Women's Lives*, Buckingham, Open University Press.

Harré, R. and Secord, P.F. (1972) *The Explanation of Social Behaviour*, Oxford, Basil Blackwell.

Henwood, K., Griffen, C. and Phoenix, A. (1998) *Standpoints and Differences: Essays in the Practice of Feminist Psychology*, London, Sage.

Hepburn, A. (2003) *An Introduction to Critical Social Psychology*, London, Sage.

Hollway, W. (2006) *Social Psychology Matters*, Maidenhead, Open University Press/Milton Keynes, the Open University.

Howitt, D. (1991) *Concerning Psychology: Psychology Applied to Social Issues*, Milton Keynes, Open University Press.

Jones, D. and Elcock, J. (2001) *History and Theories of Psychology: A Critical Perspective*, London, Arnold.

Shotland, R.L. and Straw, M.K. (1976) 'Bystander response to an assault: When a man attacks a woman', *Journal of Personality and Social Psychology*, vol. 34, pp. 990–9.

Sloan, T. (ed.) (2000) *Critical Psychology: Voices for Change*, Basingstoke, Macmillan Press.

Smith, J.A., Harré, R. and Van Langenhove, L. (eds) (1995a) *Rethinking Psychology*, London, Sage.

Smith, J.A., Harré, R. and Van Langenhove, L. (eds) (1995b) *Rethinking Methods in Psychology*, London, Sage.

Stanley, L. and Wise, S. (1983) *Breaking Out: Feminist Consciousness and Feminist Research*, London, Routledge and Keegan Paul.

Tuffin, K. (2005) *Understanding Critical Social Psychology*, London, Sage.

Ussher, J. (2000) 'Critical psychology in the mainstream: A struggle for survival' in Sloan (ed.) (2000).

Willig, C. (2001) *Introducing Qualitative Research in Psychology: Adventures in Theory and Method*, Buckingham, Open University Press.

Further reading

Howitt, D. (1991) *Concerning Psychology: Psychology Applied to Social Issues*, Milton Keynes, Open University Press.
This book takes psychology to task for its failure to make a meaningful contribution to our understanding of many social problems.

Stainton-Rogers, W. (2003) *Social Psychology: Experimental and Critical Approaches*, Buckingham, Open University Press.
This book contrasts experimental social psychology with a critical approach based in a social constructionist epistemology.

Tuffin, K. (2004) *Introduction to Critical Social Psychology*, London, Sage.
This book focuses particularly upon discursive psychology as a 'critical' perspective, but the first two chapters provide a good discussion of more general methodological issues.

Willig, C. (2001) *Introducing Qualitative Research in Psychology: Adventures in Theory and Method*, Buckingham, Open University Press.
A very readable book covering a range of qualitative methods. The first chapter orients the reader to important methodological debates and sources of critique.

Chapter 8

Individual differences

by Trevor Butt, University of Huddersfield

Introduction

When we open any standard psychology textbook, we find the territory
already mapped out for us. Cognitive, developmental, social and biological
psychology: all appear as separate domains. The British psychologist Don
Bannister said that we should always remind ourselves that this is a theoretical
construction and not a God-given set of facts. It is simply one way of
arranging things that could have been put together differently. We too readily
think that knowledge is discovered, but it is constructed as well as discovered
– what we think of as facts are made as well as found. Patterns of behaviour
do not lie around waiting to be picked up, they are only visible within the
searchlight of a particular theory. In this chapter, we will consider one aspect
of what has come to be called 'the psychology of individual differences':
theories of personality. We will see that there are various alternative
constructions of personality, each with its own strengths and weaknesses. We
will focus on two theoretical perspectives that illustrate sharply contrasting
approaches to issues of personality. Firstly, we will examine Hans Eysenck's
trait theory, through an extract from an original piece by Eysenck and
Rachman (1965). This reading is concerned with the description and
classification of personality in relation to neurotic disorders. Then we will look
at George Kelly's personal construct theory. This will be presented through an
extract from Salmon (2003), a proponent of Kelly's work, who has further
developed some of Kelly's ideas with particular reference to teaching and
learning.

Theories of personality developed in three separable but related strands in
psychology a century ago. These are known as the clinical, psychometric and
experimental traditions. In their different ways, they are all concerned with
trying to explain individual differences in behaviour – why it is that people act
so differently in what appear to be similar situations. It is no coincidence that
most theories of personality emerged from clinical practice. Freud, Jung,
Rogers, Kelly and Mischel were all clinicians for whom the problems of
personality came alive in the process of psychotherapy. What registers as
stressful stimuli, the different ways in which people respond to them, and the
strategies that might be used to overcome what Freud referred to in his
Introductory Lectures on Psycho-Analysis as 'neurotic misery' (Freud, 1963),
all vary from one person to another. What person A sees as a threat counts

only as a challenge to person B. While person C becomes depressed and anxious, person D develops headaches and stomach upsets. Person E finds she can usually talk herself round when she becomes anxious, but this rarely works for person F, who manages best by burying himself in work.

Personality theory flourished in tandem with the development of psychometric assessment, which tries to plot individual differences in terms of variables of cognitive ability and IQ. In personality assessment, however, it is traits that are supposedly measured. Traits have been defined as relatively enduring ways in which one individual differs from another. Cattell has contended that sixteen basic personality traits are needed to describe people adequately. Others have argued for two, three or five more superordinate and abstract dimensions. But these approaches agree that the explanation of any consistency in behaviour should take the form of placing the individual with respect to a number of trait dimensions that are thought to underpin behaviour.

The experimental tradition in psychology is undoubtedly the dominant one in academia generally. It began with behaviourism and extends to contemporary cognitive psychology. Skinner's (1974) radical behaviourism held that if we want to change people as the clinicians do, then we should aim to change their environments, not mythical inner states or traits. In his view, traits are descriptions of behaviour masquerading as explanations for it. If we say someone is aggressive, this might adequately describe their behaviour, but it does not explain it. For explanation we must look to how the environment has reinforced this behaviour. Responding to the fine grain of discriminative stimuli, each person brings to bear their reinforcement history. Skinner therefore engaged with the issues covered by personality theories, but strongly denied any internal mental factors of personality that determined individual differences. It was this experimental tradition that Mischel (1968) drew on in his critique of the 'trait and state' theories of psychometricians and clinicians. But, in contrast to Skinner, he also drew on the advances in cognitive psychology to create social learning theory, in which the environment is seen not as determining behaviour, but regulating it through the medium of an individual's cognitive schema.

Of the variants of trait theory, Eysenck's version is perhaps the boldest and most comprehensive in its range of application. Eysenck was concerned with the clinical application of his theory. He saw the science of personality as clarifying and sharpening the discredited psychiatric classification system. This attempted to categorise people, but never really succeeded in explaining why individuals suffered from different psychological disorders. His early work (Eysenck, 1947) focused on the ways in which soldiers broke down due to stress in battle. This was approached in terms of two orthogonal (that is, unrelated) dimensions: extraversion and neuroticism. While other trait theorists hope to establish a biological basis of behaviour, Eysenck claimed to have discovered the nature of this link forty years ago. He argues that both extraversion and neuroticism are behavioural expressions of differences in biologically-based temperament: these two dimensions are grounded in differences in cortical and autonomic arousal respectively. He suggests that the relationship between behavioural patterns and innate inherited brain structure is that of a phenotype and genotype in biology. In other words, what appears on the surface reflects causal factors at a neurological level. We see this critique elaborated in Reading 8.1.

One of the strengths of trait theories is that they are firmly grounded in the way people assess each other's personality in everyday life. There appears to be evidence here that people find a clear pragmatic value in assigning traits. If someone asks you to describe a friend, you are likely to find yourself talking in terms of dispositions – reliable, dependable, honest and conscientious, for example. There is a clear implication of consistency in behaviour. You are claiming that they are likely to be reliable with others, just as they have been with you. Furthermore, there is an implication of comparison with others. It is as though you are saying 'this person is more reliable than most'. We have here the definition of a trait – an enduring way in which one individual differs from another. It can be argued that people have always seen others in terms of personality types. Eysenck and Rachman show, in Reading 8.1, how the Ancient Greek typology can be reinterpreted with the help of the factor analysis that is available to contemporary trait theorists. It underlines Eysenck's case for the biological basis of personality and illustrates how such a typology transcends time and culture. The description of the types reflects accurate observation of people, even though the archaic explanation in terms of body humours can now seem nonsensical. While types, like psychiatric classifications, are discontinuous categories, traits are normally distributed in the population. Eysenck's case is that his is a scientific approach to personality that makes sense of a simplistic but compelling tendency to ascribe types. It does not attempt to capture the uniqueness of the individual; that is not the job of personality theory. A person's score on extraversion and neuroticism only indicates how he or she is likely to react in certain situations, much as in physics, a coefficient of elasticity or boiling point helps us predict the behaviour of a material under some sort of stress.

ACTIVITY 8.1

As you read the following extract, consider these points:

- What is Eysenck and Rachman's main objection to behaviourism?
- What assumptions do Eysenck and Rachman make about psychology and its purposes?
- What methodology do they consider appropriate for psychological research?
- What is the difference between 'categorical' and 'dimensional' systems?

Reading 8.1 is taken from a 1965 book, *Causes and Cures of Neurosis,* by Hans Eysenck and Stanley Rachman that relates trait theory to the causes and cures of neurosis.

'Dimensions of personality'

[...] In this Chapter we are proposing to introduce the concept of personality, and it will immediately be obvious that here we are departing, to some extent at least, from orthodox behaviourism. Most writers of that school adopt the position that the very notion of personality is unnecessary; considering that all learning proceeds on the orthodox principles of stimulus–response connection formation, they argue that personality, if the term is to be used at all, will simply correspond with the sum total of the person's behaviour. As Watson (1930) once put it quite clearly, personality 'is the sum of activities that can be discovered by actual observation for a long enough period of time to give reliable information.' For many behaviourists, therefore, there is no room for personality in a natural science type of psychology.

However, it is becoming more and more widely recognized that between stimulus and response interposes an organism, and the formula S-O-R [stimulus-organism-response] has pretty well superseded the old S-R [stimulus-response] paradigm. The recognition of the existence of an organism intervening between stimulus and response is made necessary by the very simple fact that identical stimuli applied to different organisms frequently lead to different responses, and even identical stimuli applied to the same organism do not always lead to similar responses. There are two possible causes for this, both involving the concept of an intervening organism. In the first place, individual organisms may differ with respect to their past reinforcement schedules; on this hypothesis, we are simply saying that past learning determines in part the reactions which we now make to different types of stimuli. There is nothing very novel in this, of course, and even commonsense recognizes the importance of past learning in present activities. However, the fact that this is so is incompatible with a simple-minded application of the principles of stimulus-response psychology. Equally interesting and important, and perhaps less widely recognized nowadays, is the fact that individual organisms differ innately with respect to many variables which may determine the responses to certain classes of stimuli. It is perhaps a little unfashionable to stress the importance of innate hereditary factors in behaviour, but the evidence regarding their importance is quite conclusive. [...] let us simply note that the organism is an absolutely essential part of any stimulus-response type of psychology, because it is the organism which intervenes between the stimulus and the response, and organisms differ, both with respect to past reinforcement schedules and also with respect to innate potentiality and other variables.

Assuming, then, for the moment that the concept of personality may have some scientific value, we may go on to search for the main dimensions of personality in the hope that these may be related to different types of neurotic behaviour [...]. We may also hope that the discovery of these main dimensions of personality will help us in the problem of *nosology*, or classification of neurotic disorders. Classification is an absolutely fundamental part of the scientific study of human personality; a satisfactory typology is as necessary in psychology as was Mendeleyeff's Table of the Elements in physics. This has, of course, always been recognized by psychologists, and almost everyone is acquainted with the famous typological classification into melancholics, cholerics, sanguines, and phlegmatics dating back to Galen and even earlier. As this system still has much to teach us, we will present it here as Figure 1; it immediately confronts us with one of the main problems of classification. The first of these may be phrased in terms of the question: 'Categorical or dimensional?' The famous German philosopher, Immanuel Kant, to whom this system owed much of its popularity during the last two hundred years, was quite specific in maintaining the categorical point of view, i.e. the notion that every person could be assigned to a particular category; he was a melancholic, or a phlegmatic, or a sanguine, or a choleric, but any mixtures of admixtures were inadmissible.

This notion of categories is, of course similar to the psychiatric notion of disease entities and their corresponding diagnoses; hysteria, anxiety state, paranoia, obsessional illness, and so on are often treated as categorical entities in this sense.

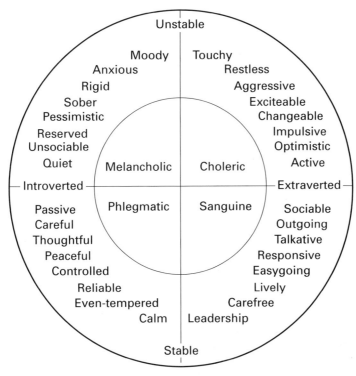

Figure 1   The inner ring shows the 'four temperaments' of Hippocrates and Galen; the outer ring shows the results of modern factor analytic studies of the intercorrelations between traits by Guilford, Cattell, Eysenck and others (Eysenck, 1963).

Opposed to this notion, we have the view that any particular position in this two-dimensional framework is due to a combination of quantitative variations along the two continua labelled 'introversion-extraversion' and 'stable-unstable'. Wundt (1903), who is the most notable proponent of Galen's system in modern times, favoured the dimensional view; he labelled the one axis 'slow-quick' instead of introversion-extraversion, and the other 'strong-weak' instead of unstable and stable.

It may be interesting to quote Wundt's very modern-sounding discussion:– 'The ancient differentiation into four temperaments ... arose from acute psychological observation of individual differences between people ... The fourfold division can be justified if we agree to postulate two principles in the individual reactivity of the affects: one of them refers to the *strength*, the other to the *speed of change* of a person's feelings. Cholerics and melancholics are inclined to strong affects, while sanguinists and phlegmatics are characterized by weak ones. A high rate of change is found in sanguinists and cholerics, a slow rate in melancholics and phlegmatics.

It is well-known that the strong temperaments ... are predestined towards the *Unluststimmungen*, while the weak ones show a happier ability to enjoy life ... The two quickly changeable temperaments ... are more susceptible to the impressions of the present; their mobility makes them respond to each new idea. The two slower temperaments, on the other hand, are more concerned with the future; failing to respond to each chance impression, they take time to pursue their own ideas.' (pp. 637–638).

There is no reason to believe that the notion of the *typology* presupposes a categorical system; both Jung and Kretschmer, who were probably the best-known typologists of the inter-war period, postulated a dimensional rather than a categorical system. The widespread notion that typologies implied discontinuities, bimodal distributions, and the like does not accurately represent the writings and views of modern typologists (Eysenck, 1960).

Most writers on the subject of personality come down in favour of either the categorical or the dimensional point of view, without basing themselves on any experimental demonstration. It is, however, not impossible to devise experimental and statistical means for verifying the one and falsifying the other hypothesis. Eysenck (1950) has tried to do this in terms of the method of *criterion analysis*, which relies on separate factor analyses of intercorrelations between tests administered to two or more criterion groups (say, normals and psychotics), and a comparison of the factors emerging with the criterion column derived by biserial correlation between the tests and the criterion. The results of this method have, in every instance, supported the doctrine of continuity, and failed to support the doctrine of categorization, even when the latter seemed most firmly entrenched, as in the case of psychosis (Eysenck, 1952).

Assuming for the moment, therefore, the doctrine of dimensionality, we are required to build up, on an experimental and statistical basis, a quantitative system of personality description (Eysenck, Eysenck and Claridge, 1960). The most widely used tool for this purpose is, of course, factor analysis, and the main results of the application of this tool are shown in Figure 1. The outer ring in this Figure shows the results of a large number of factor analytic studies of questionnaires and ratings (Eysenck, 1960). As is customary in these diagrams, the correlation between any two traits is equal to their scalar product, that is to say, in this case, the cosine of their angle of separation. The closer the two traits are together in the diagram, the higher is the observed correlation between them; the further apart are any two traits in this diagram, the lower is the correlation. If the angle between them exceeds ninety degrees, the correlation becomes negative.

Factor analysis has often been criticized on the grounds that different practitioners achieve different results, and that a method which is unreliable in the sense of failing to produce agreed results cannot be taken very seriously. Whatever may have been true twenty or thirty years ago, there can be no doubt that nowadays there is comparatively little disagreement between investigators in this field. [...] The agreement present nowadays is indeed impressive, and if failure to agree could be used as a criticism of the method of factor analysis, then the almost universal agreement existing at the present time can perhaps rightly be claimed as strong support for the usefulness of the statistical method in question.

Terms such as extraversion and introversion are used in our discussion in a sense strictly derived from empirical studies [...]; they should not be taken as having the same meaning here as they do in Jung's discussion. Jung, who is often erroneously credited with originating these terms which had been in use on the continent of Europe for several hundred years before he wrote his famous book on psychological types, has put forward a very complicated scheme of personality description; there would be no point in criticizing his scheme here. We merely wish to point out that our own use of these terms must stand and fall by empirical confirmation, and owes more to the work of factor analysts and early experimentalists like Heymans and Wiersma, than to Jung and his followers (Eysenck, 1960). A brief description of typical extreme extraverts and introverts may be useful at this point, to show the reader precisely what we mean by these terms.

The typical extravert is sociable, likes parties, has many friends, needs to have people to talk to, and does not like reading or studying by himself. He craves excitement, takes chances, often sticks his neck out, acts on the spur of the moment, and is generally an impulsive individual. He is fond of practical jokes, always has a ready answer, and generally likes change; he is carefree, easygoing, optimistic, and 'likes to laugh and be merry'. He prefers to keep moving and doing things, tends to be aggressive and loses his temper quickly; altogether his feelings are not kept under tight control, and he is not always a reliable person.

The typical introvert is a quiet, retiring sort of person, introspective, fond of books rather than people; he is reserved and distant except to intimate friends. He tends to plan ahead, 'looks before he leaps', and mistrusts the impulse of the moment. He does not like excitement, takes matters of everyday life with proper seriousness, and likes a well-ordered mode of life. He keeps his feelings under close control, seldom behaves in an aggressive manner, and does not lose his temper easily. He is reliable, somewhat pessimistic and places great value on ethical standards.

These descriptions, of course, sound almost like caricatures because they describe, as it were, the 'perfect' extravert and the 'perfect' introvert; needless to say, few people closely resemble these extremes, and the majority of people undoubtedly are somewhat in the middle. This does not necessarily detract from the importance of these typological concepts, just as little as the fact that 50 per cent of the total population have I.Qs of between 90 and 110 detracts from the importance of intelligence as a concept in psychology.

It is perhaps less necessary to give a detailed description of the typology implicit in the second major dimension of personality shown in [Figure 1]. We have there labelled the one end 'unstable'; this has often in the past been called a factor of *emotionality* or of *neuroticism*, and these terms adequately designate its meaning. At the one end we have people whose emotions are labile, strong, and easily aroused; they are moody, touchy, anxious, restless, and so forth. At the other extreme we have the people whose emotions are stable, less easily aroused, people who are calm, even-tempered, carefree, and reliable. Neurotics, needless to say, would be expected to have characteristics typical of the unstable type, normal persons typical of the stable type.

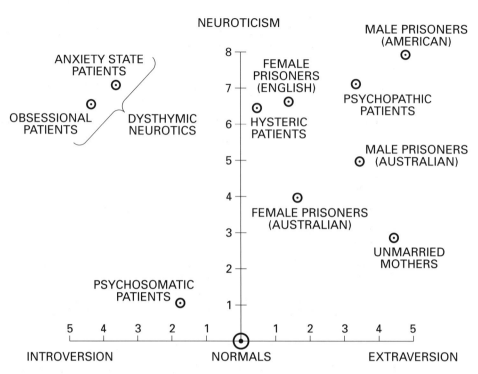

Figure 2   Position of various neurotic and criminal groups on the two factors of
             neuroticism and introversion-extraversion (Eysenck, 1964).

If we accept the principle of continuity, then we should be able to find a place for
the major psychiatric classifications of neurotic disorders within our [Figure 1].
The theory has been put forward that dysthymic neurotics suffering from anxiety,
reactive depression, obsessions, phobias, and so on would be found in the
'melancholic' quadrant, while hysterics, psychopaths, and perhaps juvenile
delinquents and criminals generally, would be found in the 'choleric' quadrant
(Eysenck, 1960). Descriptively, there seems little doubt about the truth of this
hypothesis; it is only necessary to look at the traits characterizing people in
these two quadrants to realize that they might almost have been quoted from a
psychiatric text-book, rather than being the result of factor analytic studies of
normal people. Nevertheless, experimental support would seem to be required.
Figure 2 shows the relative positions of different groups of neurotics and
criminals, with respect to scores on various questionnaires of extraversion and
neuroticism; the scales most frequently used in these studies have been the
Maudsley Personality Inventory (Eysenck, 1959), the Cattell Personality
Inventory (Cattell, 1957), and the Eysenck Personality Inventory (Eysenck and
Eysenck, 1963). To make scores comparable, these have been turned into
standard scores before plotting them in [Figure 2]. It will be seen that indeed, as
expected, patients suffering from anxiety, obsessional disorders, phobias, and
so on, i.e. patients who have been called dysthymic by Eysenck (1947), do
indeed fall into the melancholic quadrant and are strongly introverted, whereas
psychopaths and criminals generally tend to fall into the choleric quadrant and
be strongly extravert. Hysterics fall in between these two groups and are not
significantly differentiated from normals with respect to extraversion-introversion,
although they do, of course, have high scores on neuroticism. [...]

References

Cattell, R.B. (1957) *The Sixteen Personality Factor Questionnaire*, Champaign, IL, Institute for Personality and Ability Testing.

Eysenck, H.J. (1947) *Dimensions of Personality*, London, Routledge, Kegan Paul.

Eysenck, H.J. (1950) 'Criterion analysis – an application of the hypothetico-deductive method to factor analysis', *Psychological Review*, vol. 57, pp. 38–53, 17.

Eysenck, H.J. (1952) *The Scientific Study of Personality*, London, Routledge, Kegan Paul.

Eysenck, H.J. (1959) *The Maudsley Personality Inventory*, London, University of London Press/San Diego, 1962, Educ. & Indust. Testing Service.

Eysenck, H.J. (1960) *The Structure of Human Personality*, New York, Macmillan/London, Methuen.

Eysenck, H.J. (1963) 'Biological basis of personality', *Nature*, vol. 199, pp. 1031–34.

Eysenck, H.J. (1964) *Crime and Personality*, London, Routledge, Kegan Paul/Boston, Houghton Mifflin.

Eysenck, H.J. and Eysenck, S.B.G. (1963) *The Eysenck Personality Inventory*, London, University of London Press/San Diego, Educ. & Indust. Testing Service.

Eysenck, S.B.G., Eysenck, H.J. and Claridge, G. (1960) 'Dimensions of personality, psychiatric syndromes and mathematical models', *Journal of Mental Science*, vol. 106, pp. 581–9, 18, 23, 43.

Watson, J.B. (1930) *Behaviourism*, London, Kegan Paul.

Wundt, W. (1903) *Grundzuge der Physiologischen Psychologie* (5th edn), Leipzig, W. Englemann, vol. 3, no. 17.

(Eysenck and Rachman, 1965, pp. 14–21)

Commentary

We have noted that an apparent strength of trait theory is that it builds on everyday language use that gives it credibility. It uses objective measurements – personality inventories – that are derived from extensive samples of people attributing dispositions to others. But as Walter Mischel (1968) observes, the claim of a consistent and stable personality structure rests on the assumption that this represents the organisation of attributes in the ratees. Mischel goes on to argue that this assumption is in fact not justified. He cites extensive evidence that, instead, the attribution of dispositions reflects the perceptual prejudices of raters, who draw on a culturally shared trait theory to frame their observations. So, traits are not a property of people being rated, but of those doing the rating. Like beauty, traits are in the eye of the beholder. The traits that we think we find in others represent our personal construction of them. One study Mischel cited found that raters produced the same stable trait structure in people that they observed very briefly and did not know as in those that they knew well. This can only be the result of 'reading in' attributes on the flimsiest of evidence. As Chapter 4 demonstrates, people readily commit the fundamental attribution error – attributing dispositions or traits to others when this is not justified. Yet the personality questionnaires that form the basis of Eysenck's and others' trait theories are constructed from factor analytical studies that are based on this error. What seems at first glance like a strength in trait theories is transformed into a flaw.

Mischel argues that what we get from a person's own personality questionnaire is not an objective account of their behaviour, but an impression – in effect, a theory about themselves. As a respondent, you might be asked if you often have headaches, like going to parties or worry about the future. You are asked to work quickly, giving impressions rather than consulting behavioural referents for your choices. Now 'often' might mean 20 per cent of the time to me and 50 per cent of the time to you, but what gets recorded is respondents' impressions of themselves. I might tick 'Yes' to the same question that you tick 'No' to, even though you might have more headaches than me. Each question is loaded in one of the factors on which the instrument is constructed, and contributes to their score on it. These factors, as we have seen, are in turn contaminated by the fundamental attribution error. Now this does not mean that this output is meaningless. But it indicates that it tells us something about the way we perceive things and not about the existence of a trait structure that is responsible for conduct. Kelly sums this up very nicely:

> ... when I say that Professor Lindzey's left shoe is an 'introvert' everyone looks at his shoe as though this were something his shoe was responsible for. Or if I say that Professor Cattell's head is 'discursive' everyone looks over at him, as though the proposition had popped out of his head instead of mine. Don't look at his head! Don't look at that shoe! Look at me! I'm the one responsible for the statement. After you figure out what I mean you can look over there to see if you can make any sense out of shoes and heads by construing them the way I do.
>
> (Kelly, 1969, p. 72)

If we are interested in a person's theory about him- or herself, Mischel suggests that we use a procedure that is specifically designed to do just this. Mischel himself was a student of Kelly, and in this context frequently recommends both Kelly's clinical wisdom and his methods. Kelly's (1955) personal construct theory has a very different approach to personality from that of Eysenck and the other trait theorists. It is a form of phenomenology (Butt, 2004) that focuses on how things (and, particularly, other people) appear different to each individual. Each person is seen as developing a system of personal constructions of the world which is based on individual experience, and is essential in making sense of and acting in the world. Tom might see Liz as too quiet and a bit depressed. But this will be only one possible construction of her. Chris might see her as thoughtful and reflective. The traits Chris and Tom use may tell us more about them than about Liz; it is they who construe her behaviour and make sense of it in their own terms.

We can see, here, the clinical interest in a personality theory. 'Individual differences' here is about appreciating different world-views. How different individuals score on normally distributed dimensions supplied by an experimenter is of no interest. From Kelly's point of view, understanding, or putting ourselves in the position of others, is an essential step in helping them to change. As Phillida Salmon says in the final extract for this chapter, Reading 8.2, people cannot be expected to revise their construing at will. After all, a lot is at stake here. Each of us has a great deal invested in our constructions; they do not represent some detached and idle intellectual exercise. Salmon focuses on learning in the classroom, but emphasises that learning in any context requires change and is often problematic. It is not a matter of mechanistically grafting new learning on to old. It is about incorporating what we encounter into an existing system of sense-making. We might very well resist change that we apparently want when we cannot assimilate it into our existing construct system. For example, Jim may want to become more assertive, but will have difficulty in achieving this if assertive behaviour is construed by him as 'pushy', and he views himself as anything but a pushy individual.

Kelly's theory has generated a wide range of strategies for assessing personal constructions. Each one attempts to help the person articulate and express meanings that are normally beyond their reach. This is not to say that they are 'unconscious' in the psychodynamic sense of the term. It is not that they are consigned to an unconscious realm because of their disturbing quality. But much construing is pre-verbal; it goes on without us having to spell out exactly what we are doing. Kelly (1955) suggested a variety of possible strategies: the self-characterisation sketch, the role construct repertory test and the repertory grid. In Reading 8.2, Salmon describes her own development of the 'Salmon Line'.

ACTIVITY 8.2

As you read the following extract, consider these points:

- What are the features of the 'market model of education' which Salmon criticises? What are its underlying assumptions about the nature of the person and the way that people learn?

- How does personal construct psychology contrast with this?

- For what purpose was the 'Salmon Line' developed? How does it resemble Kelly's repertory grid technique? How does it differ?

Reading 8.2, by Phillida Salmon, is a discussion of personal construct psychology applied to education, learning and personal change.

READING 8.2

'A psychology for teachers'

For teachers working now in British schools at the beginning of the twenty-first century, the current educational *zeitgeist* carries little inspiration. Within a market model of education, teaching is viewed as no more than the simple delivery of a commodity: the pre-packaged bits of information that supposedly make up the school curriculum. The capacity of learners to absorb and reproduce this information in tests and examinations is the criterion of educational success. In today's society the function of the schooling system is to classify and grade its pupil intake. Through this grading young people will emerge with very different credentials: some with enhanced, others with diminished, life chances. Nor is it only pupils who are subject to classification within a hierarchy of competence. Even schools themselves must now compete with one another. Superior league tables boost pupil numbers; qualifying for specialist status brings extra money and more resources. The same competitive principle is also applied to teachers. Judgements of individual teachers as 'incompetent' or 'super' carry their own financial and career consequences.

This is a philosophy which reduces the complex processes of learning, teaching and knowing to the status of objects. Its picture of education is a picture of fixed and static entities which retain their identical character across the whole spectrum of widely different classrooms, of the huge variety of individual pupils and individual teachers. Processes in which everything is fluid and subject to varying personal meaning become simple products, predefined and easily measurable.

Current educational philosophy thus rests on a hierarchical model. All pupils are placed, through their various test performances, at some point on a scale of competence: a point which marks the fixed limits of their ability, a point beyond which they cannot go. On the assumption that learning ability is generalized and statistically distributed, young people become defined as good, average or poor learners, and learning is something that some people do well and other people do badly.

A personal construct theory alternative

In its vision of education, personal construct psychology stands in the greatest possible contrast to the current British philosophy. It is a psychology of processes, not products, of verbs rather than nouns. It sees learning, not as the reproduction of a ready-made information pack, but as the shifting of meanings within an essentially personal system of understandings. Teaching appears, in a Kellyian perspective, as the struggle to exchange understandings, to enlarge mutual comprehension between persons who may have widely different world views. 'Knowledge', far from being a standardized, externally defined entity, becomes something temporary and open to change. [...] the 'reality' status accorded to generally held assumptions cannot stand with a position which recognizes multiple realities, and the essentially provisional nature of what is known. Seen in this light, the school curriculum looks very different.

In a Kellyian perspective, a hierarchy of learning ability makes no sense. Learning, in this philosophy, is synonymous with living itself. As human beings we are all lifelong learners. While we differ hugely in what we come to know, each of us strives, in day-to-day encounters with our worlds, to understand the way things are. And for all of us, living cannot but entail experiencing what we did not anticipate. Wholly unexpected events, personal predicaments and dilemmas, the same mistake made yet again: these contingencies demand that we reflect in fundamental ways – rethink, if we can, some of our most basic assumptions. As Kelly himself vividly documented within psychotherapy, such change is seldom easy. Where our most basic sense of ourselves and our worlds seems to be at risk, we typically close ourselves off to the threat of reconstruing. Though there may be areas where new understandings seem viable, even exciting, there are others where change is strenuously resisted. Different circumstances elicit variable learning competence: we are all adept at some kinds of learning, deeply closed, even personally hostile, towards others.

If some ways of making sense seem congenial, while others appear threatening, this is because the material of learning is seldom neutral. [...] how we see things at any moment is a function of a whole system of intuitive meanings – meanings which sustain the personal projects that are our lives. Young people do not abandon their own personal projects when they enter the classroom. They bring with them their own worlds, and their personal identities within those worlds. It is in relation to that sense of themselves and their personal contexts that they hear their teachers. To a few perhaps, the material offered seems immediately interesting; it confirms the way they see things, and carries exciting possibilities for further exploration. But for others – probably many others – this classroom material may seem irrelevant, bypassing what they value, seemingly having nothing to do with them, even implicitly challenging their own deepest concerns.

Learning by inquiry

Teachers themselves are generally all too well aware of the different personal, social and cultural worlds, the multiple realities sitting side by side at classroom desks. Knowing the sense of irrelevance, even alienation, that the school curriculum can arouse, they strive to engage with pupils' personal meanings, to relate at least something of the curricular material to the urgent business of these young people's lives. The officially prescribed content to be presented in classroom work may seem to offer answers to questions that pupils seldom ask. Helping learners to achieve 'really useful knowledge' is no easy task: it stands a mile away from the facile depiction of teaching as a simple delivery of ready-made information packages.

As Kelly insisted, we all learn by asking questions. It is only by putting our uncertainties to the test – trying out the viability of our hunches, translating possibilities into actuality – that we discover something about the way things are. Of course the outcome of one enquiry typically leads to other uncertainties, and the need for further question-asking. The human quest, in Kellyian philosophy, is ongoing and lifelong. But no knowledge is ever achieved without active efforts to test out possibilities. Whereas the dominant model of learning in British schools accords pupils an essentially passive role, this philosophy demands an active participation from young people in the classroom.

A Kellyian vision of learning sees learners as necessarily being active and possessing initiative. Understandings cannot be reached through simple receptivity; pupils need to be active, argumentative, challenging. It is, as Michael Billig (1987) has tellingly shown, only through the to-and-fro of interpersonal debate that we become able to reason inwardly. Expressing personal ideas out loud, directly challenging another's opinion, playing devil's advocate: from these externalized modes come capacities to internalize – to argue with ourselves, to try out possibilities inwardly, to conduct an inner debate. This is what thinking essentially entails. And thinking, so fundamental to new understandings, can come about only in classrooms which allow space and encouragement for pupils to ask questions, and to follow up answers with further questions and challenges.

Because it allows the exploration of real questions and the active enquiries of young people, active communication between students, and between students and teachers achieves far greater dividends of understanding than the essentially short-term acquisition of unrelated facts that may result from simple teacher chalk and talk. But such methods are far from being an easy option. It is not just that in the present British educational context there are relentless pressures on teachers to produce good test results at every schooling stage. Beyond this, as Kelly was himself acutely aware, the thinking required in any new learning is difficult and often threatening.

New ways of seeing things cannot but throw a question mark over known and established ways – ways that may be buttressed by the confirmation and approval of important people. To take up the perspective entailed in what is offered, to speak in the terms, the language in which the curriculum is framed: this may seem a dangerous thing to try, a thing entailing risks to one's very identity. For 'knowledge' is never neutral; it carries the interests and concerns of particular sociocultural groupings. For school learners, the knowledge offered in their classrooms appears at first sight to 'belong' to the teachers who convey it. As such, it may seem attractive to some pupils for the very reasons that it seems alien to others.

But, as teachers often ably demonstrate, classroom knowledge is not immutable. When young people engage directly with their school curriculum, and bring their own personal issues and positions into relation with its ways of framing the world, there can be radical learning breakthroughs. And in the process whereby pupils come to enlarge their repertoires of personal meaning, the curricular material is itself altered. The understanding of English that follows from the sustained critical reflection, by themselves and their peers, on their own writings is something different from the understanding with which they began. In place of an impersonal, out-there curriculum are new meanings, personally created by those involved.

Learning poses risks

Real learning, learning that has genuinely personal implications, does not come easily. The psychotherapy clients described by Kelly do, like all serious learners, find their learning difficult and frustrating. Struggling to break out of long-established habits, familiar ways of reacting, they flounder in confusion and resistance, before, suddenly, other possibilities emerge. For this to happen, as Kelly insists, a safe, protected space is needed.

This is no less true of classroom learning. In a personal construct consulting room, clients have a place where any possible way of viewing things can be tested out without personal risk. In just the same way, young people need to be free to try out, provisionally, what it would mean to look at the world in a new kind of way. Classrooms are highly public places, with a potential, as pupils know all too well, for ridicule and humiliation. In trying out anything new, we are all apt to look clumsy and inept – to ourselves and to others who witness our performance. All this calls for a high degree of sensitivity on the part of teachers.

But there are other reasons, too, why the process of learning carries personal risks. Because any new construction has implications for other established meanings – ramifications within the whole construct system – new ways of looking at things have to be tried out first in a very tentative way. Learners needs to test out, without, as yet, commitment, what the new construction would mean for them – mean personally, that is. This is not just a matter, for instance, of working mathematically, setting out to learn the logarithmic system. It is, beyond that, a question of what it would mean to be the sort of person who does maths. Teachers need to act with delicacy, enabling their pupils to try out new material at a kind of distance, without demanding that they own it.

But what young people learn at school does not just concern curricular material. Schooling institutions do not exist in a vacuum, independent of the unequal society of which they are a part. Many teachers are committed, in their daily classroom work, to creating mutual understanding and respect. But in this they have to struggle against the racism, the sexism, heterosexism and 'injuries of class', which are endemic in the wider world in which they and their pupils live their lives. As members of this society with particular sociocultural identities, young people come, quickly and often painfully, to learn their place. Such learning is, of course, typically tacit and intuitive. It is arrived at through corridor and playground dealings, through classroom encounters, through attributions of success or failure. Even the hidden curriculum of school itself, where declared policies of equality may be contradicted by the differential treatment of its members, carries its own clear messages.

Superordinate constructs, those that stand most central to our sense of ourselves, are implicated in school learning. Most obviously, this applies to the personal identity that pupils come to acquire through their involvement, above all, with fellow-pupils. But the lessons of the classroom curriculum, if they are to be taken on personally by young people, also entail meanings which have superordinate ramifications. This makes school learning a highly complex business. What is defined in current educational philosophy as a simple act of transmission – the passing on of a predefined packet of information – appears in Kelly's philosophy as a process necessitating attention to whole networks of differentiated meaning-systems.

To take this philosophy seriously means a much larger concern than is usual with intuitive and unarticulated meanings. Without attention to such meanings, it is not possible to understand how learning occurs, and why, so often, it does not occur. For people concerned with the fundamental questions of education, Kelly's own work as a psychotherapist seems immediately relevant. Just as he strove to make explicit the intuitive levels of construing which held his clients where they were, so, to understand school learning, it is necessary to unearth, to bring into articulation, the underlying, inexplicit personal constructions of its learners. Just as Maureen Pope says [...] in relation to teacher education, so it is in the classroom; what is as yet unverbalized personal meaning must become conscious and available to reflection [(Pope, 2003)].

Exploration of construing

Until now, most explorations of personal construct systems have utilized some form or extension of Kelly's own method – the repertory grid technique [...]. The advent of this method offered a huge breakthrough in an age where psychological assessment meant forcing 'subjects' onto a psychometric bed of Procrustes. In place of generalized, preset formats which flattened and deadened human realities, grids offered access to living material, to the very terms in which people experience and engage with their own personal worlds. It enabled the elicitation of hitherto unverbalized levels of construing, and revealed the complex intuitive ramifications entailed in making human sense.

The repertory grid technique has proved widely fruitful in a huge number of psychological explorations. Yet for some kinds of educational enquiry, rather different methods may be called for. Where learning is in question, the purpose is typically not just diagnostic – even diagnostic of change over time. Those who seek to explore the learner's construing do not generally want to stop at uncovering meanings that explain why learning is or is not happening, or even how the construing involved has changed since the last time. They want to go further than just understanding: they want a method which will underpin and facilitate learning itself.

Enquiries such as these are geared towards future educational progress. The aim is to alter the very parameters of learning: to set up a course of learning within the subject's own terms. This calls for something still more flexible than the grid format. It was to meet purposes such as these that the Salmon Line

(Salmon, 1994) was developed. The name arises not merely from the egotism of its inventor, but also from its capacity to draw something lively from below the waterline. Its function, essentially, is to represent educational progression in the form of a single line: a line which allows the subject to define the personal, idiosyncratic meaning of such progression. This typically includes the curricular sphere itself, the meaning of progress within it, the evidence which would count as progress, and the kinds of experience which would enable such progress to happen. Just as importantly, it allows the identification of blocks towards positive movement.

I first used this technique many years ago in work with Hilary Claire (Salmon and Claire, 1984), in a London inner-city comprehensive school. Since the research project focused on collaborative modes of learning, we were interested in the commonality between teachers and pupils, in how they experienced the curriculum. We carried out the research with a Design and Technology teacher and his second-year class. This meant asking the teacher and each person in his class to use the line to represent this area of the curriculum. One end defined a very low level of ability in Design and Technology, the other end, the greatest possible ability. We asked the teacher to make marks along the line for each pupil in his class, according to the level of their current ability. Then we asked him why. What differentiated this pupil from that pupil, in terms of what they could and could not do? How had some individuals managed to be better than others? How far could less able pupils move up the line, and what would be needed to enable them to do so?

This way of using the line allowed this teacher's implicit theory of learning to be elicited: his sense of the curriculum, his way of evaluating progress, the expectations which guided his teaching. It also, of course, allowed us to compare his construing with that of his pupils. The group of young people who attended his classes were asked to use the line in a similar way. They marked their own positions on the line, and that of a few of their fellow pupils. We then asked them to explain their placements. Again, what could abler pupils do that less able ones could not; how had their competence come about; and what would need to happen for less able people to achieve the same level?

The outcomes of this inquiry showed a profound lack of commonality between this teacher and his pupils in how they construed the Design and Technology curriculum. On his side, the teacher saw his subject as entailing the development of designing capacity: a process in which pupils could work together to try out ideas, compare notes and challenge each other. For him, the curriculum encouraged personal creativeness, and was open to every pupil. In his perception, technical skills, and the quality of the particular article produced, were of secondary importance.

To the young people in his class, Design and Technology meant something very different. Almost universally they defined progression in the subject in terms of the quality of the object produced. They saw learning as developing from 'make-believe', practice objects, such as model bridges, to objects that were usable and 'for real', such as shelves. The finished quality of these artefacts was seen as paramount. This valuation stood in direct contrast to the teacher's priorities, which set imaginative power well above purely technical skills.

As their construing emerged from this technique, it became clear that for these pupils, the Design and Technology workshop was a kind of assembly plant in miniature. They did not see their work within it as creative, judging technical skills to be of paramount importance. In line with this perception, learning was seen as individualized, rather than involving collaboration with fellow pupils. And typically, both boys and girls saw competence as largely inborn, with female gender being an insuperable barrier.

This kind of material seems important, educationally. School learners read their own significance into what they are asked to do. They judge the progress of their work by their own criteria, and within their own, perhaps very different terms. To the extent that this happens, teacher and pupils are essentially bypassing each other. In this case, the teacher directly engaged with the lack of commonality which had emerged, making these major differences of perception the focus of class discussion. The findings of this exploration became part of the class curriculum. The wider ramifications of Design and Technology – its network of implicit connotations, its underlying significance – became the focus of group debate.

Defining a goal

In another, unpublished study (Graham, 1986) the Salmon Line was adopted to help staff at an Intermediate Treatment centre to create individualized learning programmes for the young people who were to serve their sentences there. Each young person was invited to define one goal that they hoped to achieve during their year's stay. This might be anything, from learning to control their anger, to gaining greater literacy, or improved time-keeping, or staying off drugs. One end of the line was to stand for their present position: the opposite end, for the position hoped for at the year's end. The young person was then asked to make marks along the line which would represent meaningful transitions. What would be some small, personally manageable, step, from where they are now? What would they be able to do at that point that they could not yet quite do? And what kinds of opportunity could bring that about? And so on, fleshing out the possible steps towards the ultimate goal.

When the young people had expressed their own learning goals by this means, they each, together with Beverly Graham, the researcher, met the particular staff who would be guiding their learning programme throughout the year. Together, they discussed how the resources and facilities of the centre could be used to bring about the hoped-for learning. This always resulted in modifications and extensions to the line, defining new, mutually agreed points of transition, together with realistic learning opportunities which could be set up to achieve them. And as the year progressed, and the programme began to be implemented, other changes came to be made. The meaning of the goal itself, and the increments of learning which were to add up to its achievement, altered, for the young person and his team, as time went on. This was an attempt to plan genuinely personal kinds of learning – 'really useful knowledge' – for a group for whom most institutionalized education typically carries heavily negative connotations.

More recently, the Salmon Line has proved fruitful in a project, carried out by the Language and Curriculum Access Service, Enfield (1996), which explored the way in which teachers of bilingual children constructed educational progress. In this research, the line was used in a more limited way, to elicit factors associated with positive and negative kinds of change on their own part. For one teacher, for example, the starting point was defined by the pupil appearing isolated and withdrawn, while the end point – the hoped-for outcome – represented him as socially integrated and making progress. Meaningful transition points along the way were, in order: liaison between class teachers and the Language and Curriculum Access Service team, a home visit, the gathering of accurate information, opportunities to assess language learning, and the process being kept under review. Against these facilitating conditions, the equally important potential blocks to progress were, again in order: teachers seeing the pupil as 'a cause for concern', working on inaccurate information, making assumptions, negative attitudes, and feeling pressurized to come up with the answers. Teachers working in this way felt that it contributed to the process of developing new approaches to their work, and stressed the importance of noting both steps that moved things forward and those that were real or potential blockages to movement.

[...]

References

Billig, M. (1987) *Arguing and Thinking: A Rhetorical Approach to Social Psychology*, Cambridge, Cambridge University Press.

Graham, B. (1986) *Creating Learning Programmes in Intermediate Treatment Centres*, unpublished MSc dissertation, London Institute of Education.

Language and Curriculum Access Service (LCAS), Enfield (1996) *Concerns about Progress*, London Borough of Enfield, LCAS.

Pope, M. (2003) 'Construing teaching and teacher education worldwide' in Fransella, F. (ed.) *International Handbook of Personal Construct Psychology*, Chichester, Wiley.

Salmon, P. (1994) *Girls are all very well, but...*, newsletter, European Personal Construct Association.

Salmon, P. and Claire, H. (1984) *Classroom Collaboration*, London, Routledge and Kegan Paul.

(Salmon, 2003, pp. 311–18)

Conclusion

In the two readings in this chapter, we can see a contrast both in content and style. In Eysenck and Rachman's work (Reading 8.1), there is no attempt to capture the richness of each individual; this is not the job of a personality theory as they see it. Instead they seek to map individual differences in terms of dimensions which, they claim, reflect the underlying biological basis of personality. Individual differences are thus due to differences in biological temperament that translate into behaviour. Although they argue for the clinical value of their approach, it is firmly based in the psychometric tradition that survives today chiefly in occupational rather than clinical psychology. Its interest is in discovering norms and explaining how individuals vary in relation to them. The work is written in the discourse of the natural sciences, looking for causal explanations of surface phenomena at a more micro level.

Salmon's reading (Reading 8.2), on the other hand, is based in the clinical tradition. The personal constructivism of Kelly defines personality in terms of the idiosyncratic frame of reference of each individual. It has no interest in comparing one with another, but focuses on the particular way that each person makes sense of his or her world. It is an understanding of a person's action that is sought in terms of their personal constructions. The way in which each person interprets the world is the reason why they act as they do.

So, the emphasis here is on understanding rather than scientific explanation (Butt, 2004). What the clinician wants to do is to find out why a particular person thinks, feels and acts as they do. Assessment techniques like the 'Salmon Line' are designed to help the individual articulate their bases for action. From a constructivist standpoint, it is the reconstruction of this framework of interpretation that should be the aim of any intervention.

The way people act differently in what objectively appear to be identical situations has always presented a puzzle to psychologists, and personality theories were devised in order to account for such individual differences. We should recognise, though, that this colonising of the area by personality theory creates a somewhat artificial distinction between it and social psychology. The way that we perceive others, attribute certain dispositions to them and adopt characteristic attitudes could all be thought of as features of personality. And the subtle influence of group pressure, subjective definition of the situation, and sense of identity are all likely to play a part in determining the way in which we characteristically act. Yet, these features of the social world will be difficult to define objectively, and are likely to be missed completely by any observer who is not alert to them. The influence of the social world (along with any relevant stimulus conditions that an experimentalist might look for) is downplayed when explanation is sought in terms of personality variables. Talk of individual differences bids us look inside the person for traits or states that might explain them.

The constructivist approach to personality can be seen as one that fits into a social psychology (Stringer and Bannister, 1979; Hampson, 1988; Butt, 2001, 2004). The pragmatic interests of the clinician centre on individuals and the sometimes subtle differences between them. But this does not deny that, in many ways, people in a given society are more alike than different. Kelly did not engage with where constructs come from; how it was that different people developed different systems of construction. For him, as for other psychotherapists, the issue was how to help a particular individual to change. However, he acknowledged that culture had a strong influence on the commonality in construction that we frequently see. Like other American pragmatists (for example, James, Dewey and Mead), he recognised that the individual was a product of society, not a social atom that pre-dated it. Certainly individual construction varies, but it varies within a range that is set by society. Salmon underlines this with her reference to Billig. Building on the arguments of James and Mead, Billig (1987) makes the point that what we think of as the private sphere of the mind is in fact an internalised version of the public sphere of society. We can only have internal dialogues and thoughts because we model them on conversations and dialogues we hear in the world around us. Individual construction, then, is forged out of the social construction in which we are immersed. There are indeed individual differences between people, but we must not forget the social world in which individuals are constructed.

References

Billig, M. (1987) *Arguing and Thinking: A Rhetorical Approach to Social Psychology*, Cambridge, Cambridge University Press.

Butt, T.W. (2001) 'Social action and personal constructs', *Theory and Psychology*, vol. 11, no. 1, pp. 75–95.

Butt, T.W. (2004) *Understanding People*, Basingstoke, Palgrave.

Eysenck, H.J. (1947) *Dimensions of Personality*, London, Routledge.

Eysenck, H.J. and Rachman, S. (1965) 'Dimensions of personality' in Eysenck, H.J. and Rachman, S. (eds) *Causes and Cures of Neurosis*, London, Routledge.

Freud, S. (1963) *The Complete Psychological Works of Sigmund Freud* (trans. and ed. J.Strachey in collaboration with A.Freud), vol. 16 (1916–1917), part 3, London, Hogarth Press and the Institute of Psycho-Analysis.

Kelly, G.A. (1955) *The Psychology of Personal Constructs*, New York, Norton.

Kelly, G.A. (1969) 'Man's construction of his alternatives' in Maher, B. (ed.) *Clinical Psychology and Personality: The Selected Papers of George Kelly*, London, Wiley.

Hampson, S. (1988) *The Construction of Personality* (2nd edn), London, Routledge.

Mischel, W. (1968) *Personality and Assessment*, London, Wiley.

Salmon, P. (2003) 'A psychology for teachers' in Fransella, F. (ed.) *International Handbook of Personal Construct Psychology*, Chichester, Wiley.

Skinner, B.F. (1974) *About Behaviourism*, New York, Random House.

Stringer, P. and Bannister, D. (1979) *Constructs of Sociality and Individuality*, London, Academic Press.

Further reading

Butt, T.W. (2004) *Understanding People*, Basingstoke, Palgrave.
A critical appraisal of personality theories from a constructivist perspective.

Butt, T.W. and Burr, V. (2004) *Invitation to Personal Construct Psychology* (2nd edn), London, Whurr.
A very simple guide to personal construct psychology (PCP) through everyday examples.

Fransella, F. (ed.) (2003) *International Handbook of Personal Construct Psychology*, Chichester, Wiley.
A comprehensive series of 4000-word chapters on all aspects of PCP.

Hampson, S. (1988) *The Construction of Personality* (2nd edn), London, Routledge.
Presents an argument for a constructivist approach to personality.

Matthews, G., Deary, I.J., and Whiteman, M.C. (2003) *Personality Traits* (2nd edn), Cambridge, Cambridge University Press.
Includes historical information and more recent developments in trait theory.

Chapter 9

Conclusion

By Darren Langdridge, The Open University

The settlement of social psychology

It is all too simple to portray UK social psychology as a split between an unreconstructed cognitive mainstream and a new critical (predominantly social constructionist) alternative. While it is possible to categorise social psychology in terms of the mainstream and the critical – for example, by characterising the former as informed by the natural sciences (with an emphasis on explanation and prediction, most often through experimental methods) and the latter by the social sciences (with an emphasis on understanding, most often through qualitative methods) – this is only one possible division and tends to obscure the many differences within each position as well as reify the differences between positions. However, I think it is necessary sometimes to fix terms in a debate, as long as it is done reflexively and only provisionally. This book demonstrates the complexity of the debate through the ways in which different authors engage with different perspectives in social psychology, providing a multitude of voices and, sometimes, a multitude of contrasting positions on the topics in question. Some authors seek to identify the strengths in the readings they include; others are keen to situate both historically (sometimes, but not always, with the first reading as past, second as present). Others, however, clearly aim to identify something new in the critical reading, something challenging to the mainstream rather than complementary or simply different. Whatever position is taken, the authors show the complexity of the debate and the difficult relationship between mainstream and critical.

A number of psychologists have also questioned the way in which mainstream and critical social psychologies appear, in the UK at least, to have settled into a quiet stalemate, no longer battling but also no longer dialoguing (e.g. Brown, 2002; Brown and Lunt, 2002; Good, 2000, 2002; Lunt, 2002; Langdridge, 2006; Stenner, 2002). There is a belief that in the UK, where critical social psychology has found a (somewhat) welcome home, there has been a bifurcation between mainstream and critical. Brown (2002, p. 69) describes the situation as an 'intellectual deep-freeze'. During and shortly after the 'crisis' in the 1970s things were very different; writing was full of passion and stand-up arguments between social psychologists were commonplace with real anger fuelling the debate. There was a belief among the critics that the mainstream was simply misguided, that social psychology had to be transformed, and that this could – indeed would – happen through the force of argument. Harré and Gillett (1994), two leading philosophers with a particular interest in psychology, writing long after the crisis, bemoan the co-existence of mainstream and critical (what they refer to as 'old' and 'new') thus:

> Psychology, however, has changed much more than any other of the human sciences. Not only its transformation but its lack of transformation in the last 20 years have been quite extraordinary. It is both remarkable and interesting that the old psychologies continue to exist alongside the new ones ... It is quite unique, so far as we know, in the history of science, that old, outdated, and manifestly inadequate ways of doing research, and untenable theories, have persisted alongside new and better theories and methods.
>
> (Harré and Gillett, 1994, pp. 1–2)

So, thirty years on, there is a belief that social psychology has not been transformed. Perhaps there is some truth in that. The areas of work which are generally described as mainstream (cognitive and social identity theories) remain dominant. But there has been change. For instance, the critical is, in the UK at least, now also fairly healthy, and still critical but no longer so angry. So we should ask what has happened: Why has the critique failed to demolish the mainstream? Why are there still divisions? And what can be done about the settlement in UK social psychology?

Before, moving on to address these questions directly, however, I think it is important to address some of the comments made by Harré and Gillett (1994) and, in particular, their incredulity at how – in their terms – an inferior psychology (the mainstream) can remain intact when faced with such a superior alternative (the critical). The problem for them, as I see it, lies in their judgement about the quality of the two alternatives. It appears that the criterion they use to make their judgement concerns their belief that the theoretical (philosophical) arguments of the mainstream have been destroyed by the theoretical arguments of the new. Even supposing that this were true, it is only one of many criteria with which to judge the value of a theoretical perspective in social psychology. As I discuss below, much of the work characterised as the mainstream (such as experimental research to develop predictive models) may be better suited to the broader socio-political and economic conditions in the West. That is, it may speak to the markets in which social psychological knowledge is taken up or applied in a way that is more accessible and useful than the alternatives. As the situation presently stands, the mainstream is not inferior here. Similarly, the language of science and technology, at the heart of much mainstream social psychology, may also be better suited to the needs, as presently perceived, of the consumer. Knowing that an intervention produces a 20 per cent effect may be more understandable and indeed more obviously useful than a complex and nuanced account of the experience of the same phenomenon. This is an oversimplification, of course, as there are good examples of critical work in social psychology which effect social change and many examples of mainstream work which are neither accessible nor effective, but the point remains that the criteria for making a judgement about the value of any perspective are many, such that multiple perspectives can sensibly co-exist for very good reasons even when theoretically incompatible.

Harré and Gillett (1994) have also created an oversimplified dichotomy between mainstream and critical in their statement, for the mainstream is not one homogenous thing, has not stood still for the last thirty years and has, at least to some extent, taken on board the criticisms and sought to find ways forward which accommodate aspects of the critique. For example, cognitive social psychologists and social identity theorists, while still apparently wedded to a natural science model, have in recent years recognised the way in which language is not simply representational but also performative. This has rarely meant the replacement of experiments with qualitative investigations but has sometimes resulted in the use of findings from discursive psychological studies to aid understanding of the results of experimental investigations. Many examples of the ability of the mainstream to adapt and accommodate the criticisms from other perspectives, whether discursive, phenomenological or social psychoanalytic, could be given. Still, it is important to recognise that the critics are still critical, and the target of their criticism remains work which they refer to as 'mainstream', on the grounds of the perceived a-historical, a-cultural, essentialist, dualistic, and natural scientific nature of the cognitive perspective (Langdridge, 2006). And with this in mind, it becomes important to continue to question why the criticism has not effected the fundamental change the critics would like. One answer might be that different projects are being pursued, as Taylor discusses in Chapter 1 and Chapter 3. Mainstream and critical social psychologists can co-exist because they are, in the main, attempting to do different things. Another answer is offered by Brown (2002), who suggests that the heart of the problem is the way that the standards of argument are different for mainstream and critical social psychology:

> Here is the lesson I draw: mainstream social psychology does not respond to direct argumentation. Which must mean that the standards of proof and logic that it draws upon are different to what we would usually expect ... All of this should of course not really be that surprising. Philosophers of science have long noted the ability of research programmes to absorb contradictory evidence by modifying their own auxiliary propositions and procedures. Indeed Lakatos (1974) famously described research programmes that fail to expand their range of theorems and hypotheses as 'degenerative'. Such programmes would eventually give way to more progressive research programmes. On this account, contemporary mainstream social psychology is doing very well indeed. New modification and extensions of its central propositions occur almost daily.
>
> (Brown, 2002, p. 70)

In addition, I have also noted (Langdridge, 2006) how the common categorisation of academics' own identities as cognitive or critical social psychologists plays a vital part in keeping the battle lines drawn and resisting the attack. By employing Ricoeur's (1986) political philosophy as a hermeneutic (method of interpretation), I set out to explore the way in which perspectives become ideologically entrenched, with individual positions not simply reflecting a distortion of the facts, but rather necessary components in the relationship between ideologies and utopias. That is, at a very simple level the arguments during the crisis often reflected a fundamental belief that 'the other' was completely wrong and that if only they could come to see how their perception of the world was distorted they would come to realise the truth and change. It is clearly more complex than this as the power of argument has not effected a fundamental change. The mainstream represents a core identity for many and is reproduced through organisational structures (funding bodies, journals, etc.) which tend to support mainstream research in preference to critical research. Moreover, as I have argued previously (Langdridge, 2006), the mainstream is better suited to the rational–technical nature of capitalism and the market than the utopian alternatives of critical social psychology. These alternatives instead remain visions, fantasies of the future, often fragmented and with relatively less success in convincing the funding bodies, the journals and the consumers of the value of their work. This is changing of course and some critical social psychology has been recognised through publication in leading journals and obtaining research funding, but there is still some way to go before things are equal.

But what does this settlement between mainstream and critical mean? Should we seek to integrate across the divisions or take up the fight once again? Or should we do nothing and leave well alone? Manstead and Wetherell (2005) raise a number of objections to the latter suggestion. These include: the way in which such a division can become self-reinforcing with completely separate social psychologies; the problems involved in judging the quality of research across the perspectives; and the significant difficulties for students of psychology being schooled in only mainstream or critical and not both social psychologies. So, what should be done? Well perhaps it is not necessary to return to the fight or remain with the settlement. Perhaps instead it is possible to accommodate the different perspectives, seek to recognise the value across the divisions, while also remaining critical – perhaps social psychologists can find a way to dialogue across these divisions.

Dialoguing across divisions

Koch (1993, p. 902) states that 'psychology cannot be a single or coherent discipline – whether conceived in scientific or *sui generis* terms.' Instead, he argues we should learn the lesson from other disciplines, such as physics, where the emergence of different perspectives has not led to stagnation or continual combat but rather productive dialogue. And, very recently, this has been happening in social psychology. There have been attempts – theoretically, methodologically and practically – to find ways of dialoguing across the divisions to enable movement beyond the settlement in a constructive rather than destructive way.

Brown and Lunt (2002) and Langdridge and Butt (2004) (Reading 4.2), for instance, provide different ways of escaping the intellectual deep-freeze, trying to find theoretical ways to work on a topic from a different perspective. Instead of simply regarding the findings of the other as wrong, they have sought to recognise their value by seeking to understand them from an alternative perspective. In the process, they offer up the possibility of dialogue and exchange between mainstream and critical on theoretical and methodological levels, with both learning from the other.

The 'Dialoguing Across Divisions' group, funded by the British Psychological Society, also demonstrated – in a concrete and practical way – how it is possible for psychologists to engage in productive dialogue in spite of fundamental theoretical and methodological differences (see the special issue of *The Psychologist* (2005, vol. 18, no. 9)). This group of social psychologists came together for a series of seminars to discuss similarities and differences, along with ways forward for the discipline. The group included social psychologists from different theoretical and methodological perspectives, with a view to representing a variety of perspectives from the 'so-called' mainstream and critical camps. The outcome was very positive with those present able to find ways to dialogue constructively and offer concrete suggestions for challenging the settlement. As Reicher and Taylor (2005) state:

> If one thing did come out of our meetings, it was a mutual sense of respect and a realisation that the biggest threat to intellectual progress is not arguing with each other ... but ignoring and being in ignorance of each other.
>
> (Reicher and Taylor, 2005, p. 549)

They make it clear, however, that this should not mean a return to the knock-down arguments of old but instead a turning to more nuanced discussion about similarities and differences, which are informed and constructive rather than ignorant and destructive. They recognise that most likely an intermediate position will be found where there continues to be both disagreement and agreement, some integration and also some desire to maintain clear and separate positions. This would, of course, be a real advance on the present settlement or past fighting.

There are clearly, therefore, ways of working constructively with what has been termed the mainstream and critical, and the previous seven chapters have demonstrated how productive it is to work across divisions to find new ways of understanding that recognise the contextual nature of the production of social psychological knowledge. For social psychological knowledge is not simply found, but is – like all knowledge – a product of history and culture, theory and methodology, intrinsically intertwined with the broader socio-political context in which it is located. Dialogue, with colleagues inside the discipline and also those outside, facilitates the development of theory and methodology and, most importantly, the development of the discipline more generally. Without dialogue we will either see a return to the public wrangling of yesteryear or some form of settlement with little critical engagement across perspectives. The key is in the hands of all those who contribute to the generation of knowledge in social psychology, for if we are willing to recognise the other then we will have the possibility of constructive dialogue and a discipline that is critically aware of the way in which knowledge is situated.

This book is itself a good example of dialogue. Each chapter author has sought to identify a key division in the work on a particular topic, and then to work across this division to present an overview of relevant theory and research. The chapter author may have sought to prosecute an argument in favour of one perspective, or simply highlight the differences. Regardless, all authors have had to work across different theoretical perspectives and, in the process, have demonstrated an understanding of the epistemology and methodology of the other, embedded as these are in the broader social and cultural context of the discipline in which we all work. As a result, this book has shown how it is vital to be aware of the historically and culturally, theoretically and methodologically situated nature of social psychological knowledge and also how critical understanding and creative dialogue may provide a way forward for the discipline.

References

Brown, S. (2002) 'Psychology without foundations', *History and Philosophy of Psychology*, vol. 4, no. 1, pp. 69–83.

Brown, S.D. and Lunt, P. (2002) 'A genealogy of the social identity tradition: Deleuze and Guattari and social psychology', *British Journal of Social Psychology*, no. 41, pp. 1–23.

Good, J.(2000) 'Disciplining social psychology: A case study of boundary relations in the history of the human sciences', *Journal of the History of the Behavioral Sciences*, no. 36, pp. 383–403.

Good, J. (2002) 'On the "Unsettling of social psychology": an end to the "crises" of social psychology?', *History and Philosophy of Psychology*, vol. 4, no. 1, pp. 84–92.

Harré, R. and Gillet, G. (1994) *The Discursive Mind*, London, Sage.

Koch, S. (1993) '"Psychology" or "The psychological studies"?', *American Psychologist*, no. 48, pp. 902–4.

Langdridge, D. (2006) 'Ideology and utopia: social psychology and the social imaginary of Paul Ricoeur', *Theory and Psychology*, vol. 16, no. 5, pp. 641–59.

Langdridge, D. and Butt, T.W. (2004) 'The fundamental attribution error: a phenomenological critique', *British Journal of Social Psychology*, vol. 43, no. 3, pp. 357–69.

Lunt, P. (2002) 'Middle range theory, interpretation and the traditional/critical divide in social psychology', *History and Philosophy of Psychology*, vol. 4, no.1, pp. 58–68.

Manstead, T. and Wetherell, M. (2005) 'Dialoguing across divisions', *The Psychologist*, vol. 18, no. 9, pp. 542–3.

Reicher, S. and Taylor, S. (2005) 'Similarities and differences between traditions', *The Psychologist*, vol. 18, no. 9, pp. 547–9.

Ricoeur, P. (1986) *Lectures on Ideology and Utopia* (trans. and ed. G.H. Taylor), New York, Columbia University Press.

Stenner, P. (2002) 'Social psychology and Babel', *History and Philosophy of Psychology*, vol. 4, no. 1, pp. 45–57.

Acknowledgements

Grateful acknowledgement is made to the following sources:

Chapter 2: Reading 2.1: Duck, S. (1999) 'Relating to others', Open University Press. Reproduced by kind permission of the Open University Press Publishing Company; Reading 2.2: Chodorow, N.J. (1999) 'The reproduction of mothering: psychoanalysis and the sociology of gender', University of California Press.

Chapter 3: Reading 3.1: From SOCIAL FORCES, Volume 13. Copyright © 1934 by the University of North Carolina Press. Used by permission of the publisher; Reading 3.2: Ajzen, I. (1988) 'Attitudes, personality and behaviour', Open University Press. Reproduced by kind permission of the Open University Press Publishing Company; Reading 3.3: Reprinted by permission of Sage Publications Ltd, Potter, J. and Wetherell, M. (1987) 'Discourse and social psychology: beyond attitude and behaviour'. Reprinted by permission of Sage Publications Ltd. Copyright (1987) Jonathan Potter and Margaret Wetherell.

Chapter 4: Reading 4.1: Ross, L. 'The intuitive psychologist and his shortcoming: Distortions in the attribution process', in Berkowitz, L. (ed.) (1977) *Advances in Experimental Social Psychology*, Academic Press, Inc.; Reading 4.2: Langdridge, D. and Butt, T.W. (2004) 'The fundamental attribution error: a phenomenological critique', *British Journal of Social Psychology*, vol. 43, pp. 357–69, The British Psychological Society 2004.

Chapter 5: Reading 5.1: Janis, Irving, VICTIMS OF GROUPTHINK, Copyright © 1972 by Houghton Mifflin Company. Used with permission; Reading 5.2: Potter, J. and Reicher, S. (1987) 'Discourses of community and conflict: the organization of social categories in accounts of a "riot"', *The British Journal of Social Psychology*, vol. 26, pp. 25–40, Leicester, The British Psychological Society.

Chapter 6: Reading 6.1: Tajfel, H. and Turner, J.C. (1979) 'An integrative theory on intergroup conflict' in Austin, W.G. and Worchel, S. (eds) *The Social Psychology of Intergroup Relations*. By permission of William Austin and Stephen Worchel; Reading 6.2: Billig, M. (2002) 'Henri Tajfel's "Cognitive aspects of prejudice" and the psychology of bigotry', *British Journal of Social Psychology*, vol. 41, pp. 171–188. The British Psychological Society 2002.

Chapter 7: Reading 7.1: Darley, J. and Latane, B. 'Bystander intervention in emergencies: diffusion of responsibility', *Journal of Personality and Social Psychology*, vol. 8, no. 4, 1988, pp. 377–83. Copyright © 1968 by the American Psychological Association. Adapted with permission; Reading 7.2: Cherry, F. (1995) *The Stubborn Particulars of Social Psychology*, Routledge. Copyright © Frances Cherry.

Chapter 8: Reading 8.1: Eysenck, H.J. and Rachman, S. (1965) *The Causes and Cures of Neurosis*, Routledge. By permission of Taylor & Francis Books and

Index